Stolen Honor

Stolen Honor

STIGMATIZING MUSLIM MEN IN BERLIN

Katherine Pratt Ewing

Stanford University Press
Stanford, California

Stanford University Press
Stanford, California

Printed in the United States of America on acid-free, archival-quality paper

Library of Congress Cataloging-in-Publication Data

Ewing, Katherine Pratt.
  Stolen honor : stigmatizing Muslim men in Berlin / Katherine Pratt Ewing.
    p. cm.
  Includes bibliographical references (p.   ) and index.
  ISBN 978-0-8047-5899-4 (cloth : alk. paper) — ISBN 978-0-8047-5900-7 (pbk. : alk. paper)
  1. Muslims—Germany—Berlin—Social conditions. 2. Muslims—Germany—Berlin—
Attitudes. 3. Social integration—Germany—Berlin. I. Title.
BP65.G32B474 2008
305.38'6970943155—dc22
                                2007049982

Typeset by Bruce Lundquist in 10/14 Minion

For my husband Thomas DiPrete
and our daughters Julia, Bethany, and Justine

Many immigrants come from patriarchal societies in which the honor of the woman is linked to the man, where sexual relations before marriage are forbidden and men determine how women should dress and how they should behave at home. If a woman breaks these rules, a man has lost control over his women—his wife, his sisters or his daughters. If a man can't keep control of his women, he loses his honor in the community. Honor can be cleansed, in the worst-case scenario, through murder. It's like erasing a dirty mark on the family.

—Sibylle Schreiber,
consultant on "violence in the name of honor"
for Terre des Femmes (German branch)

CONTENTS

ACKNOWLEDGMENTS

MANY PEOPLE AND INSTITUTIONS have helped make this book possible. I began working on the project while a Berlin Prize Fellow at the American Academy in Berlin in 1999. Additional support has come from the Trent Foundation, the German Academic Exchange Service (DAAD), and several sources at Duke University, including the European Studies Center, the Arts and Sciences Council, the International Affairs Committee, and the John Hope Franklin Center, as a Faculty Fellow. I also participated in a 2002 Fulbright Seminar on Immigration in Germany, where I had the opportunity to hear a myriad of voices speaking about problems of integration. These ranged from representatives of several minority communities to government officials, politicians, and scholars. A chance to write in beautiful solitude was provided by a Wildacres Residential Fellowship. I completed the final stages of manuscript preparation at the Russell Sage Foundation, well-supplied with congenial colleagues from an array of disciplines and many opportunities to exchange ideas over lunch.

I thank audiences who have heard and commented on various aspects of the argument at the Free University in Berlin, Koç University in Istanbul, and Carl von Ossietzky University in Oldenburg, Germany, and at a number of North American universities, including McMaster, Northwestern, UCLA, Harvard, Columbia, the University of Chicago, and Duke, as well as fellow participants in the SSRC-sponsored Working Group on Law and Culture. I have also benefited from the reactions and advice of students in courses at Duke and Columbia.

Many individuals have stimulated my thinking at various stages, and I cannot mention them all. In Europe, I would especially like to thank Helene

Basu, Berndt Bose, Ayse Caglar, Mehmet Sabri Erbakan, Markus Gangl, Levent Soysal, Lydia Potts, Tony Robben, and Werner Schiffauer. Deep gratitude goes to Emine Öztürk, who devoted many hours of her time over several years helping me get to know communities of Muslims in Berlin.

At Duke, I am ever grateful to my wonderful colleagues, both in the Department of Cultural Anthropology and in the wider university. Special thanks for stimulating conversations and various other kinds of support as I was struggling over the complexities of this book go to Anne Allison; Ayse Gul Altinay; Lee Baker; Miriam Cooke; Erdağ Göknar, who was an amazing teacher of the Turkish language; John Jackson; Claudia Koonz; Bruce Lawrence; Ralph Litzinger; Diane Nelson; William O'Barr; Charlie Piot; Naomi Quinn; Orin Starn; Rebecca Stein; and Deborah Thomas. I also thank several students who worked tirelessly and creatively as my research assistants, especially Attiya Ahmad, Şenay Özden, Yektan Türkyilmaz, and Elizabeth Zoe Baer. In addition to their insightful comments on the manuscript, Duke students Julia DiPrete and Marguerite Hoyler played an important role in my field research in Germany, making contacts and conducting interviews. As Americans of a younger generation, they added a perspective that otherwise would have been unavailable to me.

I also offer thanks to many colleagues at other universities in the United States, including John Bowen, Byron Good, Joan Scott, Richard Shweder, and Hakan Yavuz.

I give special thanks to Lila Abu-Lughod for taking the time to read the manuscript with her careful, critical eye. At Stanford University Press, I have been very impressed with Kate Wahl, the most enthusiastic and efficient editor I have ever met. I also appreciated the comments of the two anonymous readers for Stanford University Press, who have helped make this a better book.

Finally, I must express gratitude and love to friends and family. Special mention goes to Jan French and John French, who have been friends as well as colleagues. My husband Tom DiPrete has helped me in every way, including his scholarly perspective and endless patience, as has my eldest daughter Julia. Bethany and Justine have become German enthusiasts along the way.

Earlier versions of portions of Chapter 2 were previously published in the journal *Cultural Anthropology* and in the volume *Power and the Self*, edited by J. Mageo and B. Knauft (Cambridge University Press, 2002).

Stolen Honor

INTRODUCTION
Masculinity in a National Imaginary

Social workers estimate that thousands—perhaps tens of thousands—of Muslim women live as invisibles in Germany, their lives physically defined by the four walls of their home and ordered by four staples: the Quran, male superiority, the importance of family, violence and honor. In the middle of Germany, these women live as slaves, unseen or ignored by their German neighbors, hidden behind walls and forgotten.

Spiegel Online 2004

The percent of schoolgirls wearing headscarves in the Berlin district where Hatin [sic] was killed has gone from virtually none to about 40 percent in the past three years. Which one of today's smiling schoolgirls . . . will be next year's victim of honor?

Biehl 2005

THE COVERED MUSLIM WOMAN has become a spectacle in the Western media. Repeatedly visible on magazine covers and the front page of newspapers, she is a symbol of the challenge facing European governments that are struggling to integrate large and growing Muslim populations. For many, her headscarf is emblematic of the failure of immigrants who came to countries such as France and Germany as guestworkers to assimilate to the culture of their European hosts, even after generations of residence. Debates rage in both France and Germany over whether Muslim women and girls should be allowed to wear headscarves in public schools, with many who support a headscarf ban, arguing that the headscarf symbolizes the oppression of the Muslim woman, which a modern democracy should not condone. Many narratives by and about Muslim women portray them as victims of male brutality who must be rescued from traditional, oppressive male morality, which is imagined as a total control

1

over female bodies and actions. Memoirs by women who have escaped forced marriages, attempted honor killings (murder of a family member to preserve the family's reputation), and other violence are taken up by publishers and reviewers and become international best sellers, at least in part because they fulfill expectations that stir the moral outrage of their intended audience.[1]

With all of this attention directed at the Muslim woman as victim, no one has stopped to investigate how the Muslim man has been depicted in such accounts. Even when men are not mentioned directly, such narratives implicitly embed negative representations. These representations are particularly prominent in Europe and play a major role in the political process in many European countries, shaping public policy, citizenship legislation, and the course of elections. Though these stigmatizing images bear little relationship to the everyday practices and experiences of most men and women of Muslim background now living in Europe, the naturalization of negative stereotypes of the Muslim man has been so profound that even people who see themselves as politically and socially liberal, tolerant of difference, and cosmopolitan may not recognize the extent of this stigmatization. Why is this so? How have these negative stereotypes become so naturalized that they go unrecognized, even among many who are concerned about social equality and the rights of minorities? What is the significance of such failures of recognition?

In this book I show that the stigmatization of the masculinity of a minority such as Muslim men often goes unnoticed because of the blind spots and silences that surround this stigmatization. This sometimes invisible or implicit process of stigmatization is linked to intertwined national and transnational imaginaries that rest on a foundation of fantasy. I argue that the fantasies associated with stigmatization are enacted through national dramas of moral panic that play out in the arenas of politics and the media. A *national imaginary* is a system of cultural representations that makes the contours of the nation-state emotionally plausible,[2] in part by differentiating the nation-state from others on the basis of distinctive national cultural forms and "a strong sense of 'us' versus 'them'—a sense of exclusive belonging" (Borneman 2004: 14). A national imaginary is thus generated and sustained through an ongoing process of myth-making (Barthes 1972). The state makes claims on the loyalty of its inhabitants through identification with the nation and its specific forms of culture, a process of imagining a shared experience that simultaneously marks various forms of social difference. Thus, a "Muslim man," while recognizable on the street of any German city as an individual, likely an immigrant or the son of an immigrant, most probably from Turkey, is also seen through the lens of a socially shared fantasy that forms the context through which his visible attributes are noticed and interpreted. This social fantasy positions the Muslim man as a stigmatized "other," a positioning that affects the possibilities for the Muslim man's cultural citizenship or sense of full belonging.[3] Even more significantly, this fantasy also plays an important role in constituting a German national identity as this identity is taken up and inhabited by those who consider themselves to be German. Why would German identity be linked to a fantasy about Muslim women and their violent men?

The identity of the national subject, that is, of one who fully belongs to the nation as one of "us," rests on a discursive process in which others are defined as "not-us." In this national imaginary of belonging, the other occupies what Judith Butler has called a "zone of uninhabitability," in which the thought of inhabiting the position of the other is a threat to one's own sense of identity and is abjected with a feeling along the lines of, "I would rather die than do or be that!" (Butler 1993: 243 n. 2). *Abjection* is thus the process of maintaining a sense of wholeness and identity by casting out that which is felt to be improper or dangerous to the integrity of the self.[4] I argue that stigmatization of Muslim masculinity is a form of abjection, in which the Muslim man's sense of self and honor are represented in European national discourses as an uninhabitable way of being, for instance, a German or a Frenchman or a Norwegian. This process of abjection structures fantasy. But the Muslim man is not simply other to specific German or French or Norwegian national imaginaries. His abjection is reinforced by his positioning in a transnational imaginary in which the "modern" is constituted in opposition to the "traditional" as abjected other. As Edward Said recognized in his analysis of Orientalist discourse (1978), the Muslim stands as other in a discourse that casts the Orient as the antithesis of the West and its Enlightenment values.[5]

The national subject of a modern democracy based on equality and a respect for human rights stands as the antithesis of an abjected subject whose sense of belonging must rest on violence and the abuse of women. I show that this stigmatization is intense yet unnoticed because local cultural practices in Western countries—especially culturally specific aspects of gender and the organization of public spaces such as the nuclear family and the boundary between public and private—are confounded in public discourse with what are generally agreed to be universally applicable ideas of human rights and democracy in a kind of logical or rhetorical slippage.

When the two levels—presumably universalizable (though still historically contingent and contestable) principles such as basic human rights, freedom and autonomy, and locally specific cultural practices that vary from one European country or region to another—are confounded, minorities that do not conform to local cultural expectations are also presumed to fall outside what is expected of a citizen in a Western democracy. Through this process, other organizations of gender and family relations are identified as oppressive of women, the Muslim man is associated with this oppressive organization of gender, and he is located as other. He is stigmatized in the name of freedom, democracy, and human rights and is abjected as the antithesis of these principles. He is recognized as seeking honor and respect primarily through violence and the oppression of women, means that are incompatible with the ethical subject of a democracy. His location as other stimulates moral outrage at the violation of culturally local but assumed-to-be universal ethical assumptions about the proper organization of gender and social space, and his stigmatization goes unrecognized. Even his situation as an exploited guestworker or a minority subject to social discrimination and racism is obscured by this association with terrorism and domestic violence. The confounding of culturally particular practices and ideologies with universal principles exacerbates and justifies the stigmatization of Muslim masculinity, making it invisible even to those who are morally outraged by social inequality and discrimination.

Though negative perceptions of the Muslim man have been reinforced by the post–September 11 climate in which the Muslim man is often viewed transnationally as a potential terrorist, and though the situation of Muslims has been framed in many European countries in similar terms as a "crisis" in the media and public discourse, the specific manifestations of this crisis are somewhat different from one country to the next, even when the media and governments of the various European countries are attuned to issues facing their neighbors and closely watch steps taken to deal with various manifestations of the crisis. Each nation-state experiences the Muslim challenge in somewhat different terms because of the place that specific Muslim populations occupy within the national imaginary of the country they inhabit.

This book analyzes the structure of stigmatized masculinity as fantasy and its place in a national imaginary by focusing on an important subpopulation of Muslims in Europe, namely, Turkish immigrants and their descendants now living in Germany. In Germany, the sense of crisis has been framed as the evolution of a "parallel society" that threatens the coherence of Germany as a recently reunified state.[6] The emergence of this threatening parallel society has been attributed to a refusal of men of Turkish background to assimilate to German culture because of what is perceived as their unwillingness to give up traditional Turkish and Muslim cultural practices such as the maintenance of honor through the control of women. Some German scholars, for example, have argued that the women are eager for education and integration, but that their men hold them back and lock them up (e.g., Heitmeyer, Müller, and Schröder 1997). Furthermore, the specific manifestations of stigmatization in Germany have been shaped in part by the prominence and conflation of two sets of stereotypes: those associated with Muslims and Islam, and those associated with the Turk. Images of the Turk have a distinct and vivid history due to the often threatening presence of the Ottoman Empire at the edge of Europe over many centuries. Furthermore, Germany's long and complex history of ties to the Ottoman Empire and Turkey has also shaped representations of the Turk.

Interrogating both the sense of crisis over the integration into Germany of Turks as a Muslim minority and popular as well as scholarly explanations and proposed solutions for the crisis, I argue that the stigmatization of the Muslim man and the Turk occupies an important place in the constitution of German nationhood and subjectivity at this historical juncture. Given Germany's troubled history associated with its Nazi past, the country has been particularly preoccupied with establishing and maintaining itself as a state that exemplifies democratic values in the post–World War II period. In Germany's postwar Constitution, or Basic Law, gender equality is a key ideological site for the articulation of these democratic values. Much of the German stereotyping of Muslim men reflects a preoccupation with a Muslim organization of gender as a threat to a social order founded on these universal values as they are embedded in the Constitution. But German gender organization is itself linked to culturally and historically specific forms of personal honor, bodily discipline, and social space that mark the most intimate aspects of the relationship between the citizen and the state.

Both rural Turkish and various Islamic modes of gender organization, bodily discipline, and the maintenance of honor are in many respects at odds with these German cultural practices. However, they are not necessarily incompatible with the principles of democracy that underlie the German nation-state and its constitutional foundation. But the possibility that other gender practices might be consistent with life in a liberal democracy such as Germany is rarely considered. The alternatives are, instead, stigmatized and abjected. The confounding of the universal and the local enables and renders invisible forms of stigmatization that would be difficult to justify if they were visible and explicit.

It has been argued that "there is no single narrative of the nation" because "different groups (genders, classes, ethnicities, generations, and so on) do not experience the myriad national formations in the same way" (McClintock 1997: 93). But can we nevertheless see traces of a hegemonic national imaginary even among those who are marginalized by it, including immigrants and others marked as outsiders? I argue that not only do these stigmatizations and the social fantasies associated with them constrain the possibilities for full cultural citizenship for a stigmatized minority, but also that traces of these stigmatizations are manifest by individuals as an array of strategies for the maintenance of a positive subjectivity and identity in the face of abjection. I therefore juxtapose German social fantasies of the Muslim man with the voices of diasporic men and women of Turkish background, examining traces of stigmatization in their negotiations of public identities. My goal is to make the stigmatization of a minority masculinity visible. I demonstrate how this stigmatization is naturalized through a hegemonic discourse emotionally structured by social fantasies and how a national and transnational imaginary based on such fantasies is produced through government institutions and public culture.

NATIONAL IMAGINARIES, NATIONAL SUBJECTS, AND THE PROCESS OF ABJECTION

Where does a hegemonic national imaginary come from? A national imaginary is based, at least in part, on ideas of the state[7] that are reproduced through what Foucault called *governmentality* (Foucault 1991)—an array of practices through which the population of a modern nation-state is governed, including institutions such as schools and the police, agencies for the provision of social services, discourses, norms, and even individual self-regulation through techniques for disciplining and caring for the self. These forms of governmentality encompass more than what might formally be called "the state." They simultaneously reproduce the state and its place in a global order and locate individuals as subjects within that order,[8] regulating the most intimate details of their lives such as marriage, birth control, and kinship relations as an aspect of the state's mission to optimize the welfare and productivity of its population.[9] Forms of governmentality include institutions that minorities must negotiate every day, institutions that have the potential to shape their practices and identities. As

Aihwa Ong has demonstrated, the provision of social services to immigrants converges with other techniques of administration to constitute "particular categories of citizen-subject" (Ong 2003: 6). Often, the provision of such services is accompanied by demands for conformity to local norms and by practices of recognition and misrecognition that marginalize those who fail to conform to dominant norms.[10] These practices thus constitute a minority subject in relation to the state as it is imagined by this subject through everyday experiences of governmentality.

In Germany, social service provision and the rights of minorities to governmental services have had a significant impact on the discourse about integration. The emphasis on irreconcilable cultural difference that pervades popular discourse and that is manifest in vociferous concerns about the establishment of a parallel society stems in part from specific forms of governmentality by which minority populations are categorized and managed. Frank-Olaf Radtke (1997) has argued that migrants to Germany were turned into "ethnic minorities" by policies of the German state. These policies foregrounded language and religion in providing immigrant social services and dealt with people in terms of their ethnic identity and group membership rather than in terms of their individual circumstances. The growing number of migrants was distributed among competing welfare organizations, which provided social services, split according to differences of language and religion associated with the migrants' countries of origin. Thus, migrants from Catholic countries were handled by Catholic welfare agencies, Protestants by Protestant agencies, and Muslims (primarily from Turkey but also from the Maghreb) by nondenominational organizations with links to trade unions.

This reified perspective on cultural difference in turn shaped the research questions pursued by social advisors and scholars, who, as experts, are in a position to generate authoritative "truths" that are the basis of social projects,[11] typically framed in terms of the "difficulties and conflicts of a life between cultures" (Radtke 1997: 252). For example, detailed reports of village life in Turkey were used to demonstrate how difficult integration would inevitably be for Turkish migrants. This focus on "culture" and the difficulties of integration penetrated into popular and political discourse, contributing to xenophobic political propaganda and negative stereotypes and creating increasing pressure to restrict immigration. Family structure and gender organization have been targeted directly by institutions such as shelters for women and girls and in policies that include removing children from the care of their parents if their rights as defined in the German Constitution have been violated. In this context, the categorization of Muslims as culturally different has directly affected social policy.

Popular culture and the media—literature, newspapers, cinema, and television—also play a central role in this discursive process of shaping national and transnational imaginaries and producing identity in the contemporary world (Abu-Lughod 1993, Appadurai 1996) by generating naturalized images that delineate the realm of the possible and even the possibilities for resistance (Appadurai 1996; Foucault 1978, 1995; Butler 1989).[12] These images are often crystallized in the form of stories that embed beliefs about the origins and evolution of the nation (Shohat and Stam 1994: 118), narratives that provide variously positioned citizens with possibilities or "scripts" for individual lives, and stereotypes that characterize identities associated with many of these various social positions. In Germany there has been a growing corpus of films about and by Turkish immigrants and their offspring. This cinema is one site where the stigmatization of Turkish Muslim masculinity by German directors and even by directors of Turkish background can be traced.

Cinematic images are particularly powerful when they are consistent with other forms of knowledge that are tied to governmentality—state policies, bureaucratic expertise, and social services—as well as to the scholarly apparatus that often guides policy formation.[13] When all of these forms of knowledge production are consistent in their articulations of the plight of the Turkish or Muslim woman caught in webs of traditional patriarchy, they converge to constitute a convincing truth about the problematic integration of the Turkish other into German society, a truth often focused on representations of Turkish and Muslim gender relations and the place of masculinity in this discourse. (In Chapter 2, I examine this discursive convergence of governmental practices, scholarly apparatus, cinema, and other media that maintains a national imaginary.)

Though governmentality, the knowledge of experts, and the media are formative of subjectivities and the idea of the state, they are not in themselves sufficient to account for the emergence of a national imaginary that produces the emotional intensities associated with the threat of an immigrant Muslim population and makes the stigmatization of Muslim men unnoticeable.[14] It is not simply a coincidence that the rather diverse forces of governmentality, scholarly knowledge, and the media converge. Furthermore, as Pierre Bourdieu (1977), Sherry Ortner (2006), and other "practice theorists" stress, individuals as discursively constituted subjects nevertheless have agency to draw on diverse discourses—alternative cultural logics—as they carry out projects that both reproduce and transform existing structures. These diverse projects are clearly evident in processes of political contestation, intergenerational struggles, ethnic strife, sexual politics, and class struggles, all of which reveal profound ruptures and divisions in the social fabric. Yet there is in most nation-states most of the time a tendency for a rather remarkable coherence amidst all of this diversity and contestation, a hegemonic discourse across a range of social fields. It involves, at the very least, implicit agreements about the terms of the debate, the objects of controversy. This discourse constitutes subjects with relatively fixed identities and a delimited range of perspectives on the nation, its past and future. How is this coherence produced and reproduced out of the flux of the myriad acts, desires, and forces that make up social life?

The coherence and "truth" of a hegemonic discourse that is grounded in a national imaginary relies on the intertwining of the imagined with conditions that prevail at any particular moment (Iser 1993: 1). This intertwining generates realities with a mythological structure[15] that people emotionally invest in through the process of fantasy. Cinema and other media are often structured through a mythological process in which the identities and attributes of people, events, and objects are deprived of their specificity and turned into gestures or attributes. These abstracted individuals are dichotomized and polarized, with some being idealized and others abjected.

Abjection occurs within a discursive order that is structured by making certain things unthinkable and certain subject positions uninhabitable. Within the discursive space of a national imaginary, desires and attributes that have been abjected as not-self in the formation of a national subject may be projected onto categories of people who are viewed as other. Rhetorical associations are made among objects and concepts that may be quite dissimilar, and the attention is drawn away from inconsistencies and logical slippages. As a result of this channeling, certain objects and signifiers acquire an otherwise unaccountably powerful emotional charge,[16] often of horror, and others become nearly invisible. Hence, stigmatization through the process of abjection often goes unnoticed. Those who inhabit unthinkable subject positions are not thought about in a straightforward way.

Fantasy operates by giving the fantasizer some sort of pleasure through the imagined fulfillment of a desire. An explicit desire that is often a focus of modern identity politics is positive recognition by another, a recognition that occurs within the context of "having" a certain identity. But to take up an identity as a particular type of subject, such as a heterosexual German male, means performing that identity—in this case, masculinity—in a socially acceptable way and renouncing or disavowing other desires that may be inconsistent with that identity. Other desires and other subject positions are foreclosed, abjected, made "not-self" as part of the process of identity formation, though these abjected desires are also an important, if ambivalent, component of fantasy.

A national imaginary reflects processes by which internal differences are suppressed through the deployment of elusive objects of desire as signifiers in political discourse, often made more powerful by the mobilization of a threat to the nation (see Žižek 1989; Santner 1990; Ivy 1995; Navaro-Yashin 2002).[17] It is a commonplace that talking politics can be a potentially disruptive business in any social setting because of the emotions that such talk arouses in many of us. From the rhetoric surrounding familiar themes such as the threat of the Muslim man (especially as manifest in media focus on honor killings and the headscarf), it is clear that these signs carry powerful affect that can be seen in political speech-making, the writings of journalists, and the everyday conversations of Germans. The affect associated with such signs is linked to the ways that they evoke elusive desires.

Among the most visible public expressions of affect are moments of crisis linked with what Stanley Cohen has dubbed *moral panics*: "A condition, episode, person or group of persons emerges to become defined as a threat to societal values and interests. . . . The moral barricades are manned by editors, bishops, politicians and other right-thinking people; socially accredited experts pronounce their diagnoses and solutions" (Cohen 1980: 9). The media play an important role in a politics of anxiety associated with moral panics. I argue that such moral panics acquire their emotional force by drawing rhetorical links between a current issue and latent, historically configured social fantasies associated with a national imaginary. Moral panics are an important means by which the public renews its emotional investments in a national imaginary.

The German national imaginary in the post-1989 period of reunification has involved a reimagining of Germanness (see Borneman 1991), a remapping of homeland (Verdery 1991), and new ways of imagining nationhood. In post–World War II Germany, this process has been particularly ambivalent, especially with respect to the provision of a historical memory that prioritizes the nation, its origins, and its cultural traditions as elements of a national imaginary. Thus, there has been recurring political controversy in Germany surrounding the idea of a German *Leitkultur* (leading culture) to which immigrants might be made to conform. Yet the word is basically devoid of content since any effort to attach a specific meaning is contaminated with associations to symbols prominent during the Nazi era. As I argue in Chapter 7, *Leitkultur* thus operates as a signifier that evokes desired yet ambivalent aspects of Germanness that are threatened and produced by the presence of the immigrant. Much of the emotional force of such fantasies comes from the ways in which they trigger *jouissance.*[18] that is, pleasure associated with that which has been abjected, an unsatisfiable desire that becomes attached to politically powerful signifiers.

Both gender and the place of self within hierarchies are essential components of the process of imagining nationhood. The modern nation-state provides models for the ordering of individuals and the organization of gender as part of its educational and regulatory apparatus. The fears and desires of individuals can be powerfully evoked through perceived threats to these fundamental aspects of social order, and thus they constitute an important part of the underpinning of a national imaginary. Gender, as the fundamental social difference rooted in every individual's earliest experiences, rests on a foundation of renunciation of early desires and abjection of infantile attachments that forms the subject as a social being. Sexuality and gender organization are not merely practices to be dispassionately regulated and organized by the state. Gender and social hierarchies are fundamental aspects of our experience and identity and often serve as material for social fantasies. Even when a minority is granted full legal rights, these collective fantasies can be a source of basic challenges to the possibilities for full cultural citizenship, especially if the minority has been stigmatized and abjected.

MASCULINITY AND THE GENDERING OF THE NATION

As Simone de Beauvoir observed many years ago, "One is not born a woman, but rather becomes one" (de Beauvoir 1953: 267). Men, too, are fashioned by the cultural and political forces that converge on the particular situation of their existence. But, as de Beauvoir argued, it is woman who has been marked as other and inferior in Western thought and institutions. Following the inspiration of scholars like de Beauvoir, feminist scholars in the second half of the twentieth century set out to transform the position of women by making woman and her subordinate position an object of study. Studies of men and masculinity in the United States eventually followed, with considerable emphasis on the tensions that many men feel as they experience the pressures of conforming to the normative masculinity that has played so powerful a role in the subordination of women.[19] This normative masculinity has been characterized by heterosexuality, emotional control, aggressive social dominance, and success in the workplace.

Along with the social pressure that has accompanied the struggle for women's equality have emerged new models of masculinity that stress a move away from the "macho" toward interactional styles characterized by traits typically associated with "feminine" behavior.[20] At the same time, there has been great interest in exploring the limits of masculinity and the stigmatizations associated with homosexuality and "gender bending," within the context of the gay rights movement and the effort to normalize and celebrate alternative sexualities and gender orientations in the face of a powerful normative heterosexual masculinity.

Virtually unrecognized in this evolving discourse on masculinities, however, has been another site of stigmatization, one that is implicit in the preceding paragraph. Many of us consider ourselves "politically correct" when we criticize the dominant white male for his macho behavior and demeanor. The term *macho*, a Spanish word that has entered English as well as German and many other northern European languages, is often used as an insult in English, especially in educated and professional circles. In the United States, the form of masculinity associated with machismo is highly stigmatized and stereotyped: "As defined by U.S. society, the concept of 'machismo' has distinct negative overtones. Being macho is often associated with being a wife-beater, a philanderer, a drunk, a 'bien gallo'—a fighter, like a rooster" (Rodriguez and Gonzales 1997). What often goes unnoticed by Americans who identify themselves as politically correct is that in the United States this label was applied first to Latin American men and has contributed to their marginalization. Here is the perspective of a Hispanic journalist:

> What is macho? That depends on which side of the border you come from. Although it's not unusual for words and expressions to lose their subtlety in translation, the negative connotations of "macho" in the U.S. are troublesome to Hispanics. . . . The Hispanic "macho" is manly, responsible, hard-working, a man in charge, a patriarch. A man who expresses strength through silence. What the Yiddish language would call a "mensch." The American "macho" is a chauvinist, a brute, uncouth, selfish, loud, abrasive, capable of inflicting pain, and sexually promiscuous. (del Castillo Guilbault 1996)

"Othering" through racism and through discrimination against minorities is commonly manifested as a denigration of the masculinity of the other. Thanks to the strength and success of the civil rights movement and the accompanying rise of African American studies, many people in the United States have been sensitized to the racial stigmatization of African Americans, and the legacy of racist clichés about the hypersexed, animal-like black man has been deconstructed (see, for example, Collins 2004). Nevertheless, such stigmatizations persist, as in feminist writings that problematize African American masculinity. Though writers such as bell hooks usually locate the source of problematic expressions of masculinity such as "coolness" in the "patriarchal imperialism" of the U.S. society in which these men live (hooks 2003), they nevertheless reproduce stereotypical generalizations about the black male.

Latino studies have more recently begun to question hegemonic stereotypes of Latino men (for example, Gutmann 1996) as the discipline becomes academically established, though questioning this perspective has not yet penetrated very far into U.S. public discourse. It has been recognized that the "mistranslation" of the word *macho* has had consequences for the identity of the Latino male: "Drunkenness, abusing women, raising hell . . . are some mistaken conceptions of what macho means" (Anaya 1996: 59). Journalists seeking to disrupt this naturalized stigmatization of machismo have observed: "the uninformed often point to such behavior and call it machismo. In fact, much of this negative behavior is aped by a new generation, because as young men they are not aware that they are being conditioned. Young men acting contrary to the good of their community have not yet learned the essence of maleness" (Rodriguez and Gonzales 1997). Not only has it become an accepted stereotype that is often applied indiscriminately to all Hispanic men; it may also affect the self-esteem, identities, and behavior of Hispanic youth in the United States. As one of the founders of a group of professional Latino men whose goal is to instill positive values in young Latino men observed: "This confuses young males. . . . And some young Latinos fulfill this distorted definition of manhood by acting out a false manliness in response to living in a foreign culture where they feel emasculated by racism and a lack of educational and job opportunities" (Rodriguez and Gonzales 1997).[21] A similar unreflective stigmatization of a culturally labeled masculinity is a significant force that shapes discussions of Muslim minorities in Europe that in turn affects the possibilities for identification among Muslim men in Germany.

The stigmatization of Muslim men in terms of women's rights is a longstanding element of Western discourse. The Bush administration used the argument for women's rights as part of the justification of the war in Afghanistan, as in Laura Bush's radio address to the nation in the wake of the September 11 attacks on the World Trade Center and the Pentagon: "The fight against terrorism is also a fight for the rights and dignity of women" (Bush 2001). Statements such as this echo the arguments of earlier colonial administrators in South Asia and the Middle East, who used them to justify similar invasions and paternalistic policies (see Abu-Lughod 2002).[22] Such justifications often rhetorically equate "radical Islam," the oppression of women, and the cultural practices of Muslim men more generally.

The colonies were the site of other stigmatizations of the manhood of colonized subjects, not all of which focused on disrupting local gender roles. In some cases, representations of gendered subjectivity signified the power relationship between colonized and colonizer (Scott 1989; Stoler 1995), as in the case of the male Indian subject, who was depicted as feminine in relation to the manly Englishman. This was particularly true, for example, of the "effeminate Bengali babu," as the British characterized Bengali intellectuals in the late nineteenth century (Sinha 1995). Stigmatization is a symbolic process that creates a hierarchical relationship between self and other. But in colonial representations, there was often a profound ambivalence toward this other, a tension between the hypersexed, patriarchal savage and the effeminate, subordinate other, sometimes alternating in representations of the same other, generating an uncanny tension. This "other" masculinity is stigmatized and forms the abjected ground on which the European's dominant masculinity rests (see Bhabha 1995; Fanon 1967; Stoler 1989).

The theme of masculinity is thus deployed to stigmatize a minority as part of the process of forming a national subject. In Germany, especially during the extreme nationalism of the National Socialist period, the masculinity of the pure-blooded German was a focus of symbolic elaboration and physical discipline. The masculinity of the Jew as stigmatized other was, in contrast, denigrated, usually by representing the Jewish male as effeminate in sometimes fantastic ways. In the postwar period, the national project of shaping a democratic subject has involved a shift in the ideals of German masculinity away from a militaristic, hierarchical subjectivity toward an egalitarian orientation grounded in constitutional patriotism. Despite this reformation, there are continuities in the process of subject formation itself, founded as it is on an ever-present act of negation of forms of nationalism associated with Nazism.[23] This reformed masculine subject is also grounded on a stigmatized other—an other that has similarly been transformed so that the qualities of masculinity embodied by this other stand in contrast to those of the ideal masculine subject. At this historical juncture, the Turkish Muslim man, as a member of the currently largest minority in Germany, is a signifier that is readily at hand to embody this stigmatized masculinity.

THE TURKISH MINORITY IN GERMANY
AND THE ISSUE OF INTEGRATION

Turkish guestworkers (*Gastarbeiter*) began to flow into Germany in the 1960s to meet the demand for low-cost labor during Germany's post–World War II economic boom years. The need for a large number of foreign laborers developed suddenly with the construction of the Berlin Wall and the sealing of the border between East and West Germany in 1961. These laborers were explicitly called "guests," in contrast to the term used for foreign workers (*Fremdarbeiter*) who had been enslaved during the Nazi era (Herbert and Hunn 2001: 191). Most came directly from rural Anatolia rather than from cosmopolitan urban areas, exacerbating the cultural distance between these immigrants and an urban German population. They were meant to be a rotating, primarily male workforce and were given short-term contracts, were housed in hostels apart from established neighborhoods, and received minimal social services. But this arrangement was inefficient for employers, who preferred to renew contracts, thereby creating a more long-term labor force (O'Brien 1996). When the economy faltered in the early 1970s, the German government banned further labor recruitment, but workers already in the country were allowed to remain and to bring their families into Germany. These pragmatic responses to changing conditions led to a gradual modification of policy, without any publicly conscious decision to open the country to migration.

In the early years, these workers remained on the fringes of German society as temporary residents. At first, both Germans and the migrants themselves imagined that they would one day return to Turkey, an imaginary that has been called the *myth of return*. But by the 1980s it became clear to many of these families and to the German public that most of these migrants were in Germany to stay, and German public discourse began to frame the "problem" of their apparent lack of integration into German society. The adolescent girl who is expected to wear a headscarf, pulled out of school at a young age, kept close to home, and forced to marry a relative from Turkey became a powerful symbol of cultural and religious difference and the failure of Turks to embrace assimilation.

Though Turkey is a country with a Muslim majority and most of the Turkish migrants to Germany are of Muslim background, many Turks are quite secular in orientation.[24] Turkey became a secular state in 1924, following the collapse of the Ottoman Empire and the founding of the Turkish Republic. Old religious institutions such as the Sufi orders and schools for the training of imams were shut down.[25] Mosques came under the control of the state-run Directorate of Religious Affairs, and clothing associated with Islam and the Ottomans was banned.[26] Various institutions such as state-run schools and the military have played a central role in inculcating secularism as a core element of the state's project to modernize the population and create a Turkish national subject. In the early 1980s, a new wave of migration to Europe was triggered by the 1980 military coup in Turkey. Thousands of activists, many of them intellectuals, were imprisoned and tortured, and a significant number fled as refugees to Germany and other European countries. These refugees, many of whom were secularist leftists or actively involved in Islamic groups,[27] played a major role in establishing newspapers and other organizations for Turks in Germany. Given their institutional positioning, many of those who came as refugees have been highly visible and have disproportionately influenced public representations of the Turkish population in Germany.

The exuberant fall of the Berlin Wall in 1989 and the ensuing reunification of East and West Germany were followed by intense public debate around articulations of national identity and citizenship, including the place in the future of a united Germany of Turkish and other Muslims as Germany's largest minority. These debates about citizenship were also accompanied by expressions of xenophobia and ethnic violence that targeted the Turkish population. Anti-immigrant sentiment was especially strong in the former Eastern states, which underwent profound social and economic transformations during the reunification process. Turkish communities experienced considerable fear for their safety throughout Germany. The political rhetoric calling for foreigner-free zones (*ausländerfreie Zonen*) and a number of brutal attacks on Turkish families by neo-Nazis sharpened public awareness of integration issues and generated intensified support among liberal Germans for the competing idea of Germany as a "multicultural" society. Though the liberalization of citizenship laws, away from the principle of descent or "blood" (*jus sanguinis*) to the principle of place of birth (*jus soli*), was slow in coming—becoming law in a limited form in 2000—and restrictions on dual citizenship are still onerous, increasing numbers of second- and third-generation Turks have opted for German citizenship and are becoming more involved in the political process. But many continue to be troubled by media and political representations of Turks and Muslims as well as the "failure" of integration, a rhetoric that has been exacerbated by the increased fear of Muslims after September 11, 2001, and the rising strength of nationalist, socially conservative politicians across Europe.

Even before September 11, escalating nationalism and xenophobia in both Europe and the United States were associated with burgeoning immigrant populations. Aside from the powerful rhetorical links that are now made between Muslim immigrants and terrorism, many people fear increasing social unrest and the chaos of disintegration that a growing minority population threatens to bring. One conservative German politician, Hans-Peter Uhl of the Christian Social Union, expressed these concerns in the following terms: "Nine percent of the current German population consists of immigrants. While this percentage is relatively small, the immigrant population can be a social problem when there are too many foreigners in your workplace, in the streets, in your apartment building, and in your child's classroom. . . . There are 7 million foreigners living in Germany, and the main political question is how to integrate them into society."[28] The murder of Theo van Gogh in the Netherlands in November 2004 and the rioting of Muslim youth in France in the fall of 2005 brought discussion of the problems of integration even more fully into public discourse in many European countries. Best-selling Dutch author Leon de Winter, for example, spoke about minority problems in the Netherlands: "The problems began when the first guest workers arrived in Holland—as soon as we let people from the third world come here to work in our rich country, we had a guilt complex and somehow saw them as sacred victims. We then let them bring their wives and children over without having any clue that we were importing integration problems with which we had no experience" (Spiegel Online 2006).

Concern with the problem of immigrants is not limited to a vocal conservative wing. On the contrary, Uhl spoke as he did to an American scholarly audience (a Fulbright seminar) precisely because attention to the "question of immigration" and its problems is of concern to people across the political spectrum. Though liberals and conservatives in countries such as Germany differ sharply on how to solve the nagging problems associated with the integration of immigrants and especially Muslims into their society, and though they approach these problems in divergent ways, few question the fact that integration has thus far been fraught with problems that have escalated since the 1990s. The mainstream media, policy makers, and many scholars take as a given that integrating minorities into European society is one of Europe's primary and worsening social challenges.

Debates over how integration should be accomplished are intense. These debates are grounded, not as much in disagreements about tactics, as in fundamental principles involving competing visions of the nation, the meaning of citizenship, the nature of identity, and the desirability of difference. And there are always concerns, expressed both in the media and among scholars, about the "problems" of integration and, especially during periods of high levels of immigration, an agonized search for an understanding of why integration has thus far "failed," why the social segregation of Turks into ethnic enclaves is growing (see, for example, Heitmeyer, Müller, and Schröder 1997; Leggewie 2000) and ethnic self-identification is increasing (Münz, Siefert, and Ulrich 1997: 103), and how social policy can be legislated and adjusted to fix the perceived problems. These concerns are often manifested in firestorms of controversy around events and symbols that seem to crystallize the evidence for failure and make it visible to the public eye. Most of these points of conflict have revolved around the organization of gender, as represented by the headscarf and honor killing.

Despite all of this hand-wringing, public and political angst over the "failure" of integration cannot necessarily be taken at face value. In the case of Turks in Germany, recriminations about the failures of integration (both blame assigned to immigrants and self-blame for failed policies and inaction), so starkly expressed during controversies such as these, are out of joint with evidence from studies which have shown that Turkish immigrants in Germany have by some measures actually done quite well. For example, 55 percent of immigrants from Turkey and 93 percent of the second generation speak German well (Heckmann 1997: 3). Most members of the second generation are by a number of social, cultural, and economic measures closer to "native-born" Germans than they are to their immigrant parents (Fertig 2004; Kogan 2003).[29] Economic and sociological literature on continuing disparities in educational attainment and job mobility tends to focus explanations for these disparities on problems of measurement[30] and the obstacles to integration, usually locating the sources of these obstacles in the German educational system, legal system (especially restrictions on access to citizenship), occupational structure, and social discrimination. For first-generation guestworkers these obstacles have also included limited knowledge of German, lack of education (exacerbated by the near-total discounting of Turkish educational credentials), and the perception for many years that the stay of guestworkers was temporary, a perception that made employers unwilling to invest in on-the-job training for unskilled workers (Kogan 2003: 2). Immigrants' children who were raised in Germany continue to face some structural constraints, including a lack of social capital, geographical segregation, and discrimination due to social origin (Kogan 2003: 2). Furthermore, ambivalence about the process of integration has been pervasive at the level of policy goals, with some policies aimed at furthering acculturation and assimilation and other policies—often associated with an ideology of multiculturalism—aimed at fostering a process of minority formation, reinforcing the ethnic identity of the family and the development of minority institutions (Heckmann 1997). Thus, most quantitative empirical research locates the reasons for continuing disparities in the educational and occupational attainments of minorities in structural obstacles but also indicates that integration is nevertheless proceeding at a good pace.

In contrast to the focus among quantitative social scientists on structural barriers, public and political discourse tends to focus on "culture" as the cause of failure. The integration process is said to fail because of the cultural backwardness and religious orientation of Turkish immigrants and an associated lack of motivation, all of which contribute to these immigrants resisting assimilation when given the opportunity.[31] From this perspective, any visible tendencies of immigrants to "cling" to cultural traditions become evidence confirming this resistance. In addition to the headscarf and other practices associated with Islam or village tradition such as honor killing, Germans often point to phenomena such as the large number of satellite dishes, which receive broadcasts directly from Turkey, in Turkish neighborhoods as evidence of the unwillingness of the people in those neighborhoods to integrate. Recent rhetoric in the German media has called for legislation that would force Turks to give up certain cultural practices and become more like Germans. In this rhetoric, the concept of culture is a key term used to define the Turkish minority as outsiders.

AN ETHNOGRAPHY OF FANTASY: TRACING MASCULINITY THROUGH THE GERMAN NATIONAL IMAGINARY

Instead of asking what the "problems" of integration are or why it has "failed," as the German public is often inclined to do, or becoming mired in the ambivalence that characterizes policy debates about assimilation versus minority formation and multiculturalism, I consider who talks about integration and its failures, how they talk about it, in what contexts, and to what ends in order to examine the stigmatization of masculinity and of Muslim gender practices more generally. By asking what work such perceptions and statements are doing for those who utter them, I find that a key silence surrounds the situation of the Turkish Muslim man in Europe. This silence masks how the stigmatization of Muslim and Turkish masculinities has been used as a strategy to manage immigrants and consolidate German national identity. I delineate the intensities and silences that are produced through the practices of governmentality, public debates, and the media as manifestations of a structure of social fantasy that underlies a German national imaginary. I argue that this fantasy rests on a foundation of abjection of a social other. This German national imaginary is, therefore, a force in the constitution of cultural citizenship, distinguishing those who fully belong from those who do not. By examining how diasporic, stigmatized Turkish Muslim men deploy and resist prevailing stereotypes, I also identify how this national imaginary, with its stigmatization of Muslim masculinity, leaves its traces on those who have been abjected. I then focus on moments of national controversy and moral panic when the processes of abjection in the constitution of a German national imaginary become explicit.

This book is an ethnographic study of public culture and the discursive construction of the nation. Anthropology has ventured into novel realms of inquiry that transcend the confines of "the field" as a geographically delimited space. Questions such as the discursive constitution of a stigmatized masculinity and its relationship to a national imaginary cannot be studied solely through face-to-face interactions by simply "being there."[32] The limits of ethnography have expanded to encompass new forms of data collection and the methodological blurring of disciplinary boundaries, resulting in a productive juxtaposition of sources. Such sometimes surprising juxtapositions, along with a willingness to suspend judgment on what should be selected as data and an openness to looking at a phenomenon in many different ways, have always been the hallmark of ethnography. I thus make a number of what might be construed as startling juxtapositions—anthropological ethnographies of rural Turkey with nineteenth-century German travel diaries; newspaper articles, films, and the writings of social workers. In a quest to identify the recurrent, self-evident truths and fantasies that underlie the coherence of a national imaginary, I interweave interpretations of media and scholarly sources with analyses of conversations and interviews with men and women of Turkish background living in Germany; with knowledge of families of Turkish background gained from living with such families for short periods of time and from knowing individuals over several years; and with conversations with German students, social workers, and educators.

Part 1 focuses on the historical sources of the discursive strands that come together to naturalize representations of the Turkish man as stigmatized other and manifestations of the resulting stigmatizations in identity negotiations among men of Turkish background. I begin in Chapter 1 by tracing the roots of this positioning of the Turk and the Muslim man as other in Germany. I identify several strands, ranging across academic scholarship on the Ottoman Empire, the anthropological construct of the "honor-shame complex," nineteenth-century European travel accounts, twentieth-century Turkish efforts to construct a nation of modern cosmopolitan citizens, a transnational discourse of gender equality, and ethnographies of the Turkish village. I suggest a convergence in their representations of Turkish masculinity that naturalizes understandings of cultural difference within German discourse.

Chapter 2 draws a contrast between the cultural stereotypes that structure social fantasy and the micropolitics of everyday life by exploring the powerful theme of rescuing the Muslim woman as it has appeared in German social work literature and in cinema. I argue that these distinct genres, the former playing a significant role in the shaping of practices of governmentality that affect the lives of minorities and the latter projecting widely disseminated images into public spaces, materialize cultural difference and stigmatization.

In Chapters 3 and 4, I consider manifestations of stigmatization and abjection among men who themselves occupy the subject position of stigmatized masculinity by examining the micropolitics of the research situation itself. Chapter 3 focuses on how assumptions of cultural otherness shape the research even of scholars who seek to present the experiences of men. Drawing on interpretive perspectives gained from my own research over the course of several years in Germany between 1999 and 2005,[33] I analyze the performance and negotiation of discursively constituted identities in the interview process. I examine how men manifest tensions and ambivalences about how to inhabit conflictual identities in the face of stigmatization and the extent to which such tensions play out around issues associated with this stigmatized masculinity. In Chapter 4, I focus on honor. I consider how filmmakers and other men of Turkish background negotiate issues of reputation and self-respect in a world where the concept of honor is associated with traditional masculinity and is a primary target of stigmatization.

In Part 2 I move to a series of controversies that manifest social panic surrounding the Turkish Muslim immigrant population and expose the abjection of the Turkish and Muslim man in the German national imaginary. The rhetoric surrounding these controversies indicates that these signs carry a powerful emotional charge focused on the threat of the Muslim man that can be seen, not only in the writings of journalists, but also in the everyday conversations of Germans. These controversies emerge from a discourse that locates the Muslim man and the Turk in specific ways as other.

Chapter 5 focuses on the extensive media coverage following an honor killing in Berlin in 2005, in which a young woman was murdered by her brother or brothers because they objected to her nontraditional lifestyle. For many Germans this controversy threw into relief the extent to which Muslims were moving in the direction of a parallel society, an enclave in which the honor of the Muslim man, the foundation of his masculinity, rests on a principle of violence fundamentally incompatible with the principles of modern German citizenship.

Some of the proposed solutions to problems of integration have also generated controversy. These controversies, many of which have developed over citizenship legislation and efforts to further the integration of Muslims into German society, have become symbols that reveal the fault lines within German national identity as well as the problematic position of immigrants within German society. I foreground these controversies, which define Muslim gender practices in the German media and mark the Muslim man as other. By delineating this otherness, they also reveal the contours of cultural citizenship in Germany today.

In 2006, a controversial "Muslim Test" was developed to serve as a guideline for determining the suitability of applicants for German citizenship. The questions on this test reveal the specific points at which the essence of Germanness is seen to collide with Muslimness or Turkishness. In Chapter 6, I examine the controversy surrounding this test within the context of debates over specific Islamic practices that many in the German public find troublesome: the wearing of headscarves by female teachers and the exemption of Muslim girls from school gym classes. These controversies expose the intimate linkages among gender, bodily practices, and the state, as well their foundation in social fantasies. A German discourse of the body and notions of bodily purity are directly challenged by Muslim practices.

One particularly intense debate erupted in 2000 after a conservative German politician proposed that the idea of *Leitkultur* be a standard for assimilation.

Controversy erupted because the term evoked memories of Nazism. Chapter 7 examines this controversy and some of the social fantasies of nationhood associated with it. Notions of Germanness and the need to protect the essence of German national identity in the face of large numbers of Turkish Muslim immigrants came into sharp relief during the *Leitkultur* controversy. In this discourse, the Muslim man is often posed as a threat to the German Constitution, revealing the culturally peculiar significance of the postwar Constitution as it is used to articulate the rights of the citizen as an autonomous liberal subject. Ironically, constitutional patriotism, an ideological principle developed to guard against discriminatory forms of nationalism in the name of democracy, has become the basis for abjecting a minority by characterizing this minority as an embodiment of the nondemocratic traditional other.

MYTHOLOGIZING THE "TRADITIONAL" MAN   **Part 1**

1 IMAGINING TRADITION
The Turkish Villager

THE IMAGE OF THE OPPRESSED TURKISH MUSLIM WOMAN is a symbol for the cultural challenge of absorbing large Muslim immigrant populations into German and other European societies, just as, for two centuries, the position of women in Islam has been central to a powerful Western narrative of the quintessential otherness and inferiority of Muslim social formations. Despite Edward Said's far-reaching intervention into Western scholarship and public discourse through the delineation of the discursive structure of Orientalism (1978), the dichotomies that he challenged—between West and East, modernity and tradition, vigorous globalizing society and a civilization in decline—continue to shape conversations about the problems of integration. It is a discourse in which Muslim and Turkish models of manhood and gender organization have been reified and portrayed as utterly alien to modern society, both in Turkey and in Germany.

In this chapter I trace the genealogies of contemporary representations of Turkish and Muslim manhood, focusing on several distinct genres that have been generated by differently positioned actors operating with very different goals. These actors range from nineteenth-century Western travelers who began to visit sites within the Ottoman Empire in increasing numbers in the mid-nineteenth century, to twentieth-century anthropologists looking to describe and analyze traditional social and cultural structures and the effects of modernization on Turkish villages, to late-twentieth-century Turkish feminists and scholars concerned with equal rights for women whose perspectives have been shaped not only by transnational feminisms but also by the history of Turkish nationalism and secularism. These diverse discursive strands have converged to generate a limited range of hegemonic representations of Turkish manhood.

The convergence of these strands is not coincidental. It is the manifestation of a deeper discursive process, the juggernaut of modernity and "Western" values, which rests on the postulate that Enlightenment ideas of individual freedom and equality can be universalized and are the legitimate standard against which all other ways of life are to be judged. By tracing the history of these images of Muslim and Turkish men, my goal is to disrupt this often implicit universalized standard, to foreground the contingent nature of these images, and to indicate how they emerge from the recurrent effects of European power and its Orientalist gaze. Making explicit the continuities and shifts within this discourse also parochializes images of the modern Western man, challenging their foundation in a universalized understanding of modernity by questioning the contrasts that are made between him and the culturally backward Turkish Muslim man.

What are the dominant images that recur in media representations and everyday conversations about the Turkish Muslim minority in Germany? The most blatantly stereotypical formulations map the dichotomy of modernity-tradition onto Germany-Turkey, so that Germany is understood as modern and Turkey as traditional. This is especially common within the context of discussions of Turkish men, despite obvious manifestations of Turkish cosmopolitanism (and German traditionalism) in other contexts such as advertisements for tourism and German political debates that draw on Turkey's secularism to reinforce arguments in favor of banning the headscarf in the German classroom. Much of this discourse about the traditional man revolves around the concept of *honor*. As traditional honor is understood, it subsumes all of the dimensions that mark Turkish masculinity as not-modern: a group orientation rather than individuality, given that honor is a property of the family rather than the individual; the hierarchical control of women and submission to elders rather than equality; a gendered division of labor in which women are forced to do most of the work while men relax and socialize in order to maintain their status and dignity; violation of the autonomy of women and, hence, the basic legal principle of the free and autonomous subject. Honor is also viewed as a prime motive for violence, which is seen as a characteristic behavior of the traditional Turkish Muslim man.

The actions of Turkish men vis-à-vis their families tend to be understood as a manifestation of a traditional masculinity based on the maintenance of family honor through hierarchical authority, the control of women, and violence. For those men who have integrated into German society, however, their adaptation is usually taken as evidence that they have given up their Turkish culture and adopted a modern, egalitarian orientation and individualistic autonomy. I question this dichotomizing assumption.

Public focus on honor as the core conceptual framework for thinking about the Turkish Muslim man is in many respects a popularization of the concept of the *honor-shame complex*, which was developed within the discipline of anthropology and in the 1960s was identified as characteristic of the whole Mediterranean region (see Péristiany 1966). I begin with a discussion of the anthropological theorization of this concept of honor and provide a context for it more specifically within the ethnographic literature on the Turkish village. I then turn to earlier representations of Turkish men, looking at recurrent images that appear in histories of the Ottoman Empire and in Western travel writing. German historians have over time been quite active in scholarship on the Ottoman Empire and have viewed the Ottoman through a lens that reflected German preoccupations with national character.[1] The European travelogue is a genre that goes back more than two hundred years. In these travel writings, shifts in how men and women are represented can be identified in ways that throw into relief how historically contingent current views of traditional Turkish Muslim gender practices are.

Finally, I consider twentieth-century perspectives within Turkey itself. I look at the scholarship of Turkish gender scholars within the context of the modernizing, secularist discourse of the Turkish state, which was established in the early 1920s and has from its inception seen the transformation of gender relations to be an important component of the constitution of the modern Turkish citizen. This discourse casts traditional village life and its organization of gender in a generally negative light. Turkish feminist arguments for gender equality have gone even further and tended to emphasize the extent to which even the modernizing state has retained its patriarchal organization, often in the name of preserving Turkish culture.

ANTHROPOLOGY AND THE CONCEPT OF HONOR

Anthropological ethnographies of the Turkish village have sought to present an insider's view of village life, as if from the villager's own perspective. A recent trend within anthropology has been to return to rurally focused ethnographies in order to situate local practices and actions as integral to national and global processes. Earlier ethnographies, in contrast, were the products of a discipline that distinguished itself from sociology and history by its focus on the non-modern. The goal was to describe and analyze the social structure of a village, its culture, or both as they existed before their transformation by the forces of modernity, as if village structure and culture were timeless traditions separate from the forces of history. This approach tended to create a sharp boundary between the modern man and the traditional man and to detach the village from modernity, confining it to the boundaries of tradition or culture, thereby reinforcing the archaic quality of a traditional masculinity that was discursively linked to the village. Many of these studies addressed the question of social change associated with the growing presence of the Turkish state at the village level and the large out-migration of villagers but framed this change in terms of the loss of tradition and viewed the state as external to village life, as Yael Navaro-Yashin has pointed out (2002).[2]

Within the anthropological tradition, the honor-shame complex is an influential, if now discredited, concept that has become a stereotype of gender relations from Spain to Turkey (Herzfeld 1987: 76). In the 1960s it came to be the defining feature of a Mediterranean culture area with the publication of J. G. Péristiany's edited volume *Honour and Shame: The Values of Mediterranean Society* (1966). At that time, the discipline's organization of cultural phenomena into "culture areas" resulted in the concept of honor bearing the burden of delimiting the Mediterranean area, much as caste did for South Asia or the "big man" complex did for Melanesia. In addition to creating an artificial boundary between the Mediterranean and other areas, the concept gave rise to an overemphasis on the elements that were seen to constitute this peculiarly Mediterranean cultural complex and a neglect of other aspects of social life. The honor-shame complex became a cultural essence that sharply distinguished its practitioners from modernity, even though Péristiany's book itself focused primarily on southern Europe and drew links with the structure of honor in Western Europe more broadly. The idea of an honor-shame complex was challenged by Michael Herzfeld (1980), who argued that such terms of moral valuation must be understood within specific linguistic and social contexts and suggested that the term *honor* as a general analytic category be replaced by the more neutral concept of *reputation* (Herzfeld 1980: 348), thereby attempting to disrupt the us-them dichotomy that the term honor had come to embody. Several years later, David Gilmore (1987) revisited the concept with an edited volume in which he acknowledged that honor and shame are basic organizing mechanisms in nearly all small communities or face-to-face groups such as gangs. He nevertheless sought to maintain the distinctiveness of the Mediterranean complex by foregrounding the specific linkage of male honor and female sexuality, thereby placing an even greater analytic burden on stereotyped gender differences in the conceptualization of honor.

Carol Delaney's ethnographic study of gender organization and its cultural logic in a Turkish (Anatolian) village, *The Seed and the Soil* (1991), focused directly on concepts of gender in rural Turkey. It is an instance of the interpretive approach to culture that characterized a dominant strand of American anthropology in the 1970s. Her argument supported the idea of a regional honor-shame complex by seeing it as the manifestation of a cultural system of meaning characteristic of the monotheistic worldview that had its roots in the Middle East. (Delaney contributed a chapter to Gilmore's 1987 volume.)

Delaney argued that women are subordinated through a pervasive cultural metaphor that gives the male the active role in creation and procreation and presumes the woman to be merely the environment, the "soil," that makes the seed of procreation successful. Aside from her characterization of a single cultural metaphor as the essence of Turkish village culture, encapsulated in her title, her argument makes an interpretive leap from the idea that a man is the source of generative life force and a woman is the soil that must be fertilized and protected to the analytic label "patriarchy." Her analysis ignores the possibility that villagers draw on competing sources of meaning and a range of interpretive strategies in their everyday negotiations and activities.

The analytic bias generated by the culture area framework has passed from anthropology into the media. Even as such area-delimited conceptualizations became obsolete within anthropology, the complex came to be viewed outside of anthropology in terms of "a cultural essence, an intractable and problematic 'syndrome,'" as Amanda Weidman has concisely put it (Weidman 2003: 520).

When one looks at other ethnographically based analyses of honor and its role in the enactment of masculinity, some of the oversimplifications of the popular stereotype become apparent. Even in Péristiany's early volume, the complex as it has come to be known—in which men's honor is a group rather than an individual phenomenon and is defined in terms of men's success at controlling the sexuality of their women—was not the primary focus of analysis. The chapter by Pierre Bourdieu, for example, focused on honor as a "sentiment" that is enacted in a "dialectic of challenge and riposte" among the Kabyle of northern Algeria (Bourdieu 1966: 197), in which men jockey for self-respect and public recognition, both for themselves as individuals and for their families, through a complex set of strategies that establish and maintain honor in the face of various challenges. This dialectic is similar to the *eghoismos* (aggressive self-regard) that Herzfeld (1985) analyzed in the performance of masculinity among Cretan shepherds. Bourdieu demonstrated how the term honor actually encompasses several distinct categories among the Kabyle, only some of which focus on defending one's home and one's women.

Other ethnographic studies disrupted the idea of a unitary culture complex by foregrounding how terms glossed as "honor" are configured and used distinctively in different regions and communities. Michael Meeker (1976), for example, compared honor as a system of meaning among Black Sea Turks and Levantine Arabs and found that, though the system of meaning was similar for both, resting on a distinction between (in Arabic) *sharaf* (honor in a broad sense) and *'ard* (sexual honor), the cultural structuring of that system was significantly different in the two societies, resulting in differing relationships between the two categories that had important implications for behavior.[3] Lila Abu-Lughod's study of honor and poetry in a Bedouin society identified quite a different ideology of honor that "serves to rationalize social inequality . . . in a system that idealizes the equality of agnates and the autonomy of individuals." In this system women share these ideals, even though "their path to honor . . . is different" (Abu-Lughod 1986: 33). Furthermore, Abu-Lughod demonstrated that this ideology of honor is not all-encompassing by identifying expressions of sentiment in poetry that articulate quite a different sense of self.

Terms that can be translated roughly as "honor" abound in Turkish, beyond the two categories Meeker identified.[4] Each, of course, has its specific history and range of contexts in which it might be appropriately deployed in the negotiation of social positioning, power, and self-esteem. The term *şeref* (the Arabic *sharaf*, discussed by Meeker) is used across the Muslim world to describe a man's reputation within the community. Within the context of Islam, the term is associated with the prophet Muhammad to mean someone whose actions and orientations are moral. *Şeref* is also associated with the accomplishments of one's male kin and ancestors and can be used as a kind of class marker of social worth.

In Turkey, *şeref* has also come to be associated with performing military service, an important instance of how an apparently traditional institution was given new meaning through the intervention of state institutions in the early Republican period. The introduction of universal military service was linked to efforts to reorganize the structure of public life and the family away from a masculine public constituted of elder heads of extended households and the elite to a broader public composed of heads of nuclear families (Mardin 1969). The performance of military service became a crucial marker of adulthood for men: "In order to be recognized as equal participants in the public sphere, [men] needed only to perform military service and to establish a nuclear household" (Koğacıoğlu 2004: 127). To be fully recognized in the public sphere was to be *şeref*.

Namus is the term (equivalent to the Arabic *'ard*, according to Meeker) for sexual honor, which has as its opposite shame (*ayıp*), though a man who does not treat his wife fairly is also shameful (*ayıp*).[5] Paul Stirling characterized *namus* in the following terms: "An honourable man is ready to fight, resentful of insults, able to keep his women pure from all taint of gossip, if necessary by killing them, and incapable of underhand and deceitful practices" (Stirling 1965: 231). Though in some contexts honor overlaps with religious ideas of merit and uprightness, in others it contradicts them: "Honour requires intransigence and implacability; insults must be pursued and avenged, and never taken lying down. On the other hand, God is merciful, and it is the duty of a good Muslim likewise to be merciful, and to live in peace" (Stirling 1965: 232). In attempting to resolve quarrels, a person may draw on the principles of Islam against arguments based on honor.

When a man does resort to violence, the reasons are often far more complex than the straightforward enactment of a code of honor. The complexity of the possible sources of honor, reputation, and self-esteem that individuals may draw on as they negotiate social relationships in various contexts means that there are no simple formulas for action. Furthermore, for a man negotiating his self-esteem and reputation in a diasporic setting, it is not a matter of a dichotomous choice between the "traditional" path of honor and the "modern" path of individuality and freedom. Just as the sources of *şeref* have changed within the Turkish village as universal military service has come to be seen as a basic component of manhood (Altinay 2004), young men of Turkish background in Germany have found new sources of honor and prestige but do not necessarily experience these new ways of establishing and maintaining their reputations as involving a total rupture with the practices of an older generation.[6]

AMBIVALENT REPRESENTATIONS OF THE TURK

Just as anthropological models have shaped popular representations of the honor-shame complex and the relationship of the village to modernity by constituting the Turkish man as traditional, interpretive paradigms of historians and Orientalists over centuries have also played a role in shaping public perceptions of the Turk. Furthermore, these models have been closely intertwined with the political and economic interests of Western states. The rejection of Eurocentric histories in the wake of Said's critique of Orientalism has over the past several decades stimulated among Ottoman historians efforts to develop new models that disrupt these Eurocentric narratives[7] and has generated considerable interest in critically examining earlier interpretive frameworks. Virginia Aksan, summarizing much of this work, has described a focus in recent work by Europeanists on tracing "the sustaining myths and stereotypes of the 'terrible Turk'" that prevailed in Europe during the early Ottoman period and, among Ottomanists researching the nineteenth century, a focus on reinterpreting the "Ottoman road to the modern," including critiques of recurrent interpretive frameworks such as the "Decline Theory (part of the larger Islamic Decline model)" and the "Impact of the West" (Aksan 2007: 1). These now-challenged interpretive frameworks underlie representations of Turkish and Muslim masculinity that continue to resonate in the German national imaginary.

There are numerous recent studies of the evolution of German and other European images of the Turk through the centuries (for example, Kleinlogel 1989; Kula 1992; Kuran-Burçoğlu 2003; Soykut 2003; Spohn 1993). Nedret Kuran-Burçoğlu, for example, identified in these representations major shifts that correspond to the vicissitudes of relative military power and territorial control exercised by Europeans and Turks. Turks were typically described as slaughtering Christians en masse as they took over Constantinople in 1453. *Türkengefahr* (Turkish threat) is a stock phrase in the German language that can be traced to the penetration of the Ottoman Empire into central Europe.[8] Beginning with the early printed newssheets (*Zeitung*) that circulated in Germany in the sixteenth century, the *Türkengefahr* vied with the development of the Protestant Reformation as the top news story for a century (Kortepeter 1991: 152). The Turk was the barbarian beating at the gates of Europe. Turks are remembered for overrunning most of Hungary in 1526 and controlling it for nearly two centuries, a core element of the history of middle Europe, as is the story of how they were just barely pushed back from Austria during the Siege of Vienna in 1529, a moment that represented the farthest advance of the Ottoman Empire into central Europe. The Catholic Church was particularly strident in its depiction of the Ottoman/Turkish menace in images that were promoted throughout Europe (Soykut 2001).

The abatement of the Turkish threat opened a rhetorical space for Enlightenment and Orientalist images of the benign and exotic Turk, though these images, too, have even earlier roots. Across the centuries there has been a positive strand in secular literature, evident, for example, in fifteenth-century German Carnival plays, in which social and political critique of local conditions and injustices drew on the contrasting image of the Turkish Sultan as a just and generous ruler (Kuran-Burçoğlu 2003: 26). This perception can be seen echoed in later Enlightenment productions such as the play *Nathan de Weise* (1779) by the eighteenth-century playwright Gotthold Ephraim Lessing. Promoting a philosophy of tolerance, Lessing used a "virtuous Turk" to demonstrate that noble characters can be found in all faiths (Kuran-Burçoğlu 2003: 29). The romantic appeal of the exotic played out and spread across Europe during the eighteenth and nineteenth centuries in the "Turquerie" movement, in which all things Turkish became fashionable.

With the defeat of the Ottoman army at the second Siege of Vienna in the late seventeenth century, there was a shift in the image of the Turk that can be closely linked to representations of manhood. The fear of the unstoppable warrior and barbarian was eventually displaced in the nineteenth century by the image of the Ottoman as "the sick man of Europe,"[9] an image that is associated with theories of the decline of Ottoman and Islamic civilizations.

Echoes of early images of the Ottoman Empire can be seen in the European accounts of Turkey that were produced by the growing number of travelers to Turkey in the late seventeenth century. These accounts accompanied deepening diplomatic and commercial ties and formed an integral part of the discourse that justified European colonizing efforts by depicting foreign cultures as less civilized. Lisa Lowe has argued that English travel accounts of Turkey in the late seventeenth century "played a leading role in establishing the terms of the relationship between European and colonial cultures. The portraits of Turkish and Middle Eastern culture as alternately violent and barbaric, slovenly and lascivious, or grotesque and incomprehensible supported and permitted an ideology that justified the cultural subordination of the foreign and colonial cultures from which profits were being extracted in the form of material and goods" (Lowe 1991: 37). In the nineteenth century, Germans were similarly interested in establishing a presence in the Orient and were actively engaged in an array of ventures in the Ottoman Empire.

Nineteenth- and twentieth-century German scholarship on Islam and the Ottoman Empire reveals certain specifically German preoccupations that were manifest in representations of the Turk. Manhood was closely linked to the idea of national character and was thought to shape the vigor and viability of the nation. Nineteenth-century theories of the nature of the Ottoman Empire and Islamic civilization thus depict a certain sort of masculinity associated with national character. This can be seen in Max Weber's view of Islam as a religion of warriors with feudal patrimonial relations that were not conducive to the development of capitalism (Turner 1974).[10] This view can be linked to the paradigm of the rise and gradual decline of the Ottoman Empire over five centuries. The German Turkologist Theodor Menzel developed the concept of a Turkish heroic age, the characteristics of which "possess a decidedly national, even völkisch form, being a manifestation of a national life [which was] certainly primitive, but strong and internally united. Its basis was the 'permanent human reservoir of vigorous Turkish masses from Central Asia'" (Heywood 2002: 6–16). The German category of *Volk* (folk) was a romantic image closely tied to the idea of national character. The Austrian Ottoman historian Paul Wittek developed a theory explaining the rise of the Ottoman Empire in terms of the *ghazi* (Muslim warrior who has fought against infidels), who was "the idealized and archetypal 'heroischritterlich' Islamic march warrior figure of the Anatolian borderlands." He was "not only the social element around which the nascent Ottoman state crystallized, but an ideal figure whose ethos permeates the whole subsequent history of the Ottoman state" (Heywood 2002: 15).

This vision of the Turkish *Volk* and ethos had significant implications for German perspectives on the Turk. Kurt Hildebrandt, the Nazi historian, focused on how the scholar looking at "small states blossoming into world-empires, and then in weakness fallen in pieces, and foundering in barbarism, is compelled to come to grips with the question of the causes of such swift decay, according to their inner meaning" (Kurt Hildebrandt, 1924, *Norm und Verfall des Staates*, in Heywood 2002: 18).[11] Hildebrandt asked whether the cause lay in the political and spiritual overdevelopment of the society or in the deterioration of physical man, that is, race. The Ottoman Empire was thus a state that had had its own particular genius for a time and then decayed because of a loss of manly vigor, which could be understood as biological decay of the race.

Intimations of the theory of history that posited the decay of the Ottoman man are evident in the travel writings of the German countess and author Ida Hahn-Hahn, who summarized the history of the Ottoman state in a letter she wrote to her sister from Constantinople in 1843. She described a decline from an early "vigorous" period when the Turks were "more and more impetuous, more and more irresistible, more and more alarming for the whole West," to a period in which the "destroyers of greatness now sprang up: indolence and fondness for pleasure in the sultans; love of splendour and profusion in the whole court." She recognized decline in both Europe and the Ottoman Empire in the eighteenth century, but she saw the Ottomans in the nineteenth century as nearly moribund: "I figure to myself that the empire is sinking under a slow, very slow decline, always incident to enervated organizations" (Hahn-Hahn 1845, I: 136). Though Prussians and Austrians had come to teach the Turks European skills, "Foreign discipline, foreign science cannot pass organically into the blood, into the germ of life. For regenerating worn out natures inoculation with foreign culture is not sufficiently effective" (Hahn-Hahn 1845, I: 137). In describing items in the shops, she concluded: "that element which we estimate more highly than luxury—elegance—is totally unknown to the Turk." She suggested that on the outside "the Turkish national character has really something imposing" but that it is already dead (Hahn-Hahn 1845, I: 143).

Images of the Ottoman Empire in German travel accounts sometimes vacillated between an antique, idyllic, biblical land of unchanging inhabitants and a corrupt empire of ignorant, violent villains incapable of economic progress (Erker-Sonnabend 1987), in a manner similar to Lowe's characterization of English travel writing. Several late-nineteenth-century German writers depicted a distinctive Turkish national character—by which was meant the male personality—in similar binary terms. The Turk was frugal, modest, loyal, and charitable, except when he was stimulated to fury, brutality, and religious fanaticism in battle (Wolfgang von Oettingen, 1897, "Unter der Sonne Homers" [Under the Sun of Homer] in Erker-Sonnabend 1987: 71).

One image that persists from old Orientalist views of the Ottoman Empire is a judgment about men's attitudes toward work. Nineteenth-century German writers echoed a theme that had been a part of the European vision of Turks for centuries, emphasizing the Turkish inclination to sit, drink coffee, and chat in the "good mood of the Orient" (Rudolf Lindau, 1899, *Zwei Reisen in der Türkei* [Two Journeys in Turkey], in Erker-Sonnabend 1987: 76) or the "enervating comfort of the soul" (Franz von Werner, 1877, *Türkische Skizzen* [Turkish Sketches], in Erker-Sonnabend 1987: 78). Yet their representations contained an ambivalent mixture of envy and scorn: "If one has been sufficiently steamed, massaged, rubbed, soaped and rinsed, then follow the desired hours of the laziest tranquility. We consider such practices to be unmanly, but at least they lead to the development of a definite sense of well-being" (Wolfgang von Oettingen,

1897, "Unter der Sonne Homers," in Erker-Sonnabend 1987: 71). Von Oettingen explicitly contrasted German standards of active masculinity with the "unmanliness" of Ottoman court life.

The recognition of unmanliness and an unwillingness to work was linked to the theory of the decline of the Ottoman Empire, a decline attributed to decay in the character of its men. This link was explicit in Countess Hahn-Hahn's account, as in her sarcastic comment on a "high personage" whom she had mistakenly thought was being accompanied by a slave with a large gun: "A Turk shoot! A Turk take pleasure in strong exercise and rapid motion! Oh no! only Franks [the common designation at the time for all Europeans in Constantinople] are fools enough to call that amusement. The Turk's enjoyment, his pleasure, his diversion, is repose. The machine that is carried after him is the magic wand which transports him into the paradise of that delightful repose, is—the pipe" (Hahn-Hahn 1845, I: 152–153). She continued for several pages on the topic of the decadent character of these men: "Whosoever knows so little of the mind as the Turk, as so little activity, knows nothing of passion but its brutal side, never feels a longing but only a desire; whoever has ceased, at the same time, to be engaged in a struggle for the preservation of life, like the savage nations, but is acquainted with all the indulgences of voluptuous effeminacy—precisely like the Turk—must addict himself to opium" (Hahn-Hahn 1845, I: 153).

The widespread representation of the Ottoman Empire as lacking any respect for hard work continues to echo, perhaps unintentionally, in more recent anthropological studies of Anatolian rural society (Bellér-Hann and Hann 2000: 114). Carol Delaney's 1991 ethnography, for example, cast men in a negative light with respect to topics that reiterate old Orientalist themes. She was particularly explicit about villagers' negative attitudes about work: "Villagers must work, but they do not like to; work in any form is looked down upon. It is not seen as a way of learning about life, or as an affirmation or fulfillment of the self" (Delaney 1991: 115). Delaney also noted a gendered imbalance in work obligations: "Women shoulder the major portion of the physical work. I had hoped in vain to hire a few of the young men to help me fix my house and chop my wood; although they would help me with 'head' work, they would not condescend to do manual labor" (Delaney 1991: 115n). This observation supports Delaney's general argument that women are hardworking and oppressed by their patriarchal men.

American anthropologist Michael Meeker's insightful study of the male social and political world in a Black Sea city also, at least implicitly, judges men's

practices negatively as he describes men's concern with status and their relationship to labor: "It was just as important for a man to be seen as free from
facing chores as it was for him to be involved in some other rewarding enterprise" (Meeker 2002: 105), the result being that women did all of the farm labor
while the men dressed in business suits and socialized. His analysis places men's
practices within the context of a broader "Islamic sociality" that formed the
fabric of both the Ottoman Empire and the Republic, but the Western gaze that
values hard work and sees it lacking among these men is also present in these
observations about work.[12]

Divergent historical images of the Turk created in post–World War II German discourse a potential for deep-seated ambivalence toward the Turkish man.
The Turk could be abjected on two contradictory grounds: (1) He is an embodiment of Ottoman decay linked to laziness, a lack of manly vigor, and a distaste
for hard work, and (2) the traditional Turkish man retains the violent character
of the Turkish *ghazi* hero. This violent warrior bore features reminiscent of the
German warrior hero, who is now in the postwar era to be disavowed because
of the thorough discrediting of Nazism. Turkish masculinity must therefore be
denounced in order to buttress the new foundation of German national identity that is linked to a masculinity rooted in a respect for democracy, freedom,
and human rights as articulated in the postwar Constitution.

EUROPEAN WOMEN VIEW THE OTTOMAN HAREM

One response to Said's challenge to Orientalism and the resultant concern with
examining what previously had been naturalized representations of the Eastern
other has been an interest in women's travel writing as a window into alternative perspectives produced by subjects who were themselves in a subordinate
social position at home. Sara Mills (1991) has argued that women's travel accounts are instances of a counterhegemonic discourse that challenged colonial
representations of colonized subjects. Examining women's narratives of their
travels in the Caribbean, Aisha Khan (2003) has pointed out that these accounts
did, in many respects, reflect the hegemonic understandings of their time. Lisa
Lowe has highlighted the heterogeneity of Orientalist positions, arguing that
"each orientalist situation expresses a distinct range of concerns with difference: the conflicts and collaborations among narratives of cultural, class, and
sexual differences" (Lowe 1991: x). Several English women of the eighteenth and
nineteenth centuries used images of the Turkish woman and gender practices
to contrast their own lack of rights within marriage in England (see Melman

1992). Some of the most well-known travel narratives by German women, such as those by Ida Hahn-Hahn and Ida Pfeiffer (discussed later in this chapter), like English women's accounts, self-consciously disrupt the sexualized fantasies of the harem that characterized many male travelers' accounts. They nevertheless conformed closely to dominant German views in other ways, reflecting hegemonic understandings of race and national character that shaped their perceptions of Turkish men and gender.

Given the gender segregation characteristic of Muslim societies, early European male perspectives on Turkish family life were based primarily on hearsay because men did not usually have direct access to women. Their accounts were laced with fantasies of the harem and Ottoman male sexuality that had a powerful effect on European visions of the Orient (see Said 1978).[13] In 1879, the Englishwoman Mrs. W. M. Ramsey wrote: "Cases of brutality on the part of the man towards his wife are a hundred times commoner among the lower classes of this country [England] than they are in Turkey" (quoted in Melman 1992: 111). Similarly, Lady Mary Wortley Montagu, in *Turkish Embassy Letters* (1717–1718), saw Turkish women as a sign of liberty and freedom, in contrast to male travelers, who saw them as "a sign of enslavement and barbarism" (Lowe 1991: 45; see also Melman 1992: 85–86). Montagu often traveled around Istanbul disguised as a veiled Ottoman woman and wrote: "Tis very easy to see that they have more liberty than we have, no woman of What rank so ever being permitted to go in the street without 2 muslins. . . . 'Tis impossible for the most jealous Husband to know his Wife when he meets her, and no Man dare either touch or follow a Woman in the street" (quoted in Halsband 1965: 328). This freedom was reiterated a half century later by Lady Elizabeth Craven, a playwright who traveled alone to Istanbul in 1785. Billie Melman, whose study focused on the historical shifts in the sensibilities of these travelers, noted that Craven's perception of the freedom of Turkish women was shaped by the increasing constraints on the freedom of English women with the rise of Evangelicalism. Not only did the veil give the Turkish woman the freedom to walk on the streets; she also had a right to privacy from her husband that was notable from an Englishwoman's perspective—"the custom of putting a pair of slippers outside the door separating the *haremlik* from the *selamlik* (the men's quarters and public parts of the Turkish house), to signify the woman's wish for privacy" (Melman 1992: 87). Both Montagu and Craven were also aware of the financial rights of Muslim women, who had a guarantee of money in the event of divorce, something that neither of them had when they separated from their husbands (Melman 1992: 88).[14]

Lucy M. J. Garnett, a British folklorist and traveler, wrote of Turkish "provincial and country folk" in the early 1900s, nearly two hundred years after Lady Montagu. Like Montagu, Garnett also contested the depictions of the harem presented by "superficial [male] travellers" such as E. H. Mitchell, author of *Forty Days in the East*: "A harem . . . , far from meriting the epithets of 'detestable prison' and 'place of degradation,' . . . is, as a rule, the most cheerful and commodious division of a house" (Garnett 1909: 265–266). She argued that the harem system is, not a proof of women's degraded position, but "an outcome of the regard entertained for them by the men of their nation," shielding them from the "impertinent curiosity—to say the least—of the mixed horde, Christian, Moslem, and Jew, who throng the streets of their cities and towns" (Garnett 1909: 280, 281). She also argued that Turkish women already had "all the legal, personal and propriety rights necessary to give them a social position equal if not superior to that of European women generally" (Garnett 1909: 282–283). In fact, in a discussion of Turkish writers, Garnett used the occasion to argue that in some respects Turkish women were in a better position than European women:

> Nor are the names of women absent from this long and brilliant list of Turkish writers. During the centuries when European culture was a sealed book to them, the fair denizens of the harem not infrequently found its calm undisturbed life conducive to poetic composition; and from the fifteenth century onwards a daughter of the Osmanlis has from time to time delighted her contemporaries with her pen, and given evidence of a degree of talent entitling her to rank with the literary celebrities of her day. (Garnett 1909: 173)

Though Garnett went into great detail about everyday practices, she did not devote much space to husband-wife relationships and tended to downplay the power of the husband over his wife: "Before setting out . . . a *hanum* must, however, first obtain her husband's permission. If the *effendi* is inclined to be jealous and strict, he may object to his family being much out of doors, and permission may sometimes be refused. But in the majority of households this is merely a polite formality, and leave for an expedition is granted as soon as requested" (Garnett 1909: 272). She treated the power imbalance in divorce practices in a similar way: "a husband might appear, at first sight, to possess great privileges in the matter of divorce." But she then listed three "wise regulations" that safeguard women "against a too arbitrary exercise of this prerogative": religious restriction, social restriction, and the *nekyah*, or money payable to the wife if she is divorced (Garnett 1909: 218).

Though Garnett addressed issues surrounding the status of women, which were of pressing concern in Europe at the time as feminism emerged as a social force, her interpretation of the rights of women did not locate Turkish women as an oppressed other or demonize traditional men. She, like earlier English travel writers, rather used the Ottoman man as a model for the West to point out negative qualities of European society. Writing against a common European perspective that they are "Turks," in the sense of a non-Aryan or even a "Coloured Race" (Garnett 1909: xii), Garnett argued that the Ottomans are a "white race," a great nation with an "admixture during more than six centuries with the best white blood both of Asia and of Europe" (Garnett 1909: xiii). Of the peasant, she wrote: "Physically, a Turkish peasant is well built, healthy, and owing no doubt to his habitual abstemiousness, possesses remarkable powers of endurance" (Garnett 1909: 76).[15] Garnett thus had political reasons for her positive view of Ottoman women and the practices of Ottoman men. Counterhegemonic in her depictions of gender and the characteristics of Ottomans, she nevertheless fully participated in an Orientalist racialized discourse but sought to include the Ottoman as Western rather than Eastern.

Two German women of contrasting social position, Countess Ida Hahn-Hahn and lower-middle-class Ida Pfeiffer, published widely read accounts of their travels in Turkey in the mid-nineteenth century. I have already discussed Hahn-Hahn's perspective on the decline of Turkish civilization, which conformed closely to a dominant German discourse. Though Hahn-Hahn's descriptions of the harem contested the sexualized fantasies of European men, she was extremely critical of Turkish gender practices: "A State governed by slaves; families in which women dislike to be mothers, because they are slaves, not wives—what can be more contrary to nature, and what else can this state of things betoken but an advanced stage of decline?" (Hahn-Hahn 1845, I: 251). She compares this state of decline to that of ancient Rome.[16] Ironically, Hahn-Hahn did not draw any connections between her own rejection of motherhood (she had left her children to be cared for by others and never played a role in their upbringing) and the rejection she identified in Ottoman harem women, only branding their rejection as unnatural. She instead saw these women as listless, dull, and unproductive, in contrast to her own energetic approach to life. Both she and the harem women operated as signifiers of opposed civilizations, one on the rise and one sliding into death. But in contrast to a discourse of gender that developed in the twentieth century in the context of early feminisms, Hahn-Hahn did not emphasize that men were oppressive and that women were their victims. Rather, she saw both men and women as racially and temperamentally other, products of an unnatural civilization that would inevitably collapse.

Though Ida Pfeiffer's writings cannot generally be characterized as counter-hegemonic in her evaluations of what she saw during her travels, her Austrian publisher in his preface contrasted her account with those of many authors who have "indulged their fancy" (Pfeiffer 1852: ix), no doubt referring to the fact that her narrative, like Hahn-Hahn's, does not sexualize the harem as male accounts did. She does occasionally make statements that question prevailing representations of Turkish men: "I had many opportunities of noticing the character of the Mussulman, and found, to my great delight, that he is much better and more honest than prejudices generally allow us to believe. Even in matters of commerce and business it is better to have to do with a Turk than with a votary of any other creed, not even excepting my own" (Pfeiffer 1852: 68–69). Nevertheless, she reproduced prevailing negative assessments of Turkish gender relations, though they occasionally stand in tension with her direct observations: "As a stranger, I was allowed, without opposition, a place in the front ranks,—a trait of good breeding on the part of the Turks which many a Frank would do well to imitate. In a Turk, moreover, this politeness is doubly praiseworthy, for the fact that he looks upon my poor sex with great disrespect; indeed, according to his creed, we have not even a soul" (Pfeiffer 1852: 43).[17] Commenting on her experience of harems, she wrote: "every where I found the same idle curiosity, ignorance, and apathy. Perhaps they may be more happy than European women; I should suppose they were, to judge from their comfortable figures and their contented features" (Pfeiffer 1852: 165). Despite this mildly positive statement of the situation of harem women, Pfeiffer did not romanticize or idealize them, as she continued: "their features are so entirely without any fixed character and expression, that I do not think these women capable of deep passions or feeling either for good or evil" (Pfeiffer 1852: 165–166). On the basis of a visit to the harem of the pasha, she also wrote: "The ladies of the harem seemed to look with contempt upon employment and work of every kind; for neither here nor elsewhere did I see them do anything but sit cross-legged on carpets and cushions, drinking coffee, smoking nargilé, and gossiping with one another" (Pfeiffer 1852: 165). This observation was consistent with European stereotypes of the laziness of the male Turk and his aversion to work, as well as with the prevailing thesis of civilizational decline, in which national character and racial decay are closely linked.

In the twentieth century, after the fall of the Ottoman Empire and the sweeping reforms of Kemal Atatürk, Clare Sheridan, a British sculptor and journalist, wrote from a position critical of the assumption that the West is superior. However, in stark contrast to Lucy Garnett, who had encompassed Turkey within the white West, Sheridan deployed a common orientalizing strategy that located the Turk as the nonmodern other: "In a thousand ways the Orient has a greater sense of the values of life" and a "spiritual superiority," in contrast to "Western plans for wholesale human destruction" (Sheridan 1926: 15). Sheridan was highly critical of Turkish men: "In most countries women have to be twice as efficient as men in order to gain the grudging admission of equality. In Turkey the woman works four times harder before she is worthy to be acknowledged a worker at all"; and "Women . . . are of so little account in the Black Sea region that, if a man has five children and three are girls, he will say that he has only two!" (Sheridan 1926: 113, 116). At one point she suggested that a town was more prosperous than its neighbors because its inhabitants were Georgians, who have a capacity to fight and work, in contrast to the Turks (Sheridan 1926: 207). Sheridan's judgments echo Republican representations of the earlier Ottoman era, in which the traditional man serves as the negative contrast to the modernizing Turkish citizen.

These themes of men's oppression of women and their unwillingness to work dominate post-Republican Turkish representations of the traditional Turkish man. When looking at representations of Turkish men over centuries of northern European writing—which include scholarly ambivalence over the manliness of the Turk, racialized accounts of the decline of Ottoman civilization, and women travelers' admiration of the legal and social position of the Turkish woman—we can see a hardening of negative stereotypes in the twentieth century. It is striking how the range of representations of men and gender practices in early women's travel accounts of Turkey contrasts with a greater uniformity of perspective that developed during the twentieth century.

RESHAPING MASCULINITY: TURKISH NATIONALIST DISCOURSE AND TRANSNATIONAL FEMINISMS

Though Turkey was never a colony of one of the European powers, European expansionism nonetheless virtually dismantled the Ottoman Empire. In the process, its leaders were acutely sensitive to the gaze of the European throughout the nineteenth and early twentieth centuries. Given this sensitivity, European representations of the traditional Turkish man have played a significant role in the emerging discourse of Turkish national identity in the early twentieth century, especially as this was articulated in the self-conscious official discourse of the modernizing, secularist Turkish Republic under Atatürk. The perceived backwardness of the Turkish village was a focus of reform closely linked to the nationalist project of creating a population of modern Turkish citizens. Rural populations were targeted for modernization into a secularist national culture through the introduction of universal military service for men, the promotion of universal education, and implementation of policies intended to sever connections with an Ottoman past, such as the regulation of men's clothing.[18] The social position of women was also a key issue in this modernizing discourse, which embraced many issues articulated by the early feminist movement as a way of sharply distinguishing the new Republic from its Ottoman past. Offering equality to women provided proof of westernization and democratization to a Western gaze that had used the symbol of veiling as evidence of the oppression of Muslim women (Tekeli 1981). Though the female body was a highly visible symbol of transformation, it was the "traditional" Muslim village man who lay at the intersection of these two projects of national identity and modernization and became the primary target of transformation and also of denigration. Successive waves of feminism have contributed to this denigration.[19]

The efforts of the Turkish state to modernize have included negative depictions of the village, its inhabitants, and the backwardness of "traditional" practices. Some of the modernizing reforms enacted by Atatürk's government were intended to create a rupture with the Ottoman past through style, fashioning men and women into modern, bourgeois Turkish citizens. Not only was the village woman's headscarf explicitly attacked; everyday male practices and the gendered division of labor were also criticized. As Deniz Kandiyoti has argued, Republican efforts at modernization included a transformation of hegemonic masculinity:

> A fact about the republican dress code that is often overlooked is that Atatürk never actually outlawed the veil . . . but was ruthless when it came to the sorts of headdresses men chose to wear. In the Ottoman empire, rank, origin, and ethnicity could be read clearly in the costumes and even the colors that subject populations were allowed to wear. Similarly, men of religion could be clearly distinguished by their turbans and garments. The Western hat and tie were not merely items of fashion but became the solvent and suppressor of these differences, a uniform of secularism that also signified loyalty to the new state. (Kandiyoti 1997)

This modernization of masculinity excluded the rural villager and stereotyped him:

> This new uniformity among the elite exacerbated the visible differences between urbanites and peasants. While the modern man of the republic appeared at public functions with his bare-faced wife at his side, his rural brother was pictured, and frequently caricatured, in traditional garb with his veiled wife following forty paces behind him (preferably, he rode his donkey while she walked). The unreconstructed masculinity of tradition, the sharp age and gender hierarchies, and the oppression of women were now portrayed through rural mores and interpreted as a deficit in civilization. The civilizing mission of the village teacher and kaymakam [governor of a provincial district] . . . was portrayed as the struggle of science and enlightenment against ignorance and obscurantism. (Kandiyoti 1997)

At the same time, powerful state institutions sought to transform village men into national citizens, one of the most powerful being universal military service, which removed men from their villages for two years, subjected them to the bodily discipline of basic training, taught them how to read, and exposed them to the "civilizing mission" of the state (Altinay 2004: 70–71). Scholarly literature on economic development drew close connections between the military and socioeconomic development and suggested that young discharged soldiers would find the traditional society of the village frustrating in the face of their new level of expectations (Altinay 2004: 64), thereby pushing them to modernize and become a new kind of man.

Stereotypes of the backwardness of the Turkish village continue to play a role in policy decisions within Turkey. Carol Delaney, for instance, described how some Turkish policy analysts (see Turan 1982) have pushed to consolidate farms, which would have the effect of forcing people out of villages in search of work. She suggested that these plans were a result of "a particular kind of education in which the village way of life is seen as an impediment to modernization and Westernization" (Delaney 1991: 262).

Women's emancipation from traditional gender relationships was also a part of official state ideology, as laid out in works such as Afet Inan's *The Emancipation of the Turkish Woman* (1962). Inan created an ideological link between the emancipation of Turkish women and pre-Islamic Turkish egalitarianism, a link that was tied to the secular state's broader efforts to distance itself from Ottoman Islam. Inan was the "leading architect" of this official state ideology

(Kandiyoti 1997). The inverse of this link was the association of women's oppression with Islam.

What is now called first-wave feminism—women's activism in the late nineteenth and early twentieth centuries focused on woman suffrage—directly affected women in Turkey from the beginning of the Republican era in the context of this nationalist project. Women were given nearly equal legal status with men as early as 1924 under the new Turkish Constitution and received full suffrage in 1934, only a few years after this had been achieved in Britain and the United States. However, as Turkish feminist scholars have pointed out, the legal reforms that emancipated women did not necessarily liberate them (see Kandiyoti 1987), in the sense that the state continued to view the male-headed family as the basic social unit and promoted the monogamous nuclear family as a key component of the social order by enforcing the virtue of women.

With the rise of second-wave feminism and a preoccupation in the West with women entering the labor force and, conversely, men helping out with housework, the negative stereotypes of the traditional Turkish man that accompanied modernizing discourse intensified, as in an article that appeared in the Turkish daily newspaper *Sabah* and was picked up by the BBC and other news services. It was reported that a village imam (mosque leader—always a government employee) in eastern Turkey had begun scolding local men for leaving all household work to their wives. According to the imam: "Women do the washing, they look after the livestock, they cook. And they carry the water. When I told men to help them, they have reacted very harshly" (BBC News 2004). The article reported that villagers asked the government to remove the imam from their mosque and suggested that he was "psychologically disturbed." Though the news report did not overtly challenge the villagers' assessment of their imam, the rhetorical structure of the article did this covertly. Even calling the men "villagers" marks them as other, distant from the reader of *Sabah*. This distancing stands in tension, however, with the men's assessment that the imam was "psychologically disturbed," a quotation that gives their deployment of the language of modern psychology an amusingly incongruous tone. The title of another article, "Turkish Men Scared Off by Housework" (Agence France-Presse 2004), is also ambiguous: it echoes a complaint that even urban women have of their husbands. But it also echoes a key point of male honor: the idea that men are scared suggests a kind of emasculation that is produced by modern feminist demands for gender equality. Could there also be hints here of male nostalgia for a simpler time?

Most scholarly works that have focused on the situation of women and gender relations have emphasized the continuing domination of men in traditional gender relations, despite the government's emphasis on modernizing. Sirin Tekeli (1990), for instance, argued that Turkish state feminism, which was an important component of nationalist rhetoric, promoted gender equality and women's entry into the workplace but did not really transform gender relations in the home. Furthermore, scholars have pointed out that, paradoxically, modern state institutions like the military and other structures such as the nuclear family, while attempting to disrupt traditional orientations, including the structure of gender relationships associated with village life, also produced and reproduced patriarchal gender hierarchies, even inventing new forms, making the man the "commander" of the nuclear family (Sirman 1989; Altinay 2004: 80), beneath a veneer of gender equality.

This argument rests on a tension that feminist anthropologists have articulated between a feminist project founded on a universalizing vision of gender equality that is predicated on Western premises and the anthropological project. This universalizing feminist vision assumes that gender asymmetry in any form is inconsistent with a modern subjectivity. Most anthropologists, in contrast, challenge universals in order to nonjudgmentally represent the alternative models and practices that shape the subjective experience of another, usually avoiding a stance of moral outrage that is common in feminist writing (see Strathern 1987; Boddy 1991).

A focus on the fate of the Turkish Muslim man who has been identified as traditional and patriarchal within this universalizing feminist discourse allows a parochialization of this feminist perspective. This involves examining the assumptions that underlie the stigmatizations of Turkish masculinity, disentangling equivalences that have been drawn between headscarves and oppression, a gendered division of labor and patriarchy, honor and domination.[20] Furthermore, just as a feminist may uncover inequality even when gender equality is overtly promoted, it is also possible to identify elements of gender equality beneath a veneer of asymmetry.

Second-wave feminism emerged in Turkey in the 1980s with a new perception of the discrepancy between egalitarian state ideologies and the conditions under which most women actually lived (Sirman 1989: 17).[21] Women began to take direct political action, through campaigns against domestic violence (which became highly visible through a 1987 march in Istanbul) and other forms of protest against oppression, with the goal of creating in women a feminist "consciousness." This feminist discourse, which had been directly shaped by Western feminism,[22] relocated the family as a prime source of oppression and involved a castigation of men as the dominant figures within the family. Given the pervasiveness of the opposition between modernization and traditionalism and the tendency to associate traditionalism with village life, one effect was that the denigration of village masculinity was intensified.

This aspect of feminist discourse has become increasingly focused in recent years on the honor killing as the ultimate manifestation of domestic violence and the oppression of women in the name of honor and traditional masculinity. The campaign against honor killings has become transnational, linking activists in Turkey with those in other parts of the Middle East—which anthropologists had identified as the primary site of the honor-shame complex—and Europe, where activists have drawn public attention to the plight of migrant Muslim women who continue to be subject to honor killings. This marker of oppressive male traditionalism has, in turn, been taken up into European national discourses as evidence of the failure of Muslims to integrate successfully into European societies. This campaign reproduces the dichotomy between static, rural tradition and progressive modernity.

However, the argument that a concern with honor and the practice of honor killing are simply manifestations of traditional behavior that will eventually fade out as the countryside modernizes, a frequently reiterated element of state ideology, has been challenged in Turkey by scholars such as Ayşe Parla and Dicle Koğacioğlu. Parla challenged the assumption of early studies that honor and shame are at odds with modernity. She argued that, far from rendering the code of honor and shame obsolete, the modernizing Turkish state gave this code new significance, displacing it onto the "national family," to the extent that the virtue of women was policed through virginity exams (an internal medical examination to determine whether the hymen is intact), despite a national ideology of gender equality (Parla 2001: 87 n. 41). Koğacioğlu has argued that honor crimes and other "so-called traditional practices" should be viewed as an effect of institutions such as the court system, which plays a role in reproducing these crimes by exonerating "age old traditions": "If the so-called traditions are made and remade in relation to the actions of institutions, then the reduction and eventual extinction of honor crimes require targeted intervention on the part of the institutions. . . . The utterance of 'timeless tradition,' in other words, serves to produce its other, the modern, enlightened institution" (Koğacioğlu 2004: 120).

Perhaps the most recent denigration of village masculinity in Turkey has emerged with the rise of an urban bourgeois identity linked to cosmopolitanism and neoliberalism that has come to be called *white Turk*. Sedef Arat-Koç has argued that a popular liberal feminism linked with this bourgeois identity is currently the most visible face of feminism in Turkey in popular magazines and newspapers. She has contrasted this feminism's intense criticism of the masculinity of marginalized groups with its "uncritical attitude toward the masculinities displayed by men of privileged social class / cultural backgrounds" (Arat-Koç 2007: 54 n. 14), suggesting that the actions of the rural and the poor are viewed as a cultural characteristic of the group while problems that elite urban women experience in their relationships are viewed as resulting from characteristics of a particular man.

The Republic of Turkey as a national imaginary was founded in an act of repudiation of the Ottoman Empire. It was to be a secular state, as opposed to the site of the caliphate of Islam; it was to be a part of the modern West, as opposed to the traditional East. This repudiation was enacted in highly concrete ways: the replacement of the Ottoman script with the Roman script, the fez with the top hat and bowler, and the Ottoman patriarch presiding over a harem with the modern husband whose wife stood on equal footing with him. Throughout Turkey's history, there has been an interweaving of this modernizing Turkish nationalist discourse and an evolving transnational feminism. The refashioning of gender, with new, modern images of masculinity and femininity, rested on identities that had been condemned as part of an essentialized traditional culture. At the same time, there was "a subtle shift in the locus of 'tradition.' The unreconstructed masculinities of Ottoman patriarchy were attributed no longer to urban elites, who defined themselves as 'modern,' but increasingly to village life through portrayals of the downtrodden rural woman" (Kandiyoti 1998b: 282). The resulting images of the village man and his traditional masculinity have, in turn, reinforced German stereotypes and contribute to the marginalization of the Turkish man as traditional other in German national discourse.

CONCLUSION

The Turkish national imaginary is founded on a repudiation of tradition based on a divide between the Ottoman Empire as Eastern and traditional and the Turkish Republic as Western and modern. This discourse of modernization included a reframing of masculinity in which the Ottoman patriarch, who had been an object of European fantasy as the lustful and violent yet indolent ruler of the harem in a decaying civilization, was replaced by the modern man. The Turkish national imaginary continued to be grounded on an abjection of the traditional man, though the locus of tradition was displaced from the city to the village, generating and reproducing a rural-urban dichotomy. Given the power of arguments for the protection of women, which are often made from a position of moral outrage and the advocacy of universal human rights, and given forms of governmentality targeted at disrupting what are regarded in both Turkey and Germany as archaic social forms, representations of the Turkish man as oppressor have remained virtually unquestioned, and men's own perspectives on gender relations and family structure have not been considered. It is true that people concerned with improving the situation of Turkish immigrants in Germany have sympathetically viewed the Turkish man as a victim of exploitative working conditions, poor housing, and social discrimination; however, when the German public gaze is directed at the Turkish family, the man is usually seen as the agent of Turkish women's oppression.

The interrelated discursive strands I have discussed—anthropological models of the honor-shame complex, the Orientalist constructions of Ottoman history and European travel writing, and Turkish nationalist and feminist discourses—contribute to a contemporary German discourse that stigmatizes Turkish men and their subjectivity. The marginalization of those who display any aspects of village culture, of tradition, or even of Islamic practice, especially as manifest in the honor killing, is displaced in Germany onto men of Turkish background more generally, so that only the Turk who becomes fully German in language and culture is viewed as modern. This marginalization is reinforced, often quite vocally, by secularists of Turkish background in Germany who, though visible as representatives of the Turkish community in the media and in politics, do not necessarily represent the entire range of Turkish perspectives and experiences.

2 BETWEEN CINEMA AND SOCIAL WORK

Rescuing the Muslim Woman from the Muslim Man

THIS STORY APPEARED in the German news magazine *Der Spiegel* as part of a cover article on the headscarf controversy in Germany:

> "The purity of the woman is the honor of the man," states a Turkish proverb. The family of the eighteen-year-old Turkish girl Aylin (pseudonym) was prepared to use all legal means to maintain this purity, although the girl was the third generation living in Germany: Until she was fourteen, she was only allowed to leave the house in the company of her brother or her mother, with the exception of school.
>
> Then she was raped by her uncle, but out of shame she kept silent about the incident. Her uncle became her tormenter and made her life a living hell. He repeatedly told her mother that he had seen her spending time with boys, and the mother believed him. She threatened her daughter that if she did not stop this disgraceful behavior, the mother would get "five men to rape her, and I will hold your hands myself."
>
> When the girl began an apprenticeship, the net of familial control grew tighter. Her wages went into an account that her mother had control over. The young woman had neither an EC [European Community] card nor a passport when she turned sixteen. "That is normal—many Turkish girls do not get passports, so that they cannot run away," she said.
>
> One morning in March of this year, her mother confronted her. The uncle had decided that the girl was no longer allowed to go to work. The girl shouted, "I am cursed because you are my mother," and went to the police. For a month she has lived, disguised, somewhere in Germany. (Cziesche et al. 2003: 86–87)

This story sets up a contrast between Turks and Germans by drawing on the concept of honor to mark the Turkish family as fundamentally other. Echoing a political discourse about the threat of growing immigrant minorities and the failure of integration that has been intensifying across Europe and the United States, the story was presented to articulate an increasingly vocal concern about the refusal of Turkish Muslims to integrate into German society. Within a parallel society, it is said, honor killings are proliferating, traditionally oriented men prevent their female relatives from fully participating in German society, and a young woman's mother will support male authority under any circumstances. The presentation of this story rests on a model of Turkish and Muslim gender practices in which the young woman is victim and the men in her life are often inhumane and brutal. For the most vocal activists and experts, who have easy and repeated access to the media, the solution is to save these women by offering them shelter when they escape from their families so that they can blend into German society and be free of the parallel society's constraints. In Aylin's case, the German state stepped in and provided her with a new home, a new identity, and even a new name, thereby absorbing her into German society by completely severing ties with her past.

Even though this young woman's family had clearly broken the law, as well as Turkish and Islamic moral standards, *Der Spiegel*, a major news magazine, presented this case as typical, as if Muslims would defend the right of an uncle to rape his niece. The fact that one of Europe's biggest and most influential magazines could represent Turkish and Islamic "culture" in this way indicates how constrained German public imagination is by the force of an idea of cultural otherness. The story served as evidence of the need for the German state to protect the human rights of Muslim women against the evils of Islamic culture. Such representations encourage the sense of crisis and contribute to the moral panic associated with the idea of an invisible parallel society that is growing because Germany's large immigrant Turkish and Muslim populations refuse to integrate. The perception of a crisis demands solutions, which in turn are shaped by this panic. The solution of hiding Aylin away, carried out by the German police, is quite a drastic one, given the extensive fabric of social services in countries such as Germany. This policy of hiding young women from their families, though it may be necessary in some cases, is based on the assumption that women in Turkish families are totally vulnerable to the whims of men. What from a German perspective are identified as solutions to problems in Turkish families, such as encouraging assimilation and rescue, are likely to be perceived quite differently by Turks. In German public discourse, efforts to re-solve the contradictions of the position of the woman of Turkish background (as these contradictions are understood through this discourse) generate models of integration that directly challenge and even assault certain Turkish cultural identities, making the process of coexistence more difficult and the possibility of full cultural citizenship elusive.

Exacerbating the polarization of Turkish and German cultural difference is the fact that, facing the shock of dislocation, discrimination, and social margin-alization, many in the Turkish diasporic community, especially in the early years of the guestworker program, talked about the differences between Germans and Turks in ways that echoed—often in inverted form—many of the dichotomies that are articulated in German discourse. These dichotomies include an ori-entation toward rural tradition rather than urban modernity, an emphasis on interdependence and hierarchy rather than autonomy and equality, and a focus on the group rather than the individual. In what could be called a *rural Turkish discourse*, the same terms stand as opposites, but their significance is inverted. This parallel stems from the power of these dichotomies within Turkey itself, where the villager has been marginalized as traditional within a modernizing discourse. Zafer Şenocak, a German writer of Turkish background, recognized this reproduction of the dichotomous terms of German discourse in the work of the well-known Turkish author Emine Sevgi Özdamar, who herself had come to Germany as a guestworker. He criticized the tendency of her book *Das Leben ist eine Karawanserei* (Life Is a Caravanserai) (1992) (the first book written in Ger-man by a Turkish immigrant to reach a broad German public) to reproduce the "fairy tale orientalism of the German public" (Jordan 2003: 93; Şenocak 2000).

The congruence of the perspective of the German public and the first-generation Turkish guestworker community can be seen in the *myth of return*, which appears in both German and rural Turkish discourses, though the signif-icance of migration and return are very different in each. From the official Ger-man perspective, the first Turkish immigrants were in Germany as temporary guestworkers; from the perspective of the Turkish villager, the stay in Germany was termed a kind of exile (Turkish: *gurbet*) (Delaney 1990: 523). In one docu-mentary by a filmmaker of Turkish background, *Mein Vater der Gastarbeiter* (My Father the Guestworker) (Yavuz 1994), the camera cuts back and forth be-tween nostalgically portrayed bucolic farm scenes and harsh shots of heavy in-dustrial zones and elevated urban highways, a familiar cliché in diasporic films (see Naficy 2001). The father portrayed in the film had never brought his family

to Germany during the many years he had been a guestworker before rejoin-
ing them in their village. When he revisits Germany in the 1990s and tries to
gain access to the factory where he had worked in order to get his son a job, he
is coldly refused admittance and feels betrayed, saying, "I gave them the best
years of my life." In this rural Turkish discourse, which is also colored by the
rural-urban dichotomies of Turkish modernist discourse, the safe Turkish village stands as the opposite of the threatening German metropolis.[1] The practicing Muslim confronts a godless and inhumane secularist society. The points of
view of dislocated guestworkers who were responsible for the welfare of their
families under the difficult conditions that faced them when they came to Germany had little public representation: the former villager is the subaltern who
can rarely speak in publicly audible ways, whose actions are interpreted through
the multiple discursive filters of Orientalism, Turkish and German secularisms,
feminism, and Islamic reform.[2] The parallel structures of Turkish and German
discourses, founded on the tradition-modernity dichotomy, make it particularly
difficult for migrants to resist the negative positions into which they are cast.

Though some of Germany's immigrant population, especially among first-
generation former guestworkers, might recognize aspects of their own past in
this rural Turkish discourse, migrants of Turkish background hold an array of
alternative perspectives and subject positions. For example, one anthropologist, in field research among guestworkers who had returned to their villages
for the summer, heard them report to their neighbors that they had actually
found German society quite moral (Magnarella 1998: 165), thereby disrupting
an element of rural Turkish discourse. In addition to the various perspectives
of second- and third-generation Turks in Germany, many Turks have migrated
to the country under circumstances quite different from the circumstances
of those who came under the guestworker program, including a wave of immigrants, many highly educated, who entered for political reasons during the
1980s.[3] Nevertheless, their subject positions are colored by the conjunction of
a hegemonic German discourse and a modernizing discourse in Turkey that
locates the Turkish migrant as other. Those of Turkish background who seek to
integrate into German society are often forced to choose between a "Turkish"
identity and a "German" identity even as they are confronted with marginalization through placement in inferior schools, employment discrimination, and
the effects of stigmatization.

Turks express a wide range of responses to being positioned as a stigmatized
minority and to German efforts to foster assimilation. A significant number,

especially among those who have been successful in their education and careers, view themselves as cosmopolitan and, in Berlin, may identify themselves as "Berliners." A significant portion of the second and third generation face poor job prospects, feel marginalized, and seek other sources of self-esteem such as groups of friends, athletic clubs, and street gangs. Still others turn to Islam.

I focus in this chapter on how stories like that of Aylin, caught up within a politics of representation, come to be understood as typical of gender organization within the Turkish and Muslim family, though they bear very little relationship to the micropolitics of everyday life within most families of Turkish background. I trace how cultural stereotypes play out in Germany in the different genres of cinema and social work literature. The former plays an important role in creating public images and myths; the latter is a manifestation of the scholarly apparatus that often guides policy formation and is also closely linked to other aspects of governmentality, creating a constellation of knowledge and power. I argue that these ostensibly distinct genres both naturalize a discourse based on the assumption of cultural difference. This discourse posits and constitutes homogeneous collective identities that hamper recognition of the actual heterogeneity of those who fall within the category of this collective identity; it also exacerbates miscommunications between Germans and Turks and between generations within the immigrant community, constrains social policy, and shapes the contours of accommodation and resistance to the solutions that are proposed to solve the perceived crisis. The tensions and miscommunications can be seen by tracing how people negotiate the micropolitics of everyday life, and by considering how women represent the men in their families as they describe their own experiences of growing up in a diasporic Turkish family.

THE MYTHOLOGIES OF GERMAN SOCIAL WORK

In German public culture, the scenario of the adolescent girl who is tightly controlled by her traditional Turkish family—especially her father and brothers—and finally rebels has been replayed over and over, in media accounts such as the story of Aylin, in cinema and literature, and in scholarship in the social sciences. The vignette depicting Aylin's fate appeared in the fall of 2003 in *Der Spiegel* as part of a long cover story in the wake of a decision by the Federal Constitutional Court in Germany concerning the headscarf. Though the article did not mention whether Aylin wore a headscarf, her story was presented as one piece of evidence among others that Muslim women are oppressed and that the headscarf is a symbol of their oppression and of Muslim "intolerance."

Drawing a link between the headscarf and the oppressive family that restricts the daughter's freedom is a powerful rhetorical strategy—in many ways parallel to the well-publicized headscarf struggle in France—in the politically charged debates currently going on in Germany. In Germany, conservatives and liberals alike have sought to prevent women who wear headscarves from teaching in public schools.[4] In all of these discussions, which take the struggle for women's rights as one of the hallmarks of a liberal democracy, the "problem" has been cast as one of the oppression of women in a traditional patriarchal order that has spilled over into the Western countries to which Muslim guestworkers have migrated.

A study describing the living conditions of Turkish women and girls written by Andrea Baumgartner-Karabak and Gisela Landesberger (1978), two social workers in Berlin, played an important role in shaping this discourse. Regarded at the time as "groundbreaking" (Boos-Nünning 1990: 489), it was viewed as the standard German-language work on the situation of Turkish women (Spohn 2002: 53) and included recommendations on strategies for social work with these women in Germany.[5] The authors established their authority as experts on Turkish cultural practices by spending a month in a Turkish village. From their perspective, the father makes decisions concerning the affairs of his children autocratically, with little or no input from his wife. The children, especially daughters, are treated like objects, to be traded off in marriage at the highest price possible (Baumgartner-Karabak and Landesberger 1978: 55). The writers indicate that the position of a woman is unconditional subordination to her father and husband. This male authority is justified in terms of the man's honor and the principles of Islam, which handicap and oppress women. This depiction of gender relations in the rural family is presented as if no checks on a man's arbitrary exercise of power and violence exist within the system. It is a fantasy of otherness that has echoes in the story of Aylin.

German scholars finally subjected the book to criticism in the 1990s because of its one-sided and exaggerated depictions of Turkish gender relations (see Lutz 1991; Spohn 1993, 2002). Margret Spohn, for example, pointed out that the authors were already convinced before their trip that the Turkish woman was oppressed and sought evidence of this oppression in the social structure of the Turkish village (Spohn 2002: 55). Despite the critical attention of scholars, the perspective articulated by Baumgartner-Karabak and Landesberger continued to pervade the perspective of many social workers and policy-oriented literature through the 1990s, as in the following formulation, written by Zehra Onder, a

Turkish scholar based at Bilkent University in Turkey who conducted field research in Germany in the early 1990s: "The circumstance of being torn between two cultures is most often a severe problem for Islamic families" (Onder 1996: 18). Onder made no distinction between "Islamic" and rural Turkish practices. She stated that "girls have a special negative status within the family, as well as in the Islamic environment of Turkey or among relatives and friends in Germany" (Onder 1996: 20). On the other hand,

> sons are almost invariably the favorite ones in their families. For example, if the son becomes ill, he is immediately taken to a doctor. But, if this happens to the daughter, she is usually left to her own fate . . . thousands of children, especially girls, die because of this attitude and reasoning . . . The Islamic norm-value system determines what is good and what is bad. The new social environment turns all this upside down through another value-norm system. As time elapses, a great conflict grows that can in no way be managed. (Onder 1996: 21–22)

The rhetorical structure of the article is transparent: Turkish rural culture devalues girls and overvalues boys, to the extent that girls are left to die when they become ill. This is in implicit contrast to the equal treatment of the sexes that is presumed to prevail in German society. Even the inverted relationship of Turkish to German culture is explicit: the Turkish "norm-value system" is, to quote, "upside down."

This piece of writing is a particularly unsubtle manifestation of the discourse that pervades the conversation of German social workers, government services personnel, and the schoolteachers whose job is to help Turkish children integrate into German society. Given the stereotypes about Muslim societies that dominate the Western media in the early twenty-first century, this polarized structure is plausible even to many who think of themselves as politically democratic and socially progressive. I spoke with several teachers and social workers during my research in Berlin between 1999 and 2004 and found that their attitudes toward the "problem" of Turkish integration into German society continued to be quite stereotyped, echoing the discourse of this social services–oriented literature. Most saw themselves as critical of the highly publicized racist attacks on Turks and concerned for the welfare of the Turkish population; nevertheless, their perspectives on the situation of Turkish women and integration often reflected this polarizing discourse, as illustrated by a journal entry I wrote following a conversation in the summer of 2003 with a professional woman who worked in a federal office in Berlin and had considerable contact with people from Turkey: "Her opinions about Turks seemed quite fixed. She felt that a big problem with integration is that the women are uneducated and trapped at home and so can't help their children with their schoolwork. They don't try to learn German. Her depiction of Turks seemed like an image from the early seventies." The unspoken corollary is that men are not trapped and that they are the ones who are confining their women at home.

The fact that Onder is a scholar from Turkey is a significant detail because, as I discussed in Chapter 1, modernization in Turkey over the course of the twentieth century has been shaped by a secularism that closely associated rural traditionalism, with Islam as a conservative force in a polarized political environment. Until recently, many of the Turkish educated elite, from radical left to the right, have been unreflexively secularist and supportive of state measures that strictly constrain Muslim practice. Onder's caricature of village Islam is consistent with this perspective.

Social work texts treat young Turkish women who have left their parents' homes as heroes. For example, one study is subtitled "A Long-Term Study of the Difficult Process of Finding One's Way Out of a Turkish Family" (Kultus 1998). The book's title, *Der Preis der Freiheit* (The Cost of Freedom), articulates the premise that "freedom" is something that must be bought by a young woman, paid for by her pain and struggle. Her traditional family is the repressive force that imprisons her. This book is intended as a tribute to the 743 brave Turkish women who fled their families and sought refuge in PAPATYA, a shelter for young women who wish to leave the confines and/or abuse of their Turkish families. It also highlights the importance of such public programs for facilitating Turks' adjustment to German culture. The book does include a single disclaimer to inform the reader that not all Turkish families are like the one of the book's heroine: "Not all young women of Turkish heritage in Germany leave their families under circumstances of conflict. There are also those whose parents are tolerant and who seek to let their daughters grow up in the same manner as German youth. Tolerance generally ends, however, with a girl's friendship with a young man, and with pre-marital sex" (Kultus 1998: 148). This passage implies a normative goal of the total assimilation of the Turkish young woman into German society, defined in the most liberal terms of total freedom of choice. This is, in effect, a demand for parents of Turkish background to abandon completely any effort to enforce Turkish or Islamic guidelines for the organization of gender relations and sexuality. It also implies that the German norm is one in which parents do not attempt to control or regulate their children's sexuality.

In contrast to this assimilationist view, cultural difference and multiculturalism have been emphasized in the provision of social services. Not only has the government sponsored a youth culture that celebrates hybridized art forms; both the state and private welfare organizations have, according to Frank-Olaf Radtke, actually created ethnicity and cultural difference where it otherwise would not have been salient:

> The decisive factor . . . was the emphasis on religion—a marker migrants themselves would not have used. The combination of language and religion for professional and administrative purposes created "cultures," and subsequently "ethnic groups," whose special needs the welfare organizations had to meet through particular measures . . . Migrants were no longer dealt with in their social roles as workers or family members, workless and/or homeless, pregnant, school failures, alcoholics, drug addicts, etc. but seen from an ethnological point of view as representatives of their national culture or descent. (Radtke 1997: 252)

The consequence was that intervention strategies were applied to groups rather than to individuals. Until recently, for example, minority children were often segregated by language in the schools, whether or not they needed or wanted to be. This practice found a justification in the radical cultural differences that had been posited in social work literature.

Within the genre of social work, an effort at facilitating integration was articulated at a 1996 Youth Forum in Berlin on "problems facing the migrant youth in Germany" (Soysal 2001: 17). Most of the young women participating stated that they had few problems with their parents, since many families over the years have gradually relaxed the restrictions on their daughters. Yet the forum addressed the problem of gender by calling for the emancipation of girls and dispensing with traditions (Soysal 2001: 19)—not a very balanced outcome from the perspective of respect for cultural difference. There seemed to be a discrepancy between the abstract expression of a problem with "traditional" gender practices and the specific experiences of the young women present, who did not personally experience this problem. Discussions such as this play a role in reinforcing a discourse of difference, especially when experts are involved. It becomes the lens through which individuals assess their own experiences and frame their own identities—even when they see themselves as exceptional. In this frame, the project of women is to liberate themselves from traditional practices while men must be persuaded or forced to yield their power and privilege within the family. The power of the state is then deployed to aid women in this struggle against men and tradition.

THE TURKISH IMMIGRANT AS SIGNIFIER

The earliest films depicting guestworkers in Germany were made by German directors. It is thus not surprising that these films would reflect German concerns and fantasies, ranging from social commentary critical of everyday practices of social discrimination and the poor working conditions immigrants faced to stories of Turkish girls and women being oppressed by their patriarchal fathers and husbands. Many of the films about guestworkers and their families have been created by German and Turkish directors in the genre of social realism. These films are saturated with the didactic function of social commentary, enabling audiences to see the texture of immigrant experience through devices of storytelling and imaging in ways that otherwise would be invisible. But this reality is illusory. The novelist Paul Auster, in a meditation on the demise of the silent film (2002), suggested that the introduction of sound and color was an aesthetic loss because the power of imagination had been supplanted by the semblance of reality. This semblance of reality, even in melodrama, results in a potentially powerful ideological tool that persuades by stirring emotion while giving the audience a sense of having witnessed firsthand that which is otherwise unfamiliar and even exotic.

The socially critical genre of film and literature focused on the oppressive working and living conditions of male and even female guestworkers in Germany was particularly characteristic of the early years of Turkish migration (for example, Fassbinder 1973; Gförer 1986).[6] The guestworker was often depicted as a powerless, economically exploited laborer who lived on the margins of German society and faced the ever-present threat of deportation. Several German directors used the guestworker as a device for depicting the exclusionary practices of German society. The viewer is asked to identify with the struggles of the victim as tragic hero, seeking to assert his or her humanity in the face of a heartless world.

One of the earliest and most famous depictions of the guestworker in Germany is Rainer Werner Fassbinder's film *Angst essen Seele auf* (Ali: Fear Eats the Soul) (1973), a melodrama that traces the development of a relationship between a young North African guestworker, Ali, and a late-middle-aged German cleaning woman, Emmi. Four years earlier, Fassbinder had directed the film *Katzelmacher* (1969), which focused on how the presence of a foreigner in a German neighborhood of young adults stimulates fantasies, rumors, and violence about the foreigner's sexuality and otherness. This earlier film communicated very little about the foreigner himself, in this case a Greek. In both films Fassbinder is ultimately more concerned with the foreigner as a trope for his own experience of otherness vis-à-vis German society.

In *Angst essen Seele auf*, Fassbinder powerfully uses the black male body to explore issues of discrimination and desire—no doubt in part because the Turkish body as signifier, being more ambiguous in its racial marking, would not have played out in quite the same way as fundamentally other. Ali's foreign body is the most salient presence in the film. This body is highly sexualized, its power able to stimulate desire in the frumpiest of women. The black body foregrounds the close ties between abjection and desire in the process of stigmatization. The transgressiveness of this desire is heightened by Emmi's age and position as a cleaning woman who dresses in ugly clothes and has grown children. Watching the emergence of her desire evokes in audiences an initial revulsion that echoes the reactions of her children and neighbors. When I show the film in a college classroom, students always express visceral reactions of disgust when Ali and Emmi begin to interact sexually. The students' disgust focuses on the idea of Emmi becoming sexually involved with such a younger man. Fassbinder has deployed a figure that allows a reaction of disgust uncensored by liberal sentiments and antiracist pieties. We then watch the failure of this relationship under the pressure of German prejudice and discrimination, and the physical collapse of Ali due to an ulcer caused by "fear" (*Angst*), which "eats the soul." Though *Angst essen Seele auf* focuses on a North African guestworker, its original title was *All Turks Are Called "Ali"* (Bingham 2003), an indication that Fassbinder certainly had the situation of Turkish guestworkers on his mind when he made the film, which was released at precisely the point when Germany was closing its borders to new immigrant guestworkers but was beginning to allow the families of current migrants to join their husbands. This early title refers to a moment in the film when one character comments that the Muslim immigrants are all viewed as Turks, and all are called Ali, foregrounding the way that migrant workers are treated as objects. In the film, only fragmentary bits of information about Ali's personal and cultural background emerge in broken German.

Fassbinder used the figure of the stigmatized other to express his personal fantasies of marginalization that stem from his own conflicted sexuality. The "ruination" of masculinity associated with homosexuality in Fassbinder's work has been closely analyzed by Kaja Silverman (1992). Fassbinder seems to have used the trope of the immigrant—the black other—as a vehicle to articulate his own sense of fear and marginalization in a social context in which normative masculinity excluded the possibility of a homosexual orientation.[7] In *Katzelmacher*, Fassbinder himself played the character of the marginalized immigrant who is beaten up by local men. In Fassbinder's two films about discrimination against an ethnic minority, it would seem that Fassbinder himself identifies with the character of the marginalized outsider who is the target of discrimination. As the title of *Katzelmacher* indicates, one of the salient signs of deviance is the imagined sexual proclivities of the outsider (the title is a term in Bavarian slang term for guestworker "implying sexual proclivities").[8] Fassbinder thus used the discursive structure of the stigmatization of an exploited minority to represent another form of stigmatized masculinity, associated with homosexuality, that he overtly disavowed. The sexuality and masculinity of the Muslim worker as outsider were already operating as signifiers in German cinema, though the foreigner's specific cultural difference was not a central focus.

Another film about the plight of the guestworker that has had a powerful effect on the German public is *Ganz unten* (At the Bottom of the Heap) (Gförer 1986), a documentary about the journalist Günter Wallraff (see Wallraff 1988). This film stimulated public discourse about inhumane working conditions and turned the situation of guestworkers into a major political issue. In the film, the worker, Ali, is understood to have left his family behind in Turkey to move to Germany and lives in a world where he communicates only with other guestworkers and his German boss. It showed how guestworkers were treated as subhuman, a subject position that is foregrounded by the fact that Ali was actually Wallraff himself disguised as a guestworker. By knowing that this Turk is actually German, the audience is forced to confront a contrast between the treatment of a German and the treatment of a Turk. Though some praised Wallraff's political and social agenda of calling attention to the plight of the guestworker, others criticized him for reproducing stereotypes of the guestworker in his disguise. Like Fassbinder, Wallraff was not concerned with the cultural particularity of the foreigner, but rather with the foreigner's position as other in Germany. In his disguise, Wallraff takes on the identity of the stigmatized other through performance of what is explicitly not-self, in a politics of journalistic exposé in which he becomes the hero of the oppressed in the face of their corrupt capitalist employers.

Several films focus on the hardships created by the practice of deportation, which always hangs over the head of the illegal immigrant and constitutes him as tragic hero. For example, in *Jannan—die Abschiebung* (Jannan—The Deportation) (van Beveren 1986), a Kurdish man flees Turkey but in Germany is confronted by gangsters, corrupt police, and a hardened bureaucracy. He finally commits suicide as he faces deportation. The deportation theme is also central to *Drachenfutter* (Dragon Chow) (Schütte 1987), a story of young immigrant men of different ethnicities who join forces to establish a restaurant, and to *Die Kümmeltürkin Geht* (The Spice Lady Leaves) (Meerapfel 1985), about a woman who is deported after living in Berlin for fourteen years. In each case, the central characters are represented sympathetically in terms of their class position as marginalized outsiders.

CINEMA REPRESENTATIONS OF THE TURKISH WOMEN

Film representations of the first generation of Turkish men are curiously dichotomized. Either these men are guestworkers who are represented as the exploited victims of German capitalism, an underclass, or they are Muslim foreigners who are represented in negative terms as the oppressors of their women because of their traditional culture. This is, in effect, a shift of focus from class position to cultural difference. As Turkish wives and daughters eventually followed these men to Germany, the cinematic gaze shifted in emphasis to representations of the plight of these women.[9] In addition to reflecting the demographic change that followed the 1973 shift in immigration policy away from guestworkers toward family reunification, this shift parallels a turn in feminist theory to culture as a source of oppression, a shift that I discussed in Chapter 1 in connection with feminism in Turkey.[10] This feminist agenda, when taken up into popular discourse, generated a focus on gender exploitation as a cultural practice; and this focus seemed to have displaced the media's focus on labor exploitation and class difference as characterizing the experience of Muslim immigrants. With the transition in German public discourse to a concern with Muslim gender practices, Muslim women became the oppressed class. Within this logic, Muslim men moved from being an economically exploited underclass to being the exploiters. Their inferiority was no longer a product of the inequities of a German social order but was treated as an essential attribute of Turkish traditionalism and understood to be a cultural inferiority.

Once families began to join the guestworkers after 1973, films that depicted some of the difficulties facing these families appeared. The 1979 children's film *Metin* (Draeger 1979), for example, focused on latchkey children whose parents work as laborers all day. There is little depiction of cultural difference, except for language barriers and a scene in which a German girl who has befriended Metin dresses up like a Turkish girl and is taunted by other German children. In this film the relationship between husband and wife is presented as a partnership in which both work hard. But by the late 1980s the image of the exploited guestworker as victim was joined by, and to a large extent supplanted by, a focus, not on the difficulties facing Turkish families struggling to find a place in German society, but on the plight of the Turkish Muslim woman. The otherness of Turkish and Muslim gender practices was emphasized. The image of the Turkish man shifted away from the figure of the exploited guestworker as victim, and other facets of his collective character were developed in the media. When gender and family relations were foregrounded, the moral balance of diasporic masculinity shifted. When it comes to the Turkish Muslim family, the man is viewed as traditional and violent toward women.

The image of the young woman whose family deprives her of her freedom and rights was a central part of the limited repertoire of images of Turkish immigrants that filmmakers constructed. As in the social policy literature, the dominant theme was a clash of cultures. In the film *40 Quadratmeter Deutschland* (Forty Square Meters of Germany) (1986) by Tevfik Başer,[11] a Turkish guestworker brings his bride from his home village in Turkey to his small flat in urban Germany. The film is a relentless depiction of confinement: the husband works long hours while his wife endures solitary days locked in a claustrophobic apartment and increasingly struggles against her culture and her husband. The film makes it clear that her husband's actions arise from the patriarchal culture of rural Turkey, magnified by his fear of an alien and threatening German world. He controls her life completely, and she has no other social contacts. When he suddenly dies of a seizure, she cautiously waddles, very pregnant, into the freedom of the German world outside her door. Though directed by a Turkish filmmaker who had himself moved to Germany,[12] the film is highly stereotyped in its representations of Turkish villagers who have migrated to Germany and reproduces the discourse of the Turkish intellectual and professional urban elite who sees the villager in negative terms as traditional other (see Göktürk 2001: 141).

In the film *Yasemin* (1988), a box-office hit in Germany by the German director Hark Bohm, Yasemin becomes the focus of the affections of the German boy Jan. Her father increasingly restricts her activities, pulling her out of school despite her academic promise and keeping her under constant surveillance. When he tries to send her "back" to Turkey, a place where she has never lived, she flees with Jan. The filmmaker based his depictions of Turkish life and customs on the diaries of two young girls he met while doing research for the film (Pflaum 2002). One German review described the director of *Yasemin*: "Without taking sides, he deals with the seemingly irreconcilable differences between traditional, patriarchal Muslim values and those of contemporary German society" (Pflaum 2002). Though the film acknowledges some of the German prejudices that make integration difficult, its emphasis is on the freedom that German society offers. This is very much a one-sided perspective. Katie Trumpener, in her study of German cinema, summarizes the film's message in a way that foregrounds the parallel between German and Turkish myths of return: "Here it is not the Germans who agitate to send the Turks back to where they came from. . . . Instead it is the Turks themselves who threaten to send back their own Germanicized children, and concerned, caring bureaucrats who must take Turkish children away from their parents, for their own good" (Trumpener 1989: 24).

Yasemin stresses the gulf dividing the social spaces that the main character must cross as she passes back and forth between school and home, transforming her body by hitching up and lowering her skirt, removing and donning her village-style headscarf. Openness and freedom are contrasted with closed spaces and confinement; the value of the self who may freely choose a spouse is contrasted with the value of the group that arranges marriages within the group; education and career ambition contrast with the foreclosing of possibilities for women.

The body itself is inscribed in particularly obvious ways in these films, with posture marking identity. In *40 Quadratmeter Deutschland* the female protagonist walks with hunched shoulders and eyes cast down. Yasemin, in contrast, carries herself with an assertive, sometimes even defiant posture. In *Auf Eigenen Füssen* (On One's Own Feet) (Horst and Lottman 1987), a film of similar structure to *Yasemin*, the daughter defies her father's desire to marry her off by running away to live with some German friends; but her Turkish identity is also marked by the hunched-over posture, even when she is hanging out with her German friends. Only at the end of the film, when she is alone at work in her photography studio, free of her father at last, does she stand up straight.

It could be argued that these images simply depict the reality of the situation young Turkish women faced in the early phase of diasporic experience, a reality that some women such as Aylin (of the *Der Spiegel* article that began this chapter) continue to face a generation later. I have personally met and written about women whose experiences have closely paralleled Yasemin's (see Ewing 2002), an experience that would seem to further confirm the film's accuracy. Melodrama laced with realism encourages such a reading. But it is now startling to me how closely the stories and choices of some of the young women I have known followed the "script" of films like *Yasemin* and others of similar structure such as *Auf Eigenen Füssen*, suggesting that young women's perceptions of their situations and their decision to run away were themselves being shaped by circulating representations such as those the films present. This genre of film, its themes echoed by representations in other media and the knowledge/power constellations of governmentality as manifested in social services, "scripts" the possibilities and choices of young women. To use an old phrase of Clifford Geertz, such images operate as a model "for" as well as a model "of" reality, in a process that naturalizes the film images (Geertz 1973).[13]

Running away thereby becomes thinkable for young women, a kind of cultural practice. Nergis, a young Turkish woman whom I met in the Netherlands in 1997 just after she had run away from her husband, explained: "Within the past three to four years, lots of girls have begun to run away. This is the first generation that is growing up and knows Dutch society. They don't want to live in the closed Turkish community, which doesn't even know what it is like in Turkey today—they live the way Turkey was in the 1960s. They don't want education, especially for the girls." This view, that the diaspora community was rigidly holding onto customs that had changed in Turkey, was a commonly repeated observation that I heard from a wide range of people of Turkish background, both in the Netherlands and in Germany, over several years. It reproduced the perception of an unbridgeable gap between Turkish culture and German or Dutch culture. This *perception* of an unbridgeable gap may in many cases serve to *reproduce* this gap. As I discuss later in this chapter, Nergis's own family quickly, within the space of a few days, accommodated to her desires and even changed their whole approach to managing a younger daughter. This suggests that her parents were potentially more flexible than they had seemed and that there could have been other options, other scripts, along the way, had the discursive environment been different.

The encapsulation of Turks as a "traditional" ethnic minority is reinforced by marriage patterns that are encouraged by immigration law, even as these marriage patterns are perceived within Germany and other countries to which Turks and other Muslims have migrated as a "natural" or "traditional" pattern that is difficult to make Turks give up. Marriage choices are a key strategizing response to the barriers to migration imposed by immigration laws. This response has roots in preexisting cultural practices but is not simply a reproduction of those practices. They become a tactic for maximizing migration opportunities, not just a manifestation of "tradition." In Nergis's case, the parents' intense pressure on their daughter to make what they themselves would likely have considered an unsuitable match had they been in Turkey stemmed in part from the pressure they were experiencing from relatives in Turkey who saw the marriage as an opportunity for their son to migrate to the Netherlands.

Young women are thus interpreting the actions of their parents in terms of cultural stereotypes and inevitabilities instead of recognizing the complex sources of those actions. In response, they act out their part in the script by running away. This intergenerational misinterpretation is a central theme in the 1996 film *Ben Annemin Kiziyim* (I'm My Mother's Daughter) by Seyhan Derin. Derin, the daughter of a guestworker, ran away from home at age fifteen. Her situation illustrates the classic pattern that is so clearly and stereotypically represented in the German media as a manifestation of Turkish culture: she and two sisters fled from an authoritarian father who had threatened to send them "back" to Turkey after their oldest sister eloped with a German boy. Thirteen years later, as a young director, she made this documentary film, which depicts a reconciliation with her parents that occurred through the process of making the film. The film demonstrates retrospectively the negative effects on Derin's family of the congruent polarizations of German and rural Turkish discourses. As Derin and her family work through their reconciliation before the camera, the audience sees how these polarizations had constrained Derin's possibilities for identity formation as an adolescent and how her parents' relationship had been, not a manifestation of Turkish gender inequality, but rather an effect of the stresses of migration and discrimination in Germany. From a German perspective, Derin is a prime example of successful integration—a well-educated and successful young filmmaker, an embodiment of the cultural hybrid. Yet she had been living a life of total rupture with her past and her parents.

In the film, Derin and her mother visit the family village in Turkey. It is in this liminal space and time that misunderstandings are overcome through new kinds of interactions. In the village, Derin's aunt tells her that everyone thought she and her sisters had run off to become prostitutes when they left home. In village discourse, becoming a prostitute is the most corrupting, dishonoring fate that one can imagine. What from a German perspective was seen as successful hybridity was, from the perspective of her relatives, an abomination.

Through the process of filmmaking, Derin was able to accept an identity as her mother's daughter that she had previously disavowed. Near the end of the film, she contrasts her new insights into her mother's strengths and independence with the image she had carried around of her mother, which had been based on stereotypes formed in Germany. Derin narrates (in Turkish): "The image of a self-sufficient and independent village woman blatantly contradicts my image formed in Germany of a mother who was withdrawn into herself and obediently accepted the conditions of life, a picture that gradually becomes blurred before my eye." Before the experience of making the film, Derin had known little of her mother, seeing her as someone who had most of the time been overshadowed by her father, "caught up in traditions which I could not accept as valid for me."

Derin's film account provides further evidence for the importance of disentangling explanations based on "culture" from those based on the structural constraints of the immigration situation and the dynamics of the ongoing decisions made within a particular family. But it also allows us to go further and recognize that difficulties within the family are often a consequence of the stresses of the migration itself and of the challenging circumstances of life in Germany. In her voice-over, Derin describes her father: he worked in a German mine until he was so badly injured that he became completely disabled; he incurred large gambling debts; he drank too much and then was cold to the family. Instead of being gentle, he imposed arbitrary rules. In a difficult situation, he sought to maintain control by becoming authoritarian.[14]

This reaction is itself a cultural process, but not simply a manifestation of "culture." When guestworkers commiserated and strategized, seeking solutions to the difficulties that threatened them, they drew on a range of resources and understandings, many but not all of which they had brought with them from Turkey. To identify such an active, dynamic process is quite different from merely saying that they acted in these ways because of their "culture," which is understood as preexisting rules for action that they must give up if they are to assimilate. But a German discourse that attributes to Turkish culture all evidence of what to German eyes is vice also encourages misrecognition by the men themselves. In the legal system, the "cultural defense" argument, as when a man commits a murder and then claims that his "culture" made him do it, is often used in precisely this way.[15]

FOCUSING ON MEN

The plot of a number of films such as *Yasemin* and *40 Quadratmeter Deutschland* is based on the oppression of Turkish women and their possibilities for liberation in German society. At the moment a woman gains her freedom in one way or another, her father, husband, or other male relative is vanquished. As the villain in the dramatic structure, he is not the focus of an audience's sympathies, and his defeat is presented as well-deserved. However, it is possible to read these films against the grain of this interpretation and focus on the men themselves. From this angle, one can see depictions of the man's shame and humiliation, even in films by German directors. This presentation of well-deserved humiliation is an instance of the abjection of Turkish masculinity, as this abjected masculinity is linked to honor and tradition.

In *Auf Eigenen Füssen*, for example, the seventeen-year-old girl Esma is to be married to a Turkish man without her consent. She leaves home, finds a place in a youth home, and begins training to become a photographer. But her father, whose honor is threatened by her having left home, kidnaps her and finds another husband for her. He is shamed by his daughter's behavior and loses his status in the gym where he has worked as a coach for many years. The father is depicted as enraged by his daughter's escape and concerned only with his own honor, not his daughter's happiness. He repeatedly calls her a whore. At one point, the mother says, "She's not a whore," an indication that the father's perception is distorted by his excessive concern with honor. As in many German representations, the mother's perspective is closer to a German one, a sign that women are more readily able to assimilate into German society. This is a "message film" with little subtlety of character development. The father appears to experience no inner conflict about his struggle with his daughter—only a determination to prevail and restore his honor and humiliation at his failure. The male characters act as foils to emphasize the plight of the young woman.

Yasemin, with its similar plot, also presents images that conform to popular stereotypes of the Turkish Muslim man. We see in a father's struggles to control his daughter's sexuality an oscillation between gentleness and sudden violence reminiscent of nineteenth-century German travelers' accounts of the Turkish man. At the end of the film, Yasemin resists the force of her cousin and father by grabbing a knife and threatening to kill herself. Her father helplessly watches her run off with her German boyfriend, shamed before his fellow guestworkers, who had been urging him to let her die.

Both *Auf Eigenen Füssen* and *Yasemin* depict second-generation men as well as those of the first generation. These young men are presented as simply carrying through with traditional gender relationships in the family. In *Auf Eigenen Füssen*, Esma's brother helps their father get her back after she has run away, kidnapping her from the youth home where she is living. The young men in *Yasemin* also appear unconflicted about their roles as traditional Turkish men, concerned only with successfully maintaining their personal honor and the family's honor.

But in comparison with *Auf Eigenen Füssen*, the depiction of men in *Yasemin* is rather more nuanced. The shame and emasculation of the men in Yasemin's family are particularly visible, as in the final confrontation between Yasemin and her father when he backs down in front of the other men. Yasemin's brother-in-law is sexually impotent and, to hide his failure to bloody the sheets on his wedding night, he accuses his bride of not being a virgin. This move to protect his own sense of manhood has disastrous consequences for both his wife and for her sister Yasemin, whose father drastically curtails Yasemin's life to prevent her from dishonoring the family in the same way. When Yasemin confronts her brother-in-law with his lie, he erupts in fury, also impotent, threatening to hit her with a wooden crate but instead smashing a piece of furniture and running from the room after Yasemin grabs a knife to fend him off.

We can see a similar humiliation of the traditional man who confronts a woman seeking escape at the end of the Turkish film *Berlin in Berlin* (1993), a Turkish-German coproduction directed by the prominent Turkish filmmaker Sinan Çetin. The film was intended for both German and Turkish markets and has been the object of considerable critical and scholarly attention. Angelica Fenner (2000), for example, examines the shifting spectatorial positionings structured into the film, positionings that reflect the range of intended viewers. The depiction of Turkish male subjectivity is somewhat more nuanced than in earlier films; but Çetin, whose early politically conscious films sought to negotiate the profound divide within Turkish society between rural-urban, religious-secular, and traditional-modern, has been criticized more recently for focusing on box-office successes that reproduce mainstream ethnic, class, and gender discourses instead of disrupting them (Fenner 2000: 110). According to Fenner, "he seems to offer up an image of Turkish emigres that caters to a European viewership harboring stereotypical expectations about a singular Turkish identity" (Fenner 2000: 111). Fenner identifies elements of the film that also disrupt stereotypes, such as the striking physical resemblance between the Turkish and German antagonists, which "evince[s] the arbitrary nature of ethnic difference" (Fenner 2000: 114); however, the impact of such elements must be assessed within the context of the whole film. Michelle Mattson has suggested for the German television *Krimmi* (crime show) that such elements may simply function to assuage the guilt of the hegemonic subject position by providing markers of a liberal perspective, thereby reinforcing the dominant stereotypes (Mattson 1999: 161).

The film *Berlin in Berlin* opens on a Berlin construction site, where a young German engineer, Thomas, becomes fascinated with Dilber, the wife of a Turkish construction worker who brings her husband his lunch every day. He secretly photographs her, and when the husband discovers the photos in Thomas's office, he accuses his wife of adultery. The next time she arrives at the construction site to deliver his lunch, Thomas intervenes and unintentionally impales the husband on a metal rod, killing him. Though the incident is officially declared an accident, Thomas tracks down Dilber, ostensibly to apologize to her. He is chased by her brothers-in-law, who threaten to kill him in order to restore the family honor, and Thomas slips into an open door to evade them. When he realizes that he is actually in the apartment of Dilber's family, he hides but is finally discovered by Murtuz, one of the brothers-in-law. Murtuz is about to kill him when the grandmother intervenes and declares that Islam and the rules of hospitality forbid the murder of a guest. Thomas becomes a prisoner within the apartment and gradually is included in the daily life of the family, but the threat of murder hangs over him if he steps outside the apartment. Murtuz, who as the eldest brother is entitled to marry his dead brother's wife, competes with Thomas for Dilber. Dilber, after rejecting Murtuz's advances, is shown contemplating the photographs that Thomas had taken of her.

The filmmaker leads the viewer into a perspective focused solely on rescuing the Turkish woman. At the end of the film, the traditional men in her family are dragged into a more egalitarian, modern social order when she proclaims her right to be with a German man. But if we read the film from the perspective of Turkish male honor and pride, we see that these traditionally portrayed men are humiliated: Dilber finally asks Murtuz to allow her to leave with Thomas, saying to Murtuz: "I'm leaving because I want to live. You haven't the right to kill me. I don't even know him. Let me go. I'm leaving because I want to live" (translation from Fenner 2000: 130). She as woman thus represents the modern subject who demands freedom from the traditional man, whose masculinity rests on a foundation of honor grounded in violence. Murtuz is clearly vanquished as he gives up and lets her go.

In the films discussed, women are depicted as dominated, with the husband or father showing little or no regard for women's concerns or desires. Tevfik Başer's 1986 film *40 Quadratmeter Deutschland*, discussed earlier, was regarded at the time of its release as a definitive portrait of a Turkish issue in Germany presented from the perspective of a Turkish director. As one author has commented, however, the film is "a reactionary example of a cliché-laden portrayal of Turkish fellow citizens" (Farzanefar 2005: 1; see also Göktürk 2001). If we view this film not through the lens of the oppressed woman but through that of the man, examining how his self-esteem, honor, and sexuality are depicted, it is a model of the process of emasculation in the diaspora. The husband locks his wife in the apartment when he goes to work because he is afraid of what will happen to her in this alien city. His control over her thus stems from a position of weakness and uncertainty vis-à-vis the broader German society. When he decides he wants to have sex with his wife while she is on her hands and knees scrubbing the floor, he simply mounts her from the rear, animal-like, and the rest of the scene shows her suffering through it. The audience is thereby prompted to view his sexual relations with his wife as self-serving and oppressive, as verging on rape, since we are not shown instances of mutual sexuality.

The liberation of this confined Turkish woman is linked to her husband's death. Near the end of the film, he is stricken with an epileptic seizure while taking a shower and falls dead. It is not a heroic death, but one of total weakness and emasculation: he is shown nude, with his flaccid penis exposed. He is completely humiliated in the gaze of the viewer. Given the concern among Muslims for proper bodily covering, such exposure is particularly shameful. The image of the Turkish man lying naked on a German bathroom floor stands in stark contrast to that of his wife, who timidly emerges, nine months pregnant, into the bright daylight of the German world outside her apartment. Though the Turkish director Başer is as condemning of rural Turkish gender practices and masculinity as are many German directors, he has also gone to even greater lengths to depict the abasement of Turkish masculinity by including a scene of full frontal nudity. This raises the question of whether Başer was at the same time communicating a sense of something lost in the transition to modernity.

HYBRIDITY AS A SOLUTION TO THE "CULTURAL GAP"

In articulating the problem of assimilation and how to accomplish it, a number of German institutions and discursive practices promote and support those youth who feel a part of German culture. This is evident in the social worker's depiction of the "brave" heroine who flees her Turkish family to the safety and socialization of a German shelter, discussed earlier (Kultus 1998). In the opening scene of *Yasemin*, the title character is dressed in a karate outfit and engaged in hand-to-hand combat with a German boy in an after-school karate class, though under the watchful eye of her male cousin. For Germans, secular Turkish youth who participate in cosmopolitan youth culture are the intermediaries between traditional Turks and German society; some are a sign of the success of integration, while others, who drop out of school or get caught up in violence and crime, are a sign of failure, reflections of their families' failure to appreciate the value of a good education and assimilation.

In a discursive environment in which cultural difference is dichotomized and social activists have denounced multiculturalism as a policy that encourages the maintenance of a parallel society, a popular solution to the problem of integration has been a celebration of *hybridity*, understood as the fusion of two distinct cultures into new, creative and dynamic forms, an idea originally popularized in the United States and Britain. There have been numerous scholarly critiques of this concept (see, for example, Young 1995; Werbner 1997); for Germany, Leslie Adelson has argued that the theme of "betweeness" functions to reinforce mutually exclusive collective identities (Adelson 2003: 131). Certainly the concept of hybridity is not a good model for analyzing how people caught between cultures actually negotiate identity, because it does not explain how individuals manage inconsistency through a variety of strategies that generate multiple, contextualized identities (Ewing 2003). Nevertheless, it is not simply an analytic tool that can be challenged and discarded. Though talk of hybridity among minorities in Europe does not stretch back in time as do the ideologies of "creolization" and "*mestizaje*" in discourses of national identity in Latin America, hybridity as a sign and an identity marker has nonetheless become a part of popular culture and, along with the principle of multiculturalism, an ideological force in political discourse.[16] The concept has been important for valorizing the identities of those who successfully occupy culturally "in-between" spaces, such as the Turkish girl who takes up boxing or the successful Turkish-German entrepreneur. The "hybrid" and the related model of a "hyphenated identity" have become cultural productions projected by the media, to be adopted or rejected by individuals, alongside other possible identities.[17] Commonly, it is the women who are to be redeemed through hybrid strategies, which rescue them from the oppressive strategies of their fathers and brothers.

The concepts of hybridity, hyphenation, and multiculturalism are consciously used by "German-Turkish" culture producers born in Germany. A popular Berlin radio program, for example, is called "Multikulti." But, as Asye Caglar has argued, though German-Turkish rap is celebrated by rappers as the voice of the street against the power of the "center" (Caglar 1998: 249, 251), German state-sponsored institutions such as youth clubs actively support and popularize such groups. She further points out that "a community worker tone and terminology all find their way into German-Turks' rap" (Caglar 1998: 252), addressing social problems such as racism, drug abuse, and violence and reinscribing existing categories and status rather than negotiating new scripts of identity.[18] The political message of the rap group Cartel, for example, is "to mobilize the masses against arson attacks, racism, xenophobia, exclusion, drug trade, drug abuse, materialism, capitalism, and antagonism between Kurds and Turks" (Kaya 2001: 185).[19] This "social work scenario" (Göktürk 2001: 133) also characterizes films such as *Yasemin*, a perspective particularly evident in the scene in which Yasemin's teacher comes to her father's grocery store to try to persuade him to allow Yasemin to return to school.

In recent years young German directors of Turkish background have projected an idea of hybridity in their production of a burgeoning number of films that depict the lives of youth from the second and third generations and are construed as resistant to the German discursive positioning of Turks. These films have been celebrated as the "neo-neo" German cinema.[20] Deniz Göktürk has traced in them a shift from the social realism of a "cinema of duty" toward the "pleasures of hybridity" (Göktürk 2001: 3). This shift follows a trend that had been identified for black British cinema of the 1990s (Malik 1996). A similar celebration of hybridity can be seen in Ayhan Kaya's ethnographic study of working-class Turkish "hip-hop youth" in Berlin. Kaya contests sociological representations of German-Turkish youth as a "lost generation" or "in-between," preferring to emphasize the creativity and cultural richness associated with bricolage and hybridity (Kaya 2001: 82). Though voicing the perspectives and the raw choices that many Turkish youth face, many of these images (like those of other genres of popular culture such as hip hop) also reinscribe the dichotomies of the dominant discourse as they seek to disrupt stereotypical media representations. In *Aprilkinder* (Yavuz 1998),[21] for example, three siblings are caught between cultures. The oldest son works at a demeaning job in a meatpacking plant and falls in love with a German prostitute but relinquishes her to succumb to an arranged marriage. The middle son rejects the idea of a factory job and succeeds financially through the underworld of drug dealing.

Both, however, are operating far below the middle ranks of the German status hierarchy and job ladder. The youngest sibling, a daughter, wears a Walkman to listen to pop music but is shy and fearful in public—presumably a sign of her repressive upbringing.

This generation of filmmakers, musicians, and other cosmopolitans has successfully mediated the opposition and acts as the new voice of hybrid youth. They have even become figures of mediation themselves, with their doings included in documentaries about young cosmopolitan German-Turks such as *Zwischen Kebab und Karriere* (Between Kebab and Career) (Kalinowsky and Kron 1999). Nevertheless, the images they produce do not always transcend the dichotomies they attempt to mediate in their work and lives.

Cultural production has increasingly focused on and elaborated a fluid space of integration, moving away from the dichotomies of earlier films into what Homi Bhabha has called the "third space of enunciation" (Bhabha 1994: 37). The Berliner female rapper Azize-A claims an identity in the following terms: "I attempt to erase the question 'are we Turkish or German,' and announce that we are *multi-kulti* and cosmopolitan. I want to show that we are no more sitting between the two chairs, we have got a 'third chair' between those two" (Kaya 2002: 40). As filmmakers of Turkish background establish themselves in German cinema, cinematic depictions of youth of Turkish background are showing new flexibility, but they continue to be shaped by these founding dichotomies. Even in the most celebrated of this neo-neo German cinema, the theme of the oppressed young woman remains powerful. Fatih Akin's 2004 film *Gegen die Wand* (Against the Wall; titled *Head-On* in English), which has achieved international attention, begins with the oppressed-woman theme: in order to escape from the constraints of her oppressive father, a young woman initiates a marriage of convenience with a culturally hybrid man whose life has descended into alcohol and despair. This powerful film moves between German and Turkish worlds, exploring a hybrid "third space" by disrupting the myth of a woman's escape from family into German society as well as the dichotomy between Germany as a cosmopolitan urban space and Turkey as a traditional rural space. Nevertheless, it takes off from the conventional starting point of a young woman's flight from her family, complete with the authoritarian Turkish father and the brother ready to kill her when the family is dishonored.

What are the implications of the metaphor of hybridity for representations of masculinity? Kaya, in his study of hip-hop youth in Berlin, focused on the hip-hop culture of working-class male youth who hang out in youth centers and argued that this culture brings together the cultural particularity of "attachment to homeland, religion and ethnicity" with global hip-hop music and associated forms of "coolness" (Kaya 2001: 15). As in American black youth culture, coolness involves a style of critical distance and relaxed posture that "looks very serious and masculine" (Kaya 2001: 170). Among these youth, sources of distinction associated with coolness include the experience of incarceration and use of the mobile phone, a "symbol of masculinity" (Kaya 2001: 130). This culture is inflected locally to include nostalgia for Anatolia as homeland, linguistic code-switching between German and Turkish, and Turkish interpersonal relationships. The latter include familylike authority relationships between older and younger boys within a youth group based on hierarchical relations of respect and protection (Kaya 2001: 130) and a Turkish pattern of gender relations. These young men, while having relationships with German girls, still consider local Turkish girls to be "their" women, with whom they rarely interact (Kaya 2001: 132).

Scholars such as Kaya have emphasized the creativity of this Turkish hip hop in order to disrupt the assumption that hip-hop youth are just unproductively hanging out, contesting the negative positioning in German discourse of youth of Turkish background. Nevertheless, the effects of the creative hybridity of hip hop need to be analyzed rather than merely celebrated. Studies of the effects of hip hop and rap on images of African American men in the United States suggest that gangsta imagery is a central theme because it sells, not because it represents the essence of African American male experience.[22] This imagery also creates dissension within the black community, especially with respect to the treatment of women, given that the music of some groups exhibits rampant misogyny (Watkins 2005). As bell hooks has argued, coolness among African American men in the United States has generated a problematic form of masculinity that, far from being resistant to white cultural and economic imperialism, is an effect of it (hooks 2003). It is a coolness that is intertwined with the stigmatization and marginalization of a minority. Given this tendency in some strands of hip hop to treat women as objects, what are the effects of this masculine coolness when translated through the cultural specificity of Turkish gender relations? Clearly, it is "cool" to objectify German women, but what about the treatment of Turkish women, those whom young men of Turkish descent perceive as "theirs"? How these youth treat the "Turkish girls" of their neighborhood is not simply a reflection of traditional or transitional culture, but is rather refracted through the lens of transnational coolness via symbolic icons of Turkishness and Islam.

For some Turkish parents, the threats of German society are epitomized in the very youth culture that German media and offices for integrating foreigners support—with its hybrid figures that celebrate sexuality, homosexuality, exotic fashions, alcohol, and the like. First-generation parents and community leaders may not be sensitive to what are for German authorities key differences between violence, drugs, and other illegal activities on the one hand and the rebellious but safe forms of artistic expression that neighborhood associations promote on the other. When parents in response clamp down on their children's activities for fear of losing them to the corruptions of German society, the result may be conflict and rebellion rather than communication. According to Kaya, in response to this hybrid expression of masculinity in Turkish youth groups in Berlin, "Parents try to keep their children away from the streets and the youth centres. They believe that interacting with 'deviant' German and Turkish youth will make their children disrespectful" (Kaya 2001: 136), so they try to steer those children toward the mosque.[23] For some youth, the mosque does succeed in capturing their imagination to varying degrees.

AN ISLAMIC INTEGRATION STRATEGY

Major urban centers such as Berlin have mosques representing a range of orientations to Islam. Reformist Sunni Islamic discourse has been growing among people of Turkish background in Germany, as it has in many other diasporic Muslim communities.[24] This discourse deliberately recasts and reorganizes the space of difference, offering an alternative, politically charged solution to the problem of integration that is nevertheless shaped by the discursive polarization of modernity and tradition. Most of these groups have sought to promote a discourse that recasts dichotomies of difference in quite other terms, and leaders of organizations such as Islamische Gemeinschaft Milli Görüş (IGMG) see helping families resolve the conflicts between "traditional" parents and their children raised in Germany as one of their explicit roles.[25] IGMG, for example, has articulated an approach that disrupts the orientalizing dichotomy and, they argue, promotes integration while sharply distinguishing integration on their own terms from total assimilation to German cultural practices. As an alternative to the dominant German discourse, Turkish reformist Muslims in Germany preach a renewed and purified Islam that they explicitly distance from what they see as the traditional practices of village Muslims, thereby reproducing the aspect of the modernity-tradition dichotomy that rejects village culture. A core element of this Islamic discourse is an articulation of the differences between properly Islamic gender relations and the ways in which some "traditional," "cultural" practices of Turkish men are actually un-Islamic. This discourse thus responds to the demonization of Turkish men with an alternative masculinity.

In this discourse, rural Turkish Islamic practices are considered to be a corruption of true Islam by Turkish habits, superstitions, and local culture, a position with which most Germans and many secular Turks would also agree. Reformist Muslims argue that in the village, people act out of group pressure and conformity, not out of knowledge about how to form a true relationship with God. At the same time and analogously, these Muslims reject many elements of Western consumption and popular culture, with its celebration of sexuality, violence, and the breakdown of morality and the family. This aspect of popular culture is, like the village, also viewed as a site of corruption, but of the opposite extreme—a way of life in which people act selfishly and with little guidance or moral constraint.

Between these two extremes are what reformists emphasize are the principles of true Islam, which they understand to include a freely chosen obedience to God, human rights, gender equality, respect for the body and its health, concern for the environment and the poor, and productive activity in the world. They assert that the principles of true Islam provide an alternative vision of modernity and are consistent with the principles underlying most of Western law and democracy. This discourse disrupts the German dichotomy that lines up modernity, secularism, cosmopolitanism, gender equality, and individual rights on one side and tradition, Islam, rural conservatism, patriarchy, and group conformity on the other. Islamic organizations thereby provide a position attractive to some German youth of Turkish background for resisting the identity scripts that surround them in German media, schools, and other institutions.

In practical terms, IGMG, the largest Turkish Islamic organization in Germany, founded in 1976, claims as one of its major goals the improvement of relationships between immigrant parents and their children. The organization seeks to establish social services in which young people can seek help without creating a rupture with the family. To accomplish this goal, IGMG (1) discourages marriages with relatives still in Turkey, because it feels that this increases problems in the marriage, (2) educates young women about their rights, including how to interpret the Qur'an as a defense against even the father's authority to decide the future of his daughter, and (3) provides a support structure outside the family that escapes positioning as the threatening "modern" or "Western."

A young woman with whom I talked in Berlin described how she had learned from her teachers at the mosque her family attends to resist some of the demands of her father:

> My father wants me to marry a boy in Turkey [not a relative], but I don't want him, and my mother doesn't want him. [Q: Why not?] I want someone who practices Islam and prays. Also, my father talked with him and made the decision but didn't ask me beforehand. Then when he asked me, I told him I didn't want him. I want to talk to the boy before making a decision. My father also said that the boy looked very good, but I don't think that this is a good reason. I think this boy wants to marry me because I live in Germany.
>
> My father is a person who makes a decision, and no one can change what he thinks. My father makes problems at home. This thing that my father insisted on made me psychologically ill—I couldn't listen to it anymore. I didn't want to accept my father's wish that I marry that boy. But I heard from the life of the Prophet [Muhammad] how someone should marry, and who decides. For example, the Prophet talked to his daughter, and the Prophet was emotional, in tears. He said, "I want you to marry Ali, but you must make the decision; I cannot." This is an example, so you can see that the father cannot make the decision. [Q: Did you win?] He didn't change his thinking, but he saw that he couldn't succeed. He cannot do more.

This was a woman who had had particular trouble with her father and found support within the mosque to resist him. (She emphasized, however, that most of the young women she knew had not experienced such pressure from their fathers.)

Five young women with whom I met as participants in a young women's Islamic group in Berlin discussed how their religious education was making them more aware of their rights under Islamic law. One of the women had recently married, and she said that she had known to sign a contract before marriage that gave her the right to divorce and the right to alimony. In this context, they discussed how important it is to separate Turkish custom from Islamic law or principles. One of the women also distinguished between Islamic principles and specific laws meant for particular historical situations and argued that much of German law is consistent with Islamic principles. I heard many leaders of IGMG make this point, too. A key example of this is the Qur'anic verse (2: 282) which states that two women must serve in the place of one man as a witness—a verse that many interpret to mean that the testimony of a woman is worth only half that of a man. One of the women, echoing a point that I had also heard from an IGMG leader, explained that this passage referred specifically to a business situation in which women were not typically expert at that time and thus were more likely to become uncertain or confused. In another historical context, where women were equally educated and employed, this principle would not apply.

These women characterize themselves as "conscious" Muslims who actively contest the political and media use of the headscarf as a sign of the oppression of Muslim women. They decide to cover as an act of personal choice, drawing a contrast with women who wear a headscarf out of a "habit" (Turkish: *adet*) learned in childhood and thus do so "unconsciously." As conscious Muslims, they claim self-awareness in a way that creates a tripartite social space, constituting a Western other (either non-Muslim or nonpracticing Muslim), a traditional other, and the conscious Muslim. These Muslim women stress that the headscarf enhances their freedom vis-à-vis a traditional family; their parents are not as worried about them when they go out. In many cases, youth also gain power and authority over their parents. They learn to argue that the practices advocated by Islamic reformers are true Islam and that the "village Islam" of their families has been corrupted by local culture and is practiced out of habit rather than out of a relationship with God. Among some of the families with whom I have worked, young women have often drawn their parents into their own practice, giving them books to read and teaching their mothers how to wear a headscarf properly. The young woman who resisted her father's wishes was also able to assert herself without threatening or alienating her mother.

Leaders of several Islamic organizations express a goal of educating both boys and girls for life in German society. An example of this is a series of textbooks used in a pedagogical course that includes a book devoted to recycling.[26] Recycling was discussed in the context of preserving the resources God provides, accompanied by Qur'anic verses. In IGMG and other groups, young women are encouraged to wear headscarves, while at the same they are urged to pursue higher education, especially as teachers and doctors. The men associated with IGMG whom I met spoke positively of their wives' and daughters' education and independence, encouraging them to be active professionals. Nevertheless, some women closely associated with the organization felt that it did not go far enough in promoting the equality of women within the organization itself, where the administrative hierarchy was clearly dominated by men.

This reformist Islamic discourse is adamantly refused by much of the German public, which makes no distinction between "traditional culture" and reformist Islam and perceives the consciously Muslim woman, marked by the headscarf, as the absolute other—a symbol of the antithesis of democracy, freedom, and equality. One twenty-four-year-old woman, a naturalized German citizen who came to Germany when she was eight months old, was studying at a German university and described to a German researcher her experiences of fellow students' reactions to her headscarf: "I am the only woman in the [university] department who wears a headscarf. Everyone asks me how I can speak such good German! . . . With my fellow female students . . . we study together, but it always goes the same way . . . Even a few days ago, we studied for a half hour, and then I ended up explaining, explaining, explaining and trying to justify the headscarf, everything" (Palm 2000: 39–40). She described how these classmates accused her of resisting integration and said that being religious "means you don't want to integrate yourself" into German society (Palm 2000: 40).

Some German scholars have been actively involved in shaping this attitude of the German public, including Wilhelm Heitmeyer and colleagues (Heitmeyer, Müller, and Schröder 1997), who in a book on Islamic "fundamentalism" in Germany accused Turks of resisting integration because of their involvement in Islam. Leaders of Islamic organizations with whom I have spoken have been outraged at the book's conclusions. In the *Der Spiegel* article that opened this chapter, Islam and headscarves for women are drawn into this set of contrasts: "The high value of the 'self'-responsible individual, a requirement for each democratic community, cannot be shared by the Islamic Fundamentalist because he thinks best in terms of collectives and groups" (Cziesche et al. 2003: 85). Although the case of Aylin had nothing to do with headscarves or with Islamic reformers, it is sandwiched between descriptions of two court decisions in which female students were released from required school activities, a field trip and a gym class, because participation in them violated specific *fatawa* (religious rulings). In the critical words of the *Der Spiegel* authors, the latter decision "shows how lightly German courts deal with the oppression of women by their parents in the name of religious freedom. . . . In the name of religious freedom, orthodox parents may also have the chance to confine and control Muslim girls with the blessing of the German courts—this is what the headscarf symbolizes" (Cziesche et al. 2003: 87). Aylin's story is thus used to illustrate how Muslim parents do not allow their daughters to exercise personal autonomy. Though there is no indication of what the girl who was excused from gym classes personally wished, it is implied that she, like Aylin, was being forced by her family against her will to dress modestly and thus be deprived of physical education. As presented in *Der Spiegel*, the case of Aylin serves as proof that Islamic fundamentalists do not see their women as having any right to freedom or autonomy. German representation of Islamic groups obliterates the extent to which such groups offer a path between Turkish tradition and Western materialism and consumerism for some youth of Turkish background, seeing this path as merely an extension of the rigid traditionalism of the Turk-ish villager rather than as a highly modern socio-religious movement. Young German-Turkish women who succeed in graduating from German universities and strive for careers in teaching, law, and medicine, but who also still wear headscarves, are presented as symbols of the failure of integration.

Theorists investigating reader and audience reception have stressed that au-diences do not passively accept interpellation (Radway 1984; Mankekar 1999) but are selective, recasting the representations in terms of their own desires. Devout Muslims do resist interpellation by the representations of Turkish women and girls in German-language media. They choose other scripts for their own lives. Most reformist Muslims do not reject film or television viewing as an improper activity, but they have clear criteria for deciding whether a film or TV program is "good." Aside from programming on Islamic subjects and Turkish television shows received by satellite, certain American series such as *Little House on the Prairie* are well-liked among people I know. In contrast, reformist Muslim fami-lies criticized how Turks are represented in German-language films. They were keenly aware of negative stereotypes and disliked representations of what to them felt like dark, claustrophobic Turkish homes in Germany. Young women in reformist families with whom I talked avoided films such as *Aprilkinder* (Yavuz 1998), *Gegen die Wand* (Akin 2004), and other representations of troubled Turk-ish youth, though several young men I knew had gone to see *Gegen die Wand*.

Despite the efforts of Islamic reformers to provide a viable alternative for Turkish and other Muslim youth, even the Islamic discursive position can yield a stigmatization of Turkish masculinity. One German researcher, Siegrid Nökel, who presents a positive perspective on the man who is a practicing Muslim, does so in a context that paints the Turkish man in quite negative terms. She quotes a young woman who described what led her to choose her husband:

> He had studied Islam [in Egypt]. That was also very important to me, because it let me know that he wasn't concerned only with tradition. He's really a

very worldly man. That's probably what drew me to him. That he wasn't Turkish so much as he was Muslim—I could have married a German Muslim, for that matter. And I knew that he knew himself and that he would be fair to me and treat me well, because our judge would be the prophet [Muhammad], who had never done anything wrong to a woman. With [my husband] I could depend on that; with a normal Turk, I couldn't. And it all worked out well for me. But I also know of cases where it didn't work out, where the men merely pretended. (Nökel 2002: 238)

This woman sharply distinguished adherence to Islam and "tradition," which she sought to avoid. She explicitly stated that she could not trust a "normal Turk" to treat her well. This suggests three possible characters for the "normal" Turkish man: he is ignorant, deceitful, or both. This young woman is drawn to her husband because he is educated in the scriptures and theology of Islam, not simply the common practices. Her testimony leaves the impression (or perhaps confirms a German prejudice) that a religiously educated Turkish male is an anomaly. Furthermore, her statements imply that a Turk with both education and integrity is even less typical. This theme of dishonesty and deceit is reiterated shortly thereafter in Nökel's analysis:

Overall, as is evident in many accounts, men who voluntarily adhere to an Islamic marriage ethic seem to be lucky and rare occurrences. In spite of any previous examinations, a woman can never be sure if a man who presents himself as a "true" Muslim actually is or not. Indeed, Hatice's reference to the "actor" who is solely concerned with "getting" the desired woman and then forcing her to submit to him is not at all unusual. It seems to deal instead with a far more widespread experience and fear. (Nökel 2002: 238)

Nökel avoids attacking Islam directly by drawing on the testimony of Turkish women who blame Muslim men for their perversion of the values and beliefs of Islam. Given that Nökel has posited a "problem" with integration and argued that this problem comes down to gender relations within the Turkish community, the blame must be located somewhere, and if women (the victims) and the faith are free from blame, then men remain the only viable option. Consider the following testimony from a German-Turkish woman: "It is very important to distinguish between tradition and religion. Tradition and Islam are two totally separate things" (Nökel 2002: 244). It is clear that this woman believes that Islam has been corrupted. In other words, tradition and religion bear no resemblance to one another in the realm of gender-based status and treatment.

CULTURE VERSUS THE MICROPOLITICS OF EVERYDAY LIFE

German popular discourse, Turkish rural discourse, and Islamic discourse each posit a dichotomy between urban German cosmopolitanism and rural Turkish traditionalism but identify radically different strategies for bridging this divide. I now briefly consider some of the effects of these discursive mythologies on individuals whose lives have been interpellated by them, looking at instances of young women who sought to escape the constraints of their families and at how men are represented in these instances.

The *Der Spiegel* article's account of Aylin's plight begins with a Turkish proverb, "the purity of the woman is the honor of the man," as a way of explaining the family's rationale for their treatment of Aylin. The story moves quickly from this cultural artifact to Aylin's accusation that her uncle had raped her—clearly a violation of the moral code of even the most remote Turkish village rather than a normal "cultural practice." Conversations at the Youth Forum in Berlin also invoked the concept of culture, explicitly: girls of Turkish background discussed their personal experiences and the problems they face at home. Most said that they had few problems with their own parents. A recurrent theme was to blame the "culture"—Islamic and Turkish—for the tendency of fathers and brothers to restrict girls. In other words, they did not see culture operating within their own families but imputed it to the abstract Turkish family. Other young women in the conversation objected, however, saying that nothing inherent in Turkish culture or Islam necessitated the repression of women. Instead, they put the responsibility on individual people (Soysal 2001: 18). This distinction is an important one that points to the micropolitics of the family.[27]

One young woman, "Frau B," described her negotiations with her parents as she was growing up: "I can't say if my parents were really strict or not. I must say one thing, though—things were stricter and more traditional for my older sisters. My parents seemed to develop with me. They gave me every opportunity" (Palm 2000: 38). She spoke of her parents' relationship by comparing it with the prevailing stereotype:

> It always seems like the father says what goes and what doesn't. But I know that my mother is a pretty strong woman. Everything that happened in my family—whether it was buying a new car, or something else—was discussed between them. Parents talked things over and let their children listen to them. That's how it was in my childhood. Nowadays, we all sit at the table and talk things over. A family conference at the dinner table!

> I was also fairly honest with my parents. They were pretty scared and
> shocked at times when I told them things because it was all new to them. But
> they were able to live with it. They were pleased that they heard these things
> from me and not from others . . . At the moment I have a very close guy-friend,
> and my parents are really OK with it. (Palm 2000: 38)

This was a twenty-four-year-old woman whose family moved to Germany when
she was eight years old. She was a practicing Muslim who wore a headscarf.

Norwegian anthropologist Unni Wikan, who has been conducting research
on abductions and honor killings in Scandinavia, sees the problematic aspects
of Muslim gender relations and how to deal with them in terms of a tension
between cultural, group rights as manifest in policies that support multiculturalism and the universal human rights of the individual. Wikan uses the case of
a second-generation Norwegian citizen to argue for the importance of Muslim
girls' human rights, understood to be grounded in moral individualism, to take
precedence over cultural rights. In this case, which became a big media event in
Norway, Nadia was abducted by her Moroccan parents for a forced marriage in
Morocco but was able to call the Norwegian Embassy for help. Nadia's parents
were prosecuted and sentenced in a Norwegian court. The verdict states: "The
case arises from culture conflict. . . . That they [the parents] wish to maintain
the customs of their country of birth is unobjectionable, so long as these customs do not come into conflict with Norwegian law" (Wikan 2002: 137). Variously positioned spokespeople in the Muslim community were outraged at the
verdict against Nadia's parents. The chairman of the Islamic Council stated:
"This is an insult to all Muslims. It implies that we are bushmen who do not
follow Norwegian laws and rules!" and "The charges and the verdict are an offense against the family and us Muslims. The judge is requiring us to respect
Norwegian laws, but does not show us any respect" (*Dagbladet*, November 11,
1998, quoted in Wikan 2002: 138). Given the alternatives that this verdict sets
up, one might be led to ask whether the chairman of the Islamic Council was
arguing for the right of Muslim fathers to abduct their daughters.

Wikan has played an important public role as an advocate for the rights and
safety of young women in similar situations. She herself felt that the verdict was
appropriate because it clearly prioritized the daughter's human rights over the
parents' cultural rights. She may well be right in this case, but I cannot help asking whether the outcome of such trials must be so polarized. Is it inevitable that
immigrant families be driven to such rifts in the first place? A journalist whom

Wikan cites seems to take a position different from Wikan's: he did not disagree with the sentence but wrote that the premises of the verdict were unacceptable (Wikan 2002: 138). Though Wikan does not indicate what the journalist felt an alternative premise might have been, the young women at the Berlin Youth Forum suggested one: place the responsibility for misconduct on the individual parents, and not on the "culture." The Islamic Council chairman was no doubt outraged that the court's decision posited an incompatibility between human rights and Islam in the very act of dichotomizing individual and group rights. As I mentioned earlier, the leaders of reformist Islamic organizations in Germany with whom I talked emphasized that most German laws are compatible with Islamic law, not antithetical to it.

A second alternative is to recognize that such practices are not manifestations of tradition but an outcome of modern state institutions that shape the experiences of parents and children, as well as of men and women, differently, pushing them in different directions that generate fault lines within the family that often give rise to conflict.

It is important not to assume that the illegal practices exhibited in Aylin's rape or in Nadia's abduction are typical components of the "patriarchal" Muslim family. Such an assumption locates the Muslim family as other to the abstract family implied in an ideology of gender equality. Even in hierarchical families in which the public position of the father as patriarch is crucial for maintaining the identity and status of the family and the father, actual decision-making and family dynamics are complex, fluid processes. Furthermore, German families, too, are culturally specific and do not necessarily conform to the abstract family envisioned in an ideology of gender equality as articulated in the German Constitution. Difficulties, abuse, and rebellion may arise when the father attempts to maintain exclusive power over his wife and children and are not the inevitable result of the culturally specific structure of the family, even when it is founded on hierarchy. Among immigrant families, many of the decisions that individuals make are shaped by factors such as existing structures of governmentality that immigrants confront in their daily lives and are thus not a product of a static culture they bring with them in diaspora.

A well-educated woman of Turkish background whom I knew in Germany had been married to a relative from Turkey at age eighteen and had recently divorced after fourteen years. On the basis of her experience, she felt that the power imbalance between husband and wife had more to do with the specific circumstances of migration than with Turkish culture: "There is no nationality there. It is not connected to nationality. It is a power game. And for the Turkish men who came here because of marriage from Turkey, it is just like this. This game is then turned around and the woman always says, I brought you here, so you do what I want. Yet that is not noticed at all." This woman was acutely aware of the stereotypes about Muslim gender and the patriarchal domination of men: "There are many families where of course this patriarchy rules, where the men have the say. We can't deny that. There is that. But that is not just among the Turks. It is also among the Germans." In her discussions of her marriage and the experiences of her husband, she emphasized how psychologically difficult it had been for him to migrate. He had not been at all dominant in their relationship; despite the common German stereotypes, she did not feel that her situation had been unusual.

The potentially powerful role of stereotypes and scripts stands in tension with the fluidity of actual situations of rupture, which can be analyzed by examining the micropolitics of an evolving situation. Nergis was twenty-three years old, the daughter of a Turkish guestworker in the Netherlands, when I met her in 1997, four days after she had run away from her husband.[28] She was temporarily hiding out with a mutual acquaintance she knew from work, afraid that her family would find her and kill her to maintain the family's honor.

Nergis's father had moved to the Netherlands as an unskilled worker in 1971 and brought the rest of the family in 1977, when Nergis was three years old. Engaged to a cousin in Turkey at age eleven, Nergis had, by her own account, been pushed into an arranged marriage when she was eighteen, after many years of pressure. She told stories of her mother's daily efforts to persuade her to want this marriage:

> My mother went to the *imam-hoca* [spiritual guide] to get some magic. It is something written on a piece of paper that you put into water and the writing dissolves. Then you put the water in food. I noticed one day that my mother was smiling when I came home from school. She really urged me to eat a snack, and I got suspicious. Later I looked in the cupboard and found a glass with paper in it. The next time she offered me food like that—all smiling and coaxing—I told her I would eat it upstairs in my room. I took it up and threw it out.

This was one of several similar stories of evading her mother's magic. Ultimately, however, her mother won, and Nergis was married off to a man whom she vehemently did not want to marry.

The fight with her husband that precipitated her flight was the final round in a long-term dispute over money: he was an unskilled factory worker, and she earned considerably more than he did in her work as a corporate travel agent. She and her husband had sent money that she had earned to her in-laws in Istanbul so that they could buy an apartment. One of the conditions that Nergis had insisted upon was that the apartment be in her name, since she had paid for it. They had originally agreed that it would at first be in Nergis's mother's name (her mother is the sister of her husband's mother, making Nergis and her husband first cousins) and then be transferred to her own name. The fight erupted when her husband informed her that they would not transfer the apartment to her name. When she protested, her husband said to her, "Who are you that you think they should put it in your name?" That was the last straw. She complained that they treated her like a money machine and decided at that moment that her in-laws would not suck away her money any longer. She had experienced as oppressive her husband's responses to his humiliation at being in an inferior employment situation, but he had not physically abused her.

On the day she left her husband, Nergis packed her things after he had left for work, put her suitcase in her car, and dropped her eighteen-month-old son off at her mother's house, as she usually did when she went to work. She told no one what she was doing. When she got to work and told her boss that she had no idea where she would go next, he offered to take her to stay with him and his wife. So the first two nights after she left her husband, she stayed at her boss's home. When he drove her to work each morning (she had left her own car parked in the company's locked garage), she would ride lying on the floor between the seats, covered with bags so that her relatives could not catch a glimpse of her. But on the third day, Nergis learned that her family had guessed where she was staying, and so she felt that she had to move. She went to the home of an American colleague, where I met her.

For several days Nergis's boss continued to pick her up on his way into work, hiding her on the floor of the back seat each time. He also arranged for her to meet with a lawyer, who both acted as a mediator with her family and helped her initiate divorce proceedings. In the meantime, Nergis had also enlisted the aid of many of her co-workers and myself. All were sympathetic to her plight. Her stories of coercion were outrageous from the perspective of a discourse grounded in bourgeois law and the principles of human rights and freedom. To put our actions within the frame of this discourse: a Turkish woman had become sufficiently enlightened to desire emancipation but needed help escaping her natural, traditional community, which had not yet evolved to the point of recognizing basic modern values such as equality and freedom.

It is important, however, not to simply chalk up this clash to the immigrant experience by assuming that in Turkey the traditional Turkish wife would be fully embedded in a traditional discourse.[29] On the contrary, the phenomenon of dual-career marriages is widespread in Turkey today, and many of Nergis's relatives, especially those who have moved to the major cities (as have her in-laws), follow this pattern. Many dual-career families in Turkey manage to work out reasonably stable decision-making arrangements.[30] What created a contradiction for Nergis was the fact that she was a professional who was married to an uneducated, unskilled worker (who now works on an assembly line in a pillow factory). Though in some Turkish families the wife may earn more than her husband, this difference in the status of their employment is more unusual. The discrepancy was a direct result of her immigrant status as a resident of the Netherlands. If she had lived in Turkey, her family would more likely have found her a spouse with a similar educational background. But in this case, she was used as the vehicle for bringing another relative into the Netherlands, a common fate for young women of Turkish background growing up in the Netherlands or Germany. Her situation was thus a direct product of Dutch immigration law, which forms a part of the background reality in which she lives.

Nergis had lived a highly compartmentalized life for many years. She described her position in the family as inconsistent with her life at school and at work. Her story as she told it to me was framed in terms of two compartmentalized identities: a Turkish girl whose life had been tightly circumscribed by her parents, and an educated professional woman whose career had even taken her to the Caribbean on a business trip. In Nergis's case, the situation when she ran away had not been a crisis; her husband had not physically abused her, and neither she nor her child was in any danger. But even this well-educated young woman followed the only script she knew—to run and hide. The potential for violence in the first few days after her flight was enhanced by the polarization of the situation. She really had no idea how the men in her family would react to her flight, but the well-publicized script of violence could have served as a model for them as well.

Nergis was quite powerful within her family and was actually able to arrange the outcome to her advantage. But if we consider the situation of her husband, it is likely that he experienced his situation as undermining and a challenge to his masculinity, defined in terms of being the provider and head of his family. This man was uneducated and frustrated by his low economic status vis-à-vis his wife. The clash over title to the property seemed to be an effort on his part to retain some form of dignity and status.

Because of her professional connections, Nergis was able to engage a lawyer, who functioned as a mediator between her and her family. The family made no effort to attack her, and all were able to resolve the conflict in an optimal way for Nergis. A year after I last saw Nergis, the American woman who had first introduced me to her emailed me the following message:

> She seems to be fine now—the last I heard, she had moved into her own apartment with her son, her mother takes care of her son during the day, the divorce was in process and her husband wasn't bothering her. She and her husband sold the apartment they owned jointly (which covered what they owed on it), she gave the house in Turkey to his parents, his papers were in order for Holland, and that seems to be about all he was concerned about. It's amazing how it all wound up in such a civilized manner when it was such a drama just a little over one year ago. One important factor seemed to be the *mullah* [religious leader] who acted as arbitrator. Everyone seemed to accept his word and abide by it.

Nergis's mother, who had done everything possible to persuade her to accept this marriage, thus resumed caring for her grandchild during the day and became much more flexible with her younger daughter after her experience with Nergis. A significant role was played in both creating the initial crisis and in resolving it by what the family called their *imam-hoca* (the *mullah* referred to in the email). He had initially worked to push Nergis into the marriage but switched his position and later adopted a mediating role, working alongside the lawyer to effect a resolution to the conflict.

Though Nergis's family was in many respects typical of immigrants from Turkey, the details of her situation reveal that behind what can be seen as a stereotypical situation are micropolitics that do not conform to these stereotypes. Though Nergis feared the violence of her father, brothers, or husband, her mother was actually the key player at every stage. Nergis had considerable power in her family, though she often portrayed herself as the typical Turkish girl who has been victimized by her culture and her family. Even the *imam-hoca*, who had prescribed amulets and other village treatments to force Nergis to accept her husband, demonstrated his flexibility in the end.

In retrospect, it is clear that Nergis was following a script for running away in a situation in which several factors converged to make this appear to be the only solution. But her crisis was itself an outcome of governmental policies, advice from a religious leader, and parents who were concerned with maintaining family ties with distant relatives in this diasporic situation. They drew on cultural resources to negotiate their situation, but they were not simply enacting tradition. While I have been personally involved with only two families in the midst of crises surrounding the marriage of a daughter, it was striking that in both cases, the parents did not simply respond in terms of a clear-cut set of rules or principles, but rather relied heavily on the advice of friends and religious leaders. This advice was itself fluid and variable, and ultimately they gave in to their daughter's wishes. In other situations, the outcome may be different—sometimes tragic—but it always results from the interplay of micropolitics, fluid power dynamics, and negotiation.

CONCLUSION

In this chapter I have identified some of the discursive, mythological practices that stereotype minorities and some of the rhetorical maneuvers that justify such practices in the name of a liberal sensitivity to difference. These discursive practices reify Turkish rural culture, often associate all Turks with stereotypes of village culture, and conflate reformist Islam with practices that reformist Muslims consider un-Islamic. In the field of social work, superficial reports on life in a Turkish village have been used to assess how migrants would fail to adapt to urban life in Germany, often resulting in social policies that increase segregation and make integration more difficult. This discourse also exacerbates miscommunications between Germans and Turks and between first and subsequent generations within the immigrant community. It limits the scripts available to young men and women as they negotiate their own gendered identities, sources of self-esteem and honor, and relationships with members of the opposite sex. At the heart of such miscommunications are the naturalized, stereotypical representations of Muslim men and boys, who are characterized as particularly resistant to the "democratic values" and egalitarian gender relations of modern German society as they seek to constrain their women and maintain their personal and family honor.

Men who find themselves challenged succeed in an environment in which they are socially and economically disadvantaged vis-à-vis their wives often find it especially difficult to establish an identity based on a positive masculinity. Cinema images that focus on the plight of the Turkish Muslim woman reinforce the negative aspects of this stigmatized masculinity.

Miscommunication between children and their immigrant parents leaves few options for a young woman when her family is abusive or overly restrictive. In situations in which men become violent—as may happen when they feel intensely stressed, humiliated, or personally threatened—the myth of the Turkish man who feels compelled to violently defend his honor presumes an inevitable manifestation of Turkish/Islamic culture. The young woman's last resort of running away or turning to police, courts, or German social services creates a radical rupture, driving the wedge of the German state into the Turkish family. The intrusive authority of the state and the parents' worst fears of losing their daughter to the vices of the West are confirmed.

In such ways, the images generated through these discourses can deeply affect the life trajectories of young men and women as they move into adulthood. The paths that youth from immigrant families take are shaped by the political discourses, policies, and everyday practices in which they are positioned. Some life possibilities and identities are blocked while others are promoted. By focusing on the micropolitics of everyday life—considering how individuals, no matter where they are socially positioned, operate through multiple, contextualized identities in a wide range of social situations and manage an array of contradictions and inconsistencies in their lives—one can discern the potential effects of classification and misrecognition.

3 BETWEEN MODERNITY AND TRADITION
Negotiating Stigmatization

MEN OF TURKISH BACKGROUND in Germany, whatever their orientations toward being "German," "Turkish," "hybrid," "Muslim," or any of the other categories through which they may be identified, must negotiate in their everyday lives the interpellations of a German public discourse. In this discourse, they fall all too readily into the position of threatening and/or abjected other: the husband who oppresses his wife, the brother who might murder his sister, the anti-Semite. The tradition-modernity dichotomy and all the layers of significance associated with it are routinely deployed not only in popular discourse, but also by many scholars, whose formulations, as social science, carry particular weight in the formation of policy and even of socially accepted truth. In studies of the Turkish family in Germany, a number of researchers have used analytic frameworks that maximize the contrasts between Western and traditional forms of gender, family organization, and self. The rhetorical effect of using a model based on a distinction between the independent, autonomous individual and the interdependent members of a group is to exaggerate the otherness of Turkish masculinity by assuming the historical uniqueness of the modern, Western self.

The Orientalist concept of traditional masculinity subsumes several attributes that stand in contrast to those of the Western self, the liberal subject that underlies Western notions of a democratic state. Attributes often articulated include autonomy versus heteronomy, independence versus interdependence, individual versus group, and equality versus hierarchy. The concept of the Western self is a discursive amalgam of these attributes: the autonomous, independent individual who treats others as equals. This amalgam demands of the modern subject that it display all of these attributes, though in practice the visible presence of an attribute that falls on one side of the modernity-tradition dichotomy may be taken as a sign that other attributes are also present. A researcher may thus incorrectly interpret specific interactions by taking the presence of one indicator of a traditional orientation to mean that other traditional characteristics are also present.[1]

For example, an observer may assume that a man or a woman living in a hierarchically organized extended family lacks autonomy, independence, and individuality and is therefore "traditional." Or a man's circumspection in a research setting about certain topics such as the inner workings of family life may be taken as a sign that he maintains a hierarchical relationship with his wife and does not view her as a companion. But such circumspection is often closely associated with the performance of masculinity in a public setting and is not necessarily a reflection of interactions within the family.

The research situation itself makes specific demands on its subjects (Briggs 1986). Whatever the prior relationship of the researcher to the people being studied, the very act of conducting research creates an outsider's gaze, since it entails a public audience of potential readers. Ethnographic research, whether through participant observation or interviewing, is best understood, not simply as a tool for gathering data based on explicitly articulated statements, but as a series of potentially public interactions. In these interactions, all participants enter the situation bearing preexisting identities, such as "female German researcher," "first-generation Turkish immigrant," or "laborer," and have different goals and a different array of preconceptions about how one should perform and interpret multiple, shifting identities as they interact. They negotiate a reality in the space between them (Crapanzano 1985).[2] The interview and other forms of conversation in research settings are thus key sites for the generation and negotiation of stereotypes that are interpreted through existing discourses, even among those who seek to disrupt or repudiate these stereotypes.

In this chapter, I examine the micropolitics of interaction, that is, performances of identity within the research situation in order to identify specific moments in which stereotypes are reproduced and negotiated. Are the effects of the public discourse of tradition and modernity and of the stigmatization of Turkish and Muslim men visible in how these men represent themselves to others? How do men who may be subjected to stigmatized identities in their daily lives position themselves in relation to such representations? What tactics do they use to resist and recode the stigmatizing conventions they encounter in their lives (Certeau 1984)? And how do they draw on various discourses in the process of negotiating their identities in interaction with the German or American researcher?

I begin with a reinterpretation of interview material published by the German sociologist Margret Spohn, who interviewed first-generation men who had come from Turkey as guestworkers in the early 1970s. Virtually no studies in Germany look directly at the experiences of first-generation Turkish men, apart from the work of Spohn and of anthropologist Werner Schiffauer.[3] In their studies, Spohn and Schiffauer each sought to disrupt negative stereotypes by emphasizing the diversity of individuals, partially reproducing the voices of these individuals in their analyses. Nevertheless, both Schiffauer and Spohn have, like most other researchers, taken the dichotomy between a traditional group orientation and a modern individual orientation as a starting point.[4] I focus on the interview as performance, as a presentation and negotiation of discursively constituted identities, in order to show how a theoretical framework based on the tradition-modernity dichotomy can operate as a filter that can inadvertently deepen stereotypes rather than dispel them. I then turn to my own work with second- and third-generation youth, focusing on how upwardly mobile young men articulate their relationships to the stereotypes and stigmatizations that mark them as different from the modern German citizen.

PUBLIC AND PRIVATE: MISINTERPRETING SILENCES

Margret Spohn's accounts are based on single lengthy interviews with first-generation immigrants. Her interviewing strategy evokes performances of masculinity in the presence of an unfamiliar German audience. Her material reveals men who in this formal interview situation saw themselves as representative of Turkish immigrants and thus tended to stress the public face of masculinity and the family. Much less visible, even invisible, in Spohn's material are the relationships between the interviewees' ideological self-positionings and their practices within their own families or even their performances of masculinity in contexts other than the interview setting. But even in these contextually limited accounts, one can identify tensions in the men's efforts to organize memories and opinions in the process of negotiating identity. In most cases, the task of reckoning with prevailing stereotypes and tactics for managing stigmatization are conspicuous. ğ

Spohn organized her analysis in terms of a distinction between "total interdependence" and "independence," drawing on Turkish social psychologist Çiğdem Kağitçibaşi's typology of models of family organization. Kağitçibaşi identified independence as being characteristic of the Western middle-class family, at least as an ideal, reproducing the rural-urban and tradition-modernity dichotomies characteristic of Turkish public discourse (Kağitçibaşi 2002: 5).[5] Spohn's project was thus to create a typology of the men she had interviewed. Her material is therefore useful for demonstrating how a researcher's theoretical framework can operate as a filter so that even when the goal is to present the perspectives of Turkish men themselves, often in their own words, the effect is to generate interpretations that fit the prior theoretical framework.

Spohn used her formal interview data to argue that for traditionally oriented men, whom she characterized as interdependent, the wife is important primarily in her role as mother to his children and as a bearer of his honor but is not regarded as an equal or companion. In her interviews, these interdependent men said little or nothing about their relationship with their wives, a silence that Spohn saw as characteristic of the interdependent model. She argued that in this style of family relations, a man's relationships with his father and children are more central to him than his relationships with his wife. As evidence, Spohn interpreted her interviewees' silences about their wives to mean that these men have little emotional involvement with them. Of one interviewee whom she characterized as traditional in his interdependence, she wrote: "The praise that he gives to his wife is limited to her abilities as a mother" (Spohn 2002: 262).[6] For another, "Mr. Inan portrays himself primarily as a son and not as a husband" (Spohn 2002: 250). She summarized across interviews: "Decisions are made with the approval of the father rather than of the wife. This is repeatedly noticeable during the interviews of this type: the wife emerges, if at all, only in her function as a mother, but not as the life partner with whom one negotiates and decides important things" (Spohn 2002: 278).

Spohn's interpretation does not take into account how important the boundary between public and private is within many families of Turkish background. This boundary is particularly likely to affect how Turkish men communicate about their wives in a formal interview situation. When one looks across the range of Spohn's interviewees, which included men she classified as independent as well as those she classified as interdependent, the men show a consistent reluctance to articulate emotional relationships and feelings, especially as concerned their wives. Even her most emphatically secularist, "independent-oriented" interviewee, Mr. Fener—who had become a teacher in Germany, promoted the education of his daughters and allowed them to marry Germans, and talked of liking to cook and "even wash up" (Spohn 2002:

297), thereby indicating a willingness to help his wife with housework—did not speak of any other aspects of his relationship with her. Furthermore, he spoke of the practices of cooking and washing up in response to a direct question. These practices are classic markers of an ideology of gender equality in a modern marriage that are communicated overtly and self-consciously in the media. By evoking this ideologically salient marker of gender equality, Mr. Fener positioned himself as a "modern" man, but he did not otherwise lift the veil of family privacy.

Spohn's interview with Mr. Inan offers a clear example of how responses to direct questioning about the nature of various family relationships reveal more of the etiquette of public and private than they do of the contours of these relationships, especially with respect to Mr. Inan's relationship with his wife. Mr. Inan, born in a small Turkish village in 1934, had had only a few years of schooling. At the time of the interview in 1996, he was a factory worker in Germany and lived in an apartment with his wife and four children, who had joined him in Germany in 1977 after he had been there for seven years. As with many of the other men she interviewed, Spohn concluded that his relationship with his deceased father had been and was still more significant to him than was his relationship with his wife, because much of his narrative centered on his father. One likely alternative explanation for his preoccupation with his father, however, is that he was still traumatized by his inability to be with and help his father during his last days. Mr. Inan told Spohn that his father died alone after choosing to return to Turkey. Mr. Inan's traumatization was manifest in the fact that whenever the topics of death, age, and care for the elderly came up, he said, "Don't talk about that!" (Spohn 2002: 247).

Another explanation is that it is proper to speak of one's father but not of one's wife with strangers. Mr. Inan's wife was herself present throughout the interview, and there were a number of indications that their relationship was more significant to him than he acknowledged in this context. During the interview, Mr. Inan constantly asked his wife for background information, which she supplied. This dynamic suggests a close, cooperative relationship in which he depends on her in important ways. At one point she directly intervened, contradicting him when he claimed that he sometimes helped around the house: "Not a word of that is true!" Everyone laughed loudly, and he responded: "I am always sometimes lazy. Somewhat lazy" (Spohn 2002: 252). The fact that she was able to contradict him in public and that his reaction was playful self-criticism suggests to me a flexibility in their interaction and a comfortable balance of power.

Spohn noted that it seemed important to Mr. Inan to give the interviewer the impression that he helps in the household, which she identified in the context of other interviews as a trait of a "modern" masculine identity. Given that he claimed to help in the house in response to Spohn's direct questioning, her question itself signaled a dichotomy between modern and traditional masculinities. His response, like the subsequent interchange with his wife, was clearly intended to position himself as a modern man who does not see doing housework as a threat to his masculinity. When his wife contradicted him, he stayed within this modern discursive framework and jokingly judged himself in negative terms as "lazy." In this way, he perhaps unwittingly stepped into another potential stigmatization: the lazy Turk who shirks work.

Spohn emphasized that being a husband seemed less important to Mr. Inan than being a son or a father because he provided so much information about these relationships and so little about his relationship with his wife or their decision-making processes. Nevertheless, the points in his narrative in which his relationship with his wife came up suggest that she is very important to him and is not simply dominated by him. He mentioned, without elaborating, that they had eloped because she was his stepsister and their parents had been against the marriage. At another point, he was talking about how hard it had been to be separated from his family for eight years when he first came to Germany. He described how, when he returned to Turkey, his parents were present all the time. Finally, he and his wife kissed a few times anyway and were scolded by his parents because it showed a lack of discipline (Spohn 2002: 249). He told another story about how once when he was angry with his son, she sided with the son and he angrily pointed her as well as their son toward the door (though he didn't say that she actually left). At another point in the interview, he mentioned that his wife wanted them to move to another house because of a disturbing neighbor and then exclaimed, "Oh, the costs, it costs money" (Spohn 2002: 254). These comments suggest that, like many wives, she acts as a mediator between her husband and children and plays a major role in decisions such as moving or buying a house. All of these moments indicate that Mr. Inan and his wife have a comfortable relationship that is at the center of their lives and are willing to reveal some of its contours despite the etiquette of privacy that led Spohn to conclude that other relationships were more important to him.

It is impossible to understand the significance of these men's silences about their wives without taking into account the ideological structure of the extended family. In the interviews, they were talking with a stranger, who was accompanied by a Turkish research assistant. In this context, a man's relationship with his wife would be considered a private matter that is inappropriate to discuss. It is proper to speak of one's wife only in terms of her role as a mother. It doesn't mean that his relationship with her is not important, as Spohn suggested, but rather, it is private. This practice of silence must be seen as part of an etiquette in which public and private are sharply differentiated, the latter being that which should properly be shielded from public view. Most aspects of the husband-wife relationship and interactions are not to be articulated. Even within the private spaces of the extended family, husband and wife act formally with one another in the presence of their elders as a form of respect. A man maintains his honor by referring to his wife only as the mother of his children. What he communicates says less about the interpersonal relationship between husband and wife and more about the formality of the interview situation.

Women of the same age and status are more likely to talk about their relationships with their husbands than men are to talk about their wives because female-female conversations are part of the private world, while male-male conversations are more likely to be considered public. Furthermore, it is dishonoring for a man to talk about another man's wife in public. This contrast is startlingly depicted in Fatih Akin's film *Gegen die Wand*, in which a newly married couple living in Germany visits the wife's relatives.[7] The men and women socialize separately, as is customary. In the scene, the men are planning an outing to visit prostitutes, and the new husband incites near-violence by suggesting that those present should "fuck" their wives instead—a word the other men find an affront to use in reference to their wives. The next scene shows the women freely discussing their husbands' skills (and lack thereof) in bed using graphic imagery. I experienced a similar openness regarding graphic talk about sexuality among young Muslim women in Pakistan who lived in gender-segregated families and neighborhoods and always wore burqahs. Surprised, embarrassed, and far more inhibited about discussing sexual intimacies myself, I realized that gender segregation did not mean sexual repression and that the willingness to wear a bikini on a public beach was not the same as sexual liberation. Furthermore, my expectation that people should act consistently in different contexts, a demand that one somehow be the same on the inside and the outside, was a peculiarity of my own cultural environment and its Protestant Christian–based ideologies. This expectation of consistency is not necessarily a mark of the independence or autonomy of the modern subject, but a culturally specific practice linked to social etiquette.

In the diasporic setting of Germany, many first-generation men from Turkey have adopted a modern subject position within a discourse of gender equality, ranging from being willing to say the words "my wife" in public to claiming that they participate in housework. These are some of the most explicitly articulated elements of Western gender equality. But even men who present themselves as modern or cosmopolitan tend to maintain a curtain of privacy around the intimacies of family life. It is thus difficult to infer the details of family dynamics directly from what they say, since self-positioning vis-à-vis an ideology of gender relations is not directly tied to how men interact with their wives or other family members in what they consider informal private settings. Western inferences about the total power of the husband and the powerlessness and insignificance of his wife are often ill-founded because they rest on an assumption of consistency between public and private that does not even apply particularly well to the Western family.

This ideological difference concerning the relationship between public and private in the rural Turkish family and the Western family is not elaborated in German public discourse and thus exacerbates miscommunication between the German public and Turkish minorities. Men of Turkish background may not even realize that in certain settings they are being asked to prove their modernity through the expectation that the modern man may or even should openly discuss the specifics of his relationship with his wife publicly. Maintaining such privacy is a form of honorable behavior that may never have been challenged directly by the practices of modernity because it is not explicitly articulated in popular German stereotypes of traditional honor.

ASSERTING A TRADITIONAL MASCULINITY: HIERARCHICAL AUTHORITY AND THE MICROPOLITICS OF THE FAMILY

Within hierarchically organized Turkish families, there is often a discrepancy between an overt ideology of hierarchy and more egalitarian decision-making processes that are either covert or implicit. Furthermore, even in hierarchically organized families, the ideal within the family is usually not dominance and submission, as some proponents of women's rights have been known to argue, but responsibility, love, and care on the part of the elders of the family and deference and respect on the part of the children and other subordinates. Such families have a complex and fluid political dynamic. In many families, the father maintains his public authority as the head of the extended family and primary decision-maker only by privately consulting with other family members and taking into account their attitudes, feelings, and expertise. I directly observed this dynamic within families even around relatively small decisions, and most men and women emphasized it to me when talking about their natal families.

Though this overt authority of the male head of household can be abused, most women have other social supports to draw on, especially their natal family and even their in-laws, to protect them in situations of abuse. However, women who are brought from Turkey to marry and thus have no close personal ties with anyone in their new community may lack this support network. They may have no one to help protect them if they do have an abusive husband. In such situations, when a woman cannot draw on her extended family because of the process of migration, the availability of social services and shelters for protecting women is extremely important. In German public discourse, however, the vulnerability of such women is usually attributed to traditional culture with its hierarchical structure and male authority rather than to the structure of migration and the disruption of kinship networks.

Within the hierarchically organized extended family, accommodations to individual needs and expertise go on behind the scenes rather than in full public view, especially when these accommodations violate ideological articulations of hierarchy. Such discrepancies between ideology or explicitly articulated cultural rules and everyday practices are a part of the habitus of the family and play out as the micropolitics of everyday life.

Turkish women I knew in Germany explicitly recognized and even described exploiting these differences between the ideology of the Turkish man as decision-maker within a hierarchically organized family and the more fluid negotiations of family dynamics that are evident in women-only conversations. In one conversation among several women, for example, a young woman of Turkish background who was herself the daughter of a guestworker and is now a teacher in the German city of Kiel reported that once when she had asked a Turkish woman whether her daughter could participate in a school activity, the mother had replied that she would have to ask her husband. This teacher's interpretation of this response was that the woman "just needed time to think it over." This is an instance of how women use the public face of the family and its gendered authority structure to maneuver and negotiate with outsiders. But behind the scenes, it is often the mother who actually makes the day-to-day decisions about her children. On the basis of her own experience in a Turkish family and community, the teacher felt that this episode was typical of how women negotiate decision-making. At the same time, most women also recognize the importance of maintaining the honor of their husbands, which they do by maintaining the public representation that they must defer to them. When ethnically German teachers hear a mother defer a decision in order to consult with her husband, the effect is often to reinforce the stereotype that Turkish men are authoritarian and oppressive and that women have no authority. The women in this particular conversation perceived this as the kind of moment when a Turkish woman will exploit a German stereotype of Turkish gender relations as an interactional strategy to gain maneuvering room. They are discussing an experience of knowing how to interpret as insiders, in contrast to the German discourse of otherness, which ignores the extent to which everyone uses similar maneuvers to delay making a decision or avoid confrontation.

This disjunction between public and private can be discerned in interviews with Turkish men, even when they do not articulate it explicitly. Mr. Hacıoğlu was another of Spohn's interviewees. Like Mr. Inan, he migrated in 1970 from a small Turkish village and had had little education. In 1996, the time of the interview, Mr. Hacıoğlu lived alone in an apartment, having left his wife and children behind in Turkey, and had worked in the same factory for many years, without advancement. Spohn noted that she had been particularly uncomfortable interviewing him because he treated her as a representative of the German people, the German voice (Spohn 2002: 218). Given Spohn's reaction, the feeling was probably mutual: he no doubt felt that he was functioning as the "Turkish voice," in a situation in which both he and Spohn were uncomfortable. This discomfort would suggest that he was presenting his most public face to the interviewer.

Drawing on Kağitçibaşi's typology of interdependence and independence, Spohn characterized Mr. Hacıoğlu as the prototypical interdependent Turkish immigrant man, meaning that he fully retained the values of traditional masculinity and the hierarchical organization of gender relations and the family. Evidence for this included his unquestioning assertion of this hierarchical organization and the absolute authority of the patriarch, to the extent that he declared, "when I tell my wife to die, she dies" (Spohn 2002: 229). In many of his utterances, this man does appear to conform closely to the stereotype of the Turkish patriarch who feels free to abuse other family members in an effort to impose his authority on them. He also presented the village as the protector of tradition. He persistently idealized the village and its structure of relationships, contrasting this idealization with the corruptions of the city and of Germany. He felt that he was the one who made all important decisions. He saw education and the city as disrupting these relationships, even within Turkey, so that his own sons back in Turkey resisted their father's authority "and cannot be swayed through beating" (Spohn 2002: 222). In the interview, Mr. Hacıoğlu defiantly embraced the stigmatized stereotype of the traditional villager.

Yet this voice of total authority and control may represent very little of the everyday dynamic of his relationship within the family and with his wife. In the interview these assertive statements appeared to be a performance of masculinity in his role as a voice of traditional rural Turkey. Other utterances offered at least a small window into a very different side of the power dynamics in many marriages that are organized in terms of a sharply gendered division of labor and authority. Examining some of these utterances, I place Mr. Hacıoğlu's assertions of absolute control over his wife and children within the context of other references to these relationships in which his ideological assertion of masculine authority was subordinate to other intentions in the immediate interaction. At one point, he reproduced something he had said to his wife that emphasized his experience of emasculation in Germany: "I said to my wife in Turkey: 'I go to work, then I am a man, I come home and do the women's work.' [laughs] Isn't it so? So I am the one who made this tea, I'm also the one who washes the glasses. I am the one who does everything here" (Spohn 2002: 228). This was a consequence of moving alone to Germany. In addition to manifesting his preference for a gendered division of labor, he expressed an embarrassment about his situation during the interview, when, in order to maintain his honor with respect to hospitality, he was forced to perform a woman's functions as hostess. Yet he was also expressing an appreciation of what his wife does for him. He needs her to make him feel like a man, and is willing to let her know this. In contrast to his explicit assertions of total control over his wife and children, Mr. Hacıoğlu's comments about them in other contexts indicated that these are precisely the situations over which he has little control. For example, he expressed fantasies of being all-powerful in the village and asserted that his relationship with his children has not changed as a result of his migration. Yet at another point he complained that his sons resist and even reject his authority. Given the curtain of privacy that surrounds the marital relationship, it can be inferred that his assertions about his wife's obedience may be performances of masculine authority that stand in an analogous relationship to the private dynamics of their relationship. She may not be as submissive to his authority as he suggests.

Mr. Hacıoğlu also spoke of another relationship, though we have no direct evidence of the nature and extent of the woman's power in this relationship:

that with his German girlfriend, who did not fall under the veil of privacy. Though his characterizations of this relationship were also quite ideological, he vividly conveyed an image of German women that can be used as a mirror that reflects the contours of his fantasies about women. It is important to note that, according to Spohn's interpretation, he did not try to dominate or change this girlfriend, though he lived with her for four or five years (Spohn 2002: 243). His characterization of German women suggests that he felt a kind of emasculation in this relationship, but this was expressed only in terms of the general issue of rights in a marriage:

> We were together for four or five years. But I have many children. I said to her: "I have a wife. When I say to my wife, 'Die!' Then she dies. When I say 'Stay here,' she stays here. But you are not so. I say yes, they [the Germans] are good in some ways, not good in others. If I would marry, if I would marry her, she would perhaps throw me out after two years. My salary—I would receive 3,000 regardless. He [the divorce lawyer] would take away 1,500 of that to give to her and would give 1,500 to me. What am I supposed to do with 1,500? Should I pay the rent with that or feed myself, or buy myself clothing? I could never take a vacation. (Spohn 2002: 229)

This snippet of a reported conversation includes a characterization of a woman with a mind of her own who might throw the man out, leaving him with no ability to take care of himself and his basic needs. He went on to discuss marriage more abstractly: "The girl doesn't say, 'Who is this boy? Will he protect me later or not?' She doesn't say that. She goes for three, four months, a year, two years, then she gets a divorce. Her marriage falls apart and she leaves. [unclear] But the women have many rights. There are no men's rights" (Spohn 2002: 229). As Spohn argues, this potential loss of financial control "is a strong interference in his feelings of self-worth and his masculine identity" (Spohn 2002: 229). Mr. Hacıoğlu presented a picture of a relationship in which the woman is powerful (being likely to throw him out). He felt that he was at her mercy, with no institutional safeguards to protect him. His depiction of German women may provide a window into how he interacts privately with his wife as well, at least in some contexts.

Mr. Hacıoğlu may be an example of the sort of man whom Zehra, a young woman of Turkish background whose parents had brought her to Germany when she was eight, described as "macho" only on the outside. Conversations with women are another source for gleaning the possibility of this sort of discrepancy between public performances of masculinity and gender relations within the privacy of the family. The disjunctions between the publicly presented hierarchical structure of the family dominated by its men and the private side of family dynamics is foregrounded in the following interchange, which occurred (in German) between Zehra and my daughter Julia:

> Julia: So do you think that these negative representations of Turkish men are true? Because I . . . like I said, I read many articles in which the Turks here are portrayed very negatively, that they are very strict and oppress women. Do you think that this is true? . . .
>
> Zehra: In my generation, how the men are now, you mean? For example, the men always want to wear the pants in the family.
>
> Julia: We say the same thing in English!
>
> Zehra: Yes, from the outside they look macho. But in the family they are not very macho at all. Then the women wear the pants.
>
> Julia: That is also what Deniz [a female friend of Zehra's] said. That the women always have the last word.
>
> Zehra: Yes, it was always like that, and it will always be like that. Because ultimately these men are still at their mother's feet. In many ways they are still their mothers' baby boys. And of course they like to forbid this, forbid that. Whether they actually manage to, that is a different story.

Zehra, who did not speak English, nonetheless used the word *macho* to describe the public image that Turkish men often present to the world. My own observations of family interaction, made while staying for one to two weeks with two families of Turkish background in Germany who were reformist Muslims, as well as while "hanging around" in other families, were consistent with the gendered interactions that Zehra reported. Most striking was the transformation of family spaces and interactions when visitors arrived. When these visitors were men who were not close to the family, the wife tended to disappear into the kitchen, coming out only to serve tea or dinner. Analogously, the husband would disappear when his wife or daughter had female visitors. In the case of mixed company, the home of one of the families was large enough to have two separate living rooms, while in the apartment of the other, women gathered in the small kitchen and men in the living room. Otherwise, I saw give-and-take relationships between spouses. One wife, for example, reached for her husband's cheeks and affectionately shook his head, explaining to me,

"Er ist mein Teddybär" (he's my teddy bear). He just looked a bit embarrassed and smiled.

Men vary in the extent to which their ways of talking about family and their wives are grounded in an ideology of hierarchy, which many of the first generation had grown up with in rural Turkey. In this model, the division of labor is clearly articulated, with the husband/father being the primary authority who is responsible for the family's maintenance and welfare in relationship to the outside world and the wife maintaining and supporting her husband and children in the home. How husbands and wives come to adapt to one another over the course of a marriage is negotiated within this context but is shaped by myriad factors including the specific social environment in which they live, especially the presence or absence of an extended family or other social supports, the stresses arising from employment issues and migration, and above all, the personalities and idiosyncratic needs of each spouse. But how men represent this relationship in public contexts is an entirely different matter and may itself shift from one context to another.

MANAGING STEREOTYPES

Several members of the second and third generations with whom I worked observed that their generation is more sensitive to negative stereotypes than the first generation because these stereotypes prevent them from feeling like the insiders they should be, having grown up in Germany. Conversations and interviews with young men in 2005–2006 also indicated that stereotypes have grown harsher in recent years. Given the focus in public discourse on the problematic concept of honor as a defining feature of Turkish Muslim masculinity, especially in the wake of a controversy over an honor killing in Berlin (see Chapter 5), these young people were very sensitive about how they present to the outsider their own attitudes toward sources of self-respect and honor. The young men and women I discuss here were the children of parents who had originally moved to Germany as guestworkers. They were themselves studying at gymnasiums or universities and were aspiring to become successfully middle class. They were thus particularly sensitive to stigmatization and its effects.

Mustafa and his girlfriend Hadice were students at a Berlin gymnasium. The gymnasium is the top tier of secondary school and prepares students for the *Abitur* (the highest level of high school diploma) and admission into a university.[8] Being at a gymnasium sharply distinguishes these young people from the majority of youth of Turkish background, though this particular gymnasium is located in Kreuzberg, Berlin's "Little Istanbul," and 90 percent of its students were minorities. Mustafa and Hadice talked with my research assistant Marguerite, an American student just a couple of years older than they were. At the end of this particular conversation, Hadice summed German misrepresentations of Turks and Islam and her reactions to these stereotypes:

> I think what most needs to be discussed is that many Germans are prejudiced against us. I find it really bothersome, because, from my side, I don't think that I am any sort of barbarian, and not a terrorist, either! I think I've acquired far too much culture for that, over the years. I know how real life is, and I know for that reason that so many Germans and many other people shouldn't say that all Muslims are the same, or that this is what they do. Barbarians. I don't think anyone should say that, because there are differences everywhere. One person is like this, another like that. And also the Germans. I think that the men, most German men, they don't work much, at least compared to others, to the Turks. Our men work really hard, and yet it's believed that they just get drunk. These prejudices go both ways, though. Many German men are really businessmen, and then you have to take a second look. I think it's a good thing, too, that there are differences everywhere.

Mustafa added: "I can only agree with everything that she just said."

Identities are negotiated in interaction, and the situation of talking with researchers is one that is particularly prone to inducing the experience of being interpellated into a specific subject position within a dominant Western discourse. Hadice manifested, and Mustafa echoed, this experience of interpellation in this utterance, as they spoke to an American and expressed frustration at the injustice of German stereotypes. I laid out the roots of prominent stereotypes in Chapter 1, and most of them are echoed in Hadice's statements: the Muslim/Turk as barbarian, as terrorist, as someone who doesn't work hard. She did not mention explicitly what for many men are the most intensely experienced stereotypes: Turkish men's propensity toward violence and their oppression of women as these are linked with the principle of honor, though the term *barbarian* encompasses these ideas. Her statement is a commentary on the representations that she and her peers are confronted with in the media and in their daily lives.

For many men of Turkish background, the intense stigmatization of the Muslim and the Turkish man can be seen during the interview process in their explicit concerns about negative stereotypes and their strategies for positioning themselves in relationship to these stereotypes. These men (and women) displayed an array of strategies. Hadice's comments illustrate a succession of maneuvers for managing stereotypes and demonstrate the complex process of responding to stigmatization. First, she contrasted specific stereotypes with her own self-experience and then contrasted the oversimplifications of the process of stereotyping with real life, indicating that she understood the difference. This demonstration of superior understanding and her reference to her "culture" or educational training contradict the idea that she might be a "barbarian." She also turned the tables and began to apply the stereotype to German men by saying that most of them don't work hard. But her basic strategy, one that Mustafa shared at other points in the conversation, was to emphasize individual differences, acknowledging that some people may actually fit a stereotype but that most do not.

While individuals usually drew on an array of strategies during the course of an interview or conversation, they tended to rely primarily on one approach that created a specific subject positioning. One strategy characteristic of some first-generation men, such as Mr. Hacıoğlu, was to accept the stark dichotomies between Turk and German but invert the valence of the value judgments, thereby identifying with the rural or traditional Turk. When the retention of sharp dichotomies led to inconsistencies, a person would often compartmentalize his or her perceptions and judgments, thereby obscuring the inconsistencies. Sometimes, a person would displace a negative stereotype onto another minority, such as Kurds. Another strategy, more characteristic of those born in Germany, was to accept the negative stereotypes about Turks but distinguish oneself from the majority of Turks, asserting an alternative identity. One of these alternatives was the idea of hybridity, of being a person who picks and chooses various cultural elements considered "Turkish" or "German," claiming an identity as a hybrid of all the best elements of two distinct cultures, a tactic explicitly deployed by Bulent.

Bulent: "I'm a world citizen."
My daughter met Bulent through mutual friends and went to his apartment to interview him for me. The theme of negative stereotypes came up immediately as Julia entered his apartment for their interview and mentioned an earlier meeting she had had with an unnamed young man who had grown up in Turkey before recently moving to Germany. In response to her comment that this man in Turkey "has a different opinion," Bulent interrupted her, saying: "I know this opinion. Maybe we can also get to that, why the people in Turkey

think of us like that." The conversation thus began with Bulent's concern about negative stereotypes—this one a reference to a common observation that villages in Turkey have been modernizing but that the Turkish villagers who came to Germany as guestworkers have clung to tradition and remain frozen in the past. Bulent inferred immediately that Julia had been hearing about such images from an educated urban Turk, actually misinterpreting what Julia had intended to say. This inference became clear as the conversation unfolded. In his use of the pronoun "us" here, he identified himself with German-Turks as they are negatively stereotyped by both Turks and Germans.

Bulent described himself as the son of a Turkish farmer who had moved directly to Germany from his village in the early 1970s. After two years there, his father brought his family to the new country. They lived in a Turkish ghetto in substandard housing, where Bulent was born. His parents, who received minimal schooling in Turkey, still cannot speak much German, after nearly forty years. Bulent dropped out of school and served for four years in the German military before returning to school and getting his *Abitur*. He then left home to study at the University of Kiel and was about halfway through his program at the time of the interview. At one point, he characterized himself as a "world citizen," claiming a cosmopolitan identity. Bulent thus could be said to fall into the category of what one university-educated woman of Turkish background described as those who successfully integrate and "disappear" into German society, though this had not been the case when he dropped out of school, which is what, in public discourse, is considered to be the route of the typical Turkish youth.[9]

Within the context of concern about stereotypes and how Julia might be viewing him, Bulent associated the experience of his parents as guestworkers with a popular German representation of a Turkish guestworker and seemed to identify with his parents' experience:

> I read a book that would definitely also help your mother, by Günter Wallraff. The book is called *Ganz unten* [*At the Bottom of the Heap*] . . . [he shows Julia the book].[10] That is a German author, and he dressed up like a German—I mean, like a Turk—in the eighties, contact lenses, hair black, mustache, everything dyed black, and he said, "My name is Ali." He can speak super good German—he is German—and then he said "Yeah, I Ali, I work want." He said, "I'm Turkish." And he wrote about how the Germans acted toward the Turkish workers at that time. It is very, very interesting. And he also tells about how the Turks didn't want to learn German because they didn't want to understand the insults of

the Germans. The Germans said "shitty Turks," things like that, and the Turks said, "hey if we don't learn German, then it's better because then we don't have to understand that." So that was also a reason why we were familiar with it [the German language], but we didn't learn it. Back to tradition, they all came from rural areas—they were farmers. My father was also a farmer, and very conscious of tradition. And they came here, a different tradition, a different world, a different language, culture. And they said: the thing that unifies us is our culture. We have to keep our culture. And the people here in Germany, the Turks in Germany, they are more conscious of tradition than the people in Turkey. Turkey has also let itself be led by Europe and America very much. From TV, they see, "oh they are doing that, they are wearing that."

Bulent's last point about Turkey following Europe and the United States was a criticism of the imitative nature of Turkish society. He was rebutting the common Turkish criticism, which he had read into Julia's first comments, that Turks in Germany are stuck in the past and are more conservative than Turks in Turkey by suggesting that Turkey had become too imitative.

One of Bulent's strategies for performing a positive identity in this situation, when he was acutely aware of stigmatization by Germans and Turks and potentially by Julia, was to distance both himself and his parents from prevailing stereotypes. Though Bulent portrayed the situation of his parents as guestworkers and their living conditions in Germany as typical, many of his stories focused on how his parents did not conform to the stereotypes of strict Turkish parents trapped in traditional ideas about honor, discipline, education, and respect:

Bulent: Many also say, no German man or woman, the daughter shouldn't marry a German and if she does, then maybe it is impossible in the family and they say "No, that isn't acceptable" or "you are disowned," and with men, if the boy wants to marry, then they also say no. Thank God my parents aren't like this. They say, "Marry who you want, you decide, and if you then don't want her, then it's not our fault. That is your decision. You are old enough, you decide. You marry whoever you want and that should make you happy."

Julia: And that is the opinion of your parents.

Bulent: Unfortunately that is just my parents. . . . So really few who think like that and, for example, I could also say, "Hey, I have a girlfriend." My girlfriend called me, and sometimes we were at my house. My father saw us and just said hello. . . . My brother and I, we drank. We finished school and we drank. My brother a little too much, and we were at home and he threw up in the bathroom. My father came—many other parents would have said, "I'm throwing you out, you're not allowed to drink." My father came and said to us, "Son, should I get the doctor?"

Julia: So why is their opinion different?

Bulent: My father is not religious. And from the culture. It's a little different for my father. He was also an orphan. So his mother died and he grew up alone, and then separated from his father and so on. He was basically totally alone. And of course he didn't develop that much, unfortunately he didn't, but he came to Germany and . . . he is . . . how is my father different? Actually, that's a good question. Maybe he knew. . . . I don't know. I can't really tell you that.

Bulent, like several young men I talked with, has an image of typical Turkish parents—traditional religious villagers who are more concerned with maintaining religious rules and honor and exerting authority than with the welfare of their children. He contrasted this stereotypical parent with his own family experiences, though he did not have ready answers for why his parents would be different from the stereotypical family. He did attribute some of the problems between generations to Islam, a discursive move that is common in Turkish secularist discourse:

Bulent: My father never beat me. But if I had stolen, then he definitely would have beaten me because it would have been a disgrace. If the police had brought me home because of fighting, "Here, your son," he would have beaten me. Um, but for me I can say that I never did anything like that. . . . And all the other Turkish parents who are so connected to their religion, they say, the Qur'an forbids. . . . Also among men, I know families where the man, the boy is also not allowed to have sex. Not allowed to drink alcohol, no "I'm going to the disco," and isn't allowed to. My parents always knew. We watched TV together on Saturday evening at 12:00, and my brother and I—he's somewhat younger than me—come on, let's go out. We got up, went, "Hey, where are you going?" "Yeah, to the disco." "What? At this time of night you want to go to the disco?" "Yeah! The night starts now." "Boys, watch out for each other." That's what they said: "Boys, watch out for each other."

Julia: So you have a good relationship with your parents.

Bulent: Yes, yes, definitely.

Julia: Do you think that is unusual?

> Bulent: It is pretty unusual, yes. It is pretty unusual because if I wanted to marry a German right now, I could say to my parents, "Mama, Papa, I have a German girlfriend." If I were together with her for a year, I could say, "I'm with her, I love this woman." I then could say, "I want to marry her because she's great. . . ."

He contrasted this with what he viewed as the typical reaction of Turkish parents, who place tight controls on the marriages of both sons and daughters.

At one point, late in the interview, after he had been discussing attitudes of his that he identified as markedly different from those of other Turks, he addressed explicitly his relationship to a "Turkish" identity. His comments display his conflicted relationships to various identities and the discursive contours of these identities:

> Julia: But do you feel like a part of Turkish culture here? Even though you have these opinions?" [He had been discussing what Turkish girls are like and criticizing Turkish sexual restraints.]
>
> Bulent: I still want to say—if you interviewed a hundred Turkish men, I think you wouldn't interview anyone who thinks like I do and also says that. I mean, I think this way, and I also say it. And whether I see myself as a part of the culture, hm, part is part. I'm not a Turk. I'm also not a German. I'm a German-Turk. When I'm in Germany, they say, "you're a Turk." When I'm in Turkey, they say, "You're a German-Turk." My God [*mein Gott*]. I'm a world citizen.

This formulation, an instance of a discourse about hybridity (or hybrid discourse), was repeated in similar terms by many young people of Turkish background with whom I talked in Germany.[11]

After asserting a cosmopolitan identity as world citizen and hybrid, Bulent segued immediately into what it means to be a "Turk," beginning by distancing himself from a stereotype of violence:

> I say to myself, I don't want everything that the Turks have, I don't want to start hitting when someone looks at me funny. I mean the Turks are a little, um, how should I describe it? They have it in their blood. They are also fierce. The wars from the Ottoman Empire and so on, it's—Turks have warrior blood. And fight when they have to, yes. But not over every little thing.

Yet he does not reject this violent aspect of Turkishness completely. As he spoke, he connected the violence of Turkish street youth that gives them a bad reputation with the romantic image of the fierce Ottoman warrior, which, as I described in Chapter 1, is also present in the German popular imaginary, including children's literature and film. Bulent identified with this racial image of warrior blood running through his veins, and it forms a component of his masculine identity. He seems to have worked out a way to retain this articulation of masculinity while distancing himself from what he called the trivial violence ("every little thing") of "typical" German-Turkish youth. He thus moved into a subject position based on a positive identification with the tendency to fight. He then picked up other positive elements of both Turkishness and Germanness, thinking in terms of a model of hybridity in which one selectively incorporates "parts" of each culture: "And, for example, from the Turks I take their hospitality. This friendliness. And helpfulness." This trait of hospitality is an important dimension of honor.

> And from the Germans, I really like it that everyone does everything so precisely, according to the rules. If you say, hey, this has to stand exactly like this [demonstrating with a book on the desk], then it should be like that, and not like this. Because it could happen that it slides further and then falls. I want to have it exactly like that, period. I want to be punctual. You were very punctual today. I noticed that you were here two minutes before the meeting time. And those kinds of things.

This identification with German order is also a response to a negative stereotype about Turks, who are seen to operate on "Turkish time," that is, late for appointments. After this discussion of German cultural orientations, Bulent returned to the issue of violence, starting from a perspective articulated in German educational settings:

> I want to be able to talk about my problems and not have to hit. If I just say, OK, I have a problem, then I go to the man and say, "Did you say this and that?" Of course, if he then somehow . . . I don't know. People can do anything.

These hesitations suggest that he had begun to question the universal applicability of this abstract principle. He then began to imagine a situation in which he himself would get violent, as if he were recalling an actual incident from his past. Though he did not describe the specific memory, it seemed to interrupt his train of thought:

> And if you, for example . . . it could also happen that I—I was also a soldier—that I get to the point where I say, OK good, now I'm going to hit. I'm going to get in

a fight with this man. You can't say beforehand. Maybe he says something to me, it's a sore point, and I say . . . insulted, I forget everything and then I go and hit someone. It could happen. I mean, now these are just hypotheses, but . . .

Instead of getting into specifics, Bulent backed off into the abstract ("these are just hypotheses") and returned to the safer topic of Julia's question before regrouping and moving back again to the issue of violence:

. . . whether I see myself as part of the culture. Part is part. Not completely. Because I've also met a lot of people who come from Turkey and said, you German-Turks. And I said, "What do you mean, you? Aren't we Turks?" "Hey, I didn't mean it like that, you're different." I'm not different. I'm exactly like all the others out there. I just behave differently. Of course, I myself don't like it now when Turkish boys go out on the street and prove themselves, like, "Hey, we're going to beat up all the Germans." Why? "We just want to." They don't even have an answer, why, they say, hey we want to beat people up because then we look strong. But if a Turk, I mean not all, like a working-class Turk, if you say to him, "You asshole," he says, "You called me asshole, I'm going to hit you." Just say "asshole" back. I mean, but that doesn't work. And I mean, as long as a person is insulting me, I just say, "What's wrong with you," my God.

While he rejected the orientation that he attributed to Turkish youth in Germany, which he linked to the working class and their efforts to "prove themselves" as men, he did not entirely reject the notion of violence associated with honor. He alluded to the possibility that he could "forget himself" and respond with violence but then quickly moved back to a position critical of Turkish street youth and their desire to "look strong" as a strategy for establishing their status, self-respect, and honor.

One of Bulent's strategies for managing negative stereotypes in this research setting was to articulate a model of hybridity in which he was able to explicitly pick and choose, partially identifying with being German while continuing to see himself as Turkish in other ways. But he found it difficult, at least in this interview setting, talking to an American researcher, to admit to some of his strategies for maintaining honor because of their connection to powerfully negative representations of Turkish young men. Given his association of this violence with the working class and his own goal of getting a university degree, he clearly saw himself as moving into the middle class, away from the stigmatized parallel society inhabited by working-class Turks.

Mustafa: "Will I get a spot at a university? Probably not."

Mustafa, mentioned earlier along with his girlfriend Hadice, was a seventeen-year-old student at a gymnasium in Berlin when he was interviewed in 2006. Mustafa's parents migrated from Turkey more than thirty years ago. His father had come as a guestworker and had been a laborer for ten years before becoming self-employed. The gymnasium Mustafa attended has in recent years experienced a demographic shift so that nearly all students are now "foreigners," meaning that their families are of immigrant background, though most of the students themselves were born in Germany. Such students are a group that has been among the most decisively affected by the recent economic downturn and increased suspicion of Muslims, since their identities are invested in academic and professional success, which are potentially threatened by the worsening conditions following the events of September 11, 2001.

For Muslim youth, the events surrounding September 11 and subsequent attacks in Europe marked a radical alteration in public discourse about Muslim minorities and had the potential for triggering significant changes in the political and social environments in ways that threatened their social worlds. Mustafa emphasized the sense of threat arising from the "Islamic terrorist" discourse that intensified the negative stereotypes that young men must negotiate.

Along with the aftermath of the al-Qaeda attacks, another general condition has had a major effect on Muslim youth in Germany in the past few years. This is Germany's worsening economy, which in the form of fewer opportunities for employment, hit these youth harder than any other group. As a result, the potential for new forms of stigmatization increased quite suddenly. These two circumstances have affected the identities of youth, including the extent to which they imagine themselves as "German" and "Turkish" and what they see as viable strategies for gaining respect and being successful—strategies for becoming men.

Mustafa described how this changed environment is affecting the orientation of the second and third generations to Germany and Turkey: "I would say that here in Germany, it's very difficult nowadays, especially for youth. It's difficult to find a place to study at university, to study, and then to become independent [self-employed]. I don't think that there are great opportunities here. . . . For that reason, everyone looks for the opportunity to go back [to Turkey]." Yet he also said that he felt comfortable in Germany, in contrast to Turkey, where he doesn't know "how anything works" and feels like a foreigner. He articulated the growing despair of Turkish youth:

> In Berlin, recently, it's been the case that youth simply can't control themselves—even at school. As we see in the media, there are always cases where a student hits a teacher or something like that. But it's my opinion that it's not simply a matter of the youth—it's about education. These kids go to school, in the so-called "foreigner" [*Ausländer*] schools, where 30 to 90 percent of the students are Turkish, don't have any goals, and think, "OK, I'll finish up school and then what?" Even I, a student at gymnasium, who will make Abi [*Abitur*], have doubts as to whether or not I'll get a place at a university. What are the kids from *Hauptschule* [a lower tier secondary school] supposed to think, about what they'll do later in life, about a goal? For that reason there's always the question of whether stupid youth are guilty, or the entire society. I don't think that it rests entirely on the youth. Something should be done about it. . . . Society, that means parents, it means government.

In these statements, Mustafa indicated how powerful negative representations of young men of Turkish background are, especially as these are presented in the media. In the context of this discussion of school and career success, he did not challenge these media representations. He distinguished himself from most Turkish youth because of his future *Abitur* and was critical of their violent behavior, but he nevertheless sympathized with them and identified with their situation. He himself felt anxious about the future and recognized that those who have not been academically successful have even less of a chance to establish themselves.

> Education must be somehow differently organized. With most parents it's "OK, my kid goes to school, does his homework, does this and this, that's that." They don't really care at all, most of them. It's "have you done your homework? OK." They don't actually take a look and say, "This is how it should be done. Have you done this? And this?" You go to school through the tenth grade if you're at *Hauptschule* or *Realschule*. If you're good, you go further. But even if you do go further, what then? Even when I've got my *Abitur*, what will I do? Will I get a spot at a university? Probably not. For these reasons, it's not just about the youth, I would say.

He blamed the failure and violence of youth not on their personal lack of goals or stupidity but on structural factors: the educational system, the government, "society." He put some blame on their parents, who do not push their children to concentrate on schoolwork, but he did not explicitly attribute the parents' shortcomings to their Turkish cultural background. At another point, when discussing the honor killing of Hatun Sürücü (see Chapter 5), who had attended his school, he also avoided blaming the "culture" or traditional masculinity (as did media representations) but rather attributed the killing to the murderer's "craziness."

Mustafa identified himself as a Muslim but did not seem to be actively involved in Muslim practice or organized activities. He agreed with his girlfriend Hatice's characterization of Islam as something that is a part of her but that she practices only when she has time. Protesting dominant negative stereotypes of Muslims and Islam, Mustafa, like virtually all other Muslims I have talked with, distinguished the Muslim from the "so-called Islamist":

> The people who committed the [September 11th] attack, the problem is that you simply can't call them Muslims. People who know anything ought to know, too, that someone who does something to another person, even if I were to do something to you, that that is my sin, and that I couldn't be considered a Muslim if I did it. As I said, the word is always misused. Islamist.

Mustafa saw events such as the honor killing and "Islamist" violence as aberrations that do not reflect his community, which has been unfairly stigmatized in the German media. He grounds his identity, honor, and self-respect through a tactic in which he asserts the ties between himself and other young men of Turkish background, arguing that they are honorable and that their failures are a result of the German social system, in which they are stereotyped and systematically disadvantaged. In fact, his identity as a student at a gymnasium does not preclude ties to youth who attend lower-level schools, a point made by Hermann Tertilt, who noted that in the Frankfurt street gang Turkish Power Boys, which was notoriously violent, nearly a third of the young men attended a gymnasium (Tertilt 1996).

Young men of Turkish background at the gymnasium such as Mustafa are acutely aware of their own diasporic position and the terms in which they construct and present their identities in relation to prevailing images of Turks, but they use various strategies for establishing their own identities vis-à-vis the prevailing negative representations. Mustafa focused on the difficulties facing both himself and those who were not successful and sought to disrupt negative stereotypes and popular misunderstandings.

Sezai: "Send them back!"

Seventeen-year-old Sezai, in contrast, emphasized the differences between himself and other young men of Turkish background. He was particularly vehement within the context of a classroom conversation about integration and foreigners: "Ninety percent of the foreigners here are unemployed, get money from the state, have fifteen kids who are criminals and go to *Hauptschule*. I say, send them back. Send them back! I have integrated. I don't do illegal things, and I don't plan to live off the government." When another student commented, "Germans do that, too," Sezai replied, "And we taught them to do that! Before we came, they didn't know how!"

Sezai's remarks and subsequent statements in a more private interview setting indicate that he sharply distinguished himself from his highly negative image of the majority of Turks, whom he characterized in terms that echo prevailing media representations of this problem minority that refuses to integrate: Turks refuse to work, they live off of welfare, and they don't care about education. Their children go to second-class schools and become criminals. They are, in effect, not worthy of respect. He contrasted himself with these young men by declaring that he is integrated. This would appear to be a class difference, given that Sezai has made it to the highest level of secondary school; but if so, it is a class difference in the making, because there is no clear difference between his own class background and those of young men who do not study in a gymnasium.[12] His father, like Mustafa's, was an unskilled laborer who followed his own father from rural Turkey to Germany as a guestworker. One of Sezai's strategies for asserting self-respect in the face of the powerful negative representations of Turkish young men that surround him was to maintain a sharp boundary between himself and others. For him, the fact that he attends a gymnasium is not in itself a sufficient marker of success and respect because he is also critical of the gymnasium he attends:

> Kreuzberg is truly a multicultural borough. But from its social position, it's also a fire blight. . . . And the *Gymnasiums* really aren't at *Gymnasium* level. . . . It's because the social situation here in Kreuzberg is very different from in other boroughs. Kreuzberg is a Turkish borough. And we really do have lots of problems here. . . . Of the seven hundred students here at this *Gymnasium*, I can truly say that half are trash. . . . There are many students here who always manage to get to second semester with one or two "5"'s [the lowest grade].

Sezai's vehemence in rejecting other Turkish youth may be in part a reflection of the growing despair among these young men of Turkish background, many of whom see avenues to success gradually diminishing.

Like Mustafa, Sezai saw the possibility of returning to Turkey as an increasingly attractive option. Yet neither of them saw it as a return to their homeland; they rather saw Turkey as a place where they might be able to do better financially, a vision strikingly devoid of the romantic nostalgia for a homeland that often characterizes the view of their first-generation parents or grandparents:

> And more than anything we were born here, we've grown up here. If you were to drag us back to Turkey now—no that wouldn't do anything. I said this to my father recently: "Maybe you can go back to Turkey, but we are all here, and we must stay here." That's why I said in class today that we have to integrate, no matter how. And that's why. Let's say I've studied and I've gotten my diploma. Let's say I'm thirty years old now. Then I could imagine going back with my family to Turkey and living there. If I have good opportunities here, if I can do better here than there—but if I would have a higher position there than here, then I can imagine going back and living in Turkey. But it's still unclear.

This glimmer of imagining a return to Turkey is an echo of what appears to be a newly emerging discourse among even the most "integrated" youth and is a consequence of what they perceive as the worsening conditions for Turks in Germany today. It is striking that youth such as Sezai can imagine a future of such uncertain location. It reflects a form of cosmopolitanism, of being a "citizen of the world," to echo Bulent's phrase.[13]

Yusuf: "The people at this school are bad."

Students at the lower tiers of the educational system draw on similar tactics to manage the stigmatization of Turkish and Muslim masculinity, often distinguishing themselves as different from their peers, especially when talking with an outsider. Yusuf is a tenth-grader at a *Hauptschule* in Berlin's Neukölln district, a minority-dominated area that is considered poorer and more marginalized than Kreuzberg. His goal is to work in a fitness studio after graduation. He claimed to have no interest in school, even in the school's physical education classes, but said that he works out two hours a day at the sports center. When asked what his classmates do after school, he replied: "I have no idea what they do. I'm the only one who works out. They cause trouble. Take people's bags from them, steal. . . . The people at this school are bad. There are a few nice ones, but most are not." Despite this negative assessment of his classmates, he appeared to have a relaxed, casual relationship with a number of them: as he approached a knot of his classmates who were meeting at the sports center for a school event, he walked straight up to them, gave them all high-fives, and took a long drag on a half-smoked cigarette before they went in together.

CONCLUSION

The men discussed in this chapter handle the tensions and stresses of the diasporic situation in a variety of ways. Yet all of them are acutely aware of the dominant stereotypes that stigmatize them, and they carefully position themselves to avoid abjection as they negotiate identity, masculinity, and sexuality when presenting themselves to others. In the face of humiliation by teachers and media sensationalism, they experience the divide that has been constructed between modernity and tradition and straddle it with such tactics as the displacement of stigmatization onto others, compartmentalization of identities, and various forms of identification with the modern. They struggle with issues of loyalty and respect for their parents and friends as they negotiate stigmatizations that have only intensified since the terrorist attacks of September 11, 2001.

4 RECOVERING HONOR AND RESPECT

STEREOTYPES OF TURKISH MEN rest on the contrast between the modern autonomous subject and the traditional subject who is motivated, above all, by the principle of honor. Though honor is not the rigid code for conduct that has been popularly associated with the honor-shame complex, the German word *Ehre*, like the English word *honor*, has taken on this meaning when used to refer to the practices of Muslims and Turks. In Turkish, multiple categories associated with honor, respect, and reputation can be deployed in various ways. Even in a village setting, honor and reputation can rest on competing and contradictory principles and strategies.[1] Furthermore, how a person acquires respect and maintains his or her reputation is negotiable and sensitive to changes in the social environment. There is no clear line dividing honor from respect and reputation, except in contexts of stigmatization. In this discursive context, honor is linked to what has been stigmatized as an archaic form of masculinity manifest in practices such as an excessive protection of the women in one's family and the resort to violence in the face of insult. Ironically, a concern with honor itself becomes a source of shame and stigmatization.

Honor and reputation have been subject to particularly intense renegotiation in the diasporic situation because of this stigmatization. Stigmatized honor has been associated with scripts that diasporic men of Turkish background may ambivalently identify with and enact, but only at the risk of being marginalized and abjected as other within German social spaces. The renegotiation of honor, reputation, and respect, especially with regard to sexuality and relationships with women, has been a central theme in many of the films created by directors of Turkish background. It is also a process central to the self-presentations of many of the young men I talked with in Germany. .

In this chapter, I examine the negotiation of new scripts for the maintenance of self-respect and reputation and look at how the category of honor is both deployed and repudiated in this process. I begin by asking how filmmakers of Turkish background in both Turkey and Germany have grappled with male identity in a world where traditional honor has been stigmatized. I then consider how upwardly mobile young people from families who came to Germany as guestworkers position themselves vis-à-vis issues of honor and reputation that are associated with a Turkish identity as they strive to escape marginalization and abjection in order to become successfully middle class within German society.

NOSTALGIA FOR A STIGMATIZED MASCULINITY

Families of Turkish background in Germany have ready access to Turkish TV and films. Many homes receive satellite broadcasts directly from Turkey, and the video stores in the heart of Berlin's Kreuzberg are stocked primarily with Turkish films. In Turkey, there has been a resurgence of romantic nostalgia for rural life and the stigmatized forms of masculinity and honor associated with it. For many diasporic families in Germany, this romantic nostalgia resonates with their fading attachment to the myth of return and weakening ties to their homeland.

Within Turkey, nostalgia is a powerful theme in popular culture, especially in TV and cinema, and is closely associated with the celebration of male social spaces and practices (Suner 2004). The rise of Arabesk music, which accompanied the move of rural populations to the city, is steeped in this masculine nostalgia: "The genre has remained closely bound to masculine culture. It is strongly associated with mustaches, masculine friendship, and raki-drinking, cigarette-smoking rituals" (Özbek 1997). Masculine nostalgia suffuses films like the box-office hit *Eskiya* (The Bandit) by Yavuz Turgul (1996), which drew large audiences in Turkey and among Turks in Germany. In this film, the main character chooses to resist the corruptions of modern society in favor of the disappearing values of love, honor, and respect. Honor is linked with tradition, honesty, and trustworthiness. Images of male solidarity are juxtaposed against the disruption of these relationships by the pressures of modernity and corruption. According to film scholar Asuman Suner, nostalgia for the village and the past is reinforced by "what might be called mild leftwing oppositional politics"

(Suner 2004: 309) that is critical of the excessive authority of the state and its attempts to suppress ethnic diversity and Islam in an authoritarian imposition of secularism and modernity. Media expression of nostalgia for a masculinity based on honor thus stands in tension with nationalist and feminist discourses that reject traditional gender relationships and denigrate rural masculinity.

In recent years in Turkey, the label *white Turk* has come to be associated with an urban cosmopolitan identity, popular feminism, secularism, and the denigration of traditional masculinity, while the *black Turk* stands for the traditional, conservative, and lower class (Arat-Koç 2007). Despite the salience in Turkish media of an urban cosmopolitan discourse represented by a white-Turk perspective, many have noted a resurgence of the perspective of the black Turk. This resurgence is embodied, for instance, in the success of Recep Tayyip Erdoğan as prime minister, as one columnist for the *Turkish Daily News* expressed rather starkly, defining black Turks as the Anatolian conservative electorate: "Erdogan's success story is the victory of the 'black Turks' against the 'white Turks.' It has a mathematical explanation: there are simply more 'black Turks' than 'white Turks'" (Bekdil 2005). According to sociologist Arus Yumul, there has been a "remachoisation of masculinity," a move to transform the stigma associated with the image of the black Turk into a positive image: "It is a masculinity embracing violence, aggression, and the basic constituents of 'delikanlik' [young manhood]. It involves the exaggerated display of emotions, especially grief, a characteristic from the arabesk music and culture, which began to develop among migrants and urban squatter settlements in the 1970s, and expanded beyond these neighborhoods during the 1980s" (Yumul 1999: 115).

Films made by young filmmakers in Turkey depict concerns with masculinity and power that are linked nostalgically with the themes of masculinity and honor. Zeki Demirkubuz, for example, returns repeatedly to the theme of the erosion of masculinity and power in his films. In his 1997 film *Masumiyet* (Innocence), the male characters are trapped in a small-town world where their efforts to be honorable are repeatedly frustrated. The film opens with Yusuf's release after ten years in prison, where he served time for killing his best friend. This was a friend he had made while doing his compulsory military service. But on the day they finished their service, his friend ran off with his sister, prompting Yusuf to shoot them. This act, committed to defend his honor, resulted in his imprisonment. At his release, Yusuf is fearful of the world outside the prison walls. In his transient existence, he visits his sister, who is locked in a marriage founded on hatred. She silently avoids her husband (she has been reduced to silence because Yusuf's gun not only killed her lover but also destroyed her tongue). Her husband weeps in frustration, "What have I done to deserve this?" and then beats her in what appears to be a daily occurrence. As Yusuf moves out into the world, he falls in love with a prostitute. Along with his love comes jealousy and a desire to take care of her. In a scene that utterly undermines the possibility of male honor through the protection of one's woman, she resists his efforts to "protect" her by opening herself to him graphically and crudely.

In a conversation I had with him, Demirkubuz attributed the erosion of masculinity to modernity. Far from seeing this as a problem confronting only the traditional Turkish man, he feels that it is a universal problem in Western societies: "In modernity, there are constant struggles over power, no clear authority or hierarchy, but the power struggles are there nevertheless. It's not that things are equal." But he thinks that a woman fundamentally wants a man to have power over her. This would account for the prostitute's rejection of the two men who are "in love" with her and devoted to her. They do not exert power over her and thus do not command her respect. A Turkish woman who was a part of my conversation with Demirkubuz whispered to me her reaction to his position: "This is just Turkish man-talk. When men dominate like that, it causes the petty malice that women engage in." She seemed to be enacting the conflict over masculinity that Demirkubuz had portrayed in the film.

Can we see the theme of nostalgia for a lost masculinity linked with honor carried over into German-Turkish films? What happens to the idea of honor in the gap between Turkey and Germany? Is the stereotype of honor in Germany frozen in the 1960s, just as the idea of the village has been? I suggest that a tension between the threat of emasculation and the maintenance of honor has been a key theme among Turkish-German filmmakers but has gone virtually unacknowledged because it gets translated into a problem of cultural difference, or failures to shed "tradition."

In Fatih Akin's film *Kurz und schmerzlos* (1998), a young man who feels alienated from his father's values gets caught up involuntarily in an underworld of drug violence. He at first rejects Turkish traditional culture, including Islam. Early in the film his father invites him to pray with him and he refuses. Later, he is with his father at the mosque praying, but does not carry through the prayer and eventually walks out before it is over. During the course of the film, he negotiates the tension of how to maintain honor vis-à-vis his sister's love life. He gives his best friend, a Greek Christian, the go-ahead to date his sister, thereby transcending the traditional enmity between Greeks and Turks, but responds with violence when she chooses to go out with someone else. He finally reconciles himself to this situation, accommodating a new organization of gender. But he ultimately takes up the mantle of male honor by avenging the murder of his best friend. He thus rearticulates the practice of honor instead of simply rejecting it. When he returns to his father's apartment after the killing, he joins him in prayer, indicating a repositioning of his identity and masculinity vis-à-vis his father's world.

Akin's most recent film, *Gegen die Wand* (see Chapter 2), also explores the rearticulation of masculinity in the space of diaspora. To date, this is the most successful film by a German director of Turkish background, winning the Golden Bear Award in Berlin and transcending the circumscribed domain of German domestic cinema onto the international circuit. It also gave Akin a reputation among Turkish film critics, who had previously ignored German-born Turkish directors. Though the plot takes off from a situation common in Turkish-German films, with Sibel, a young second-generation woman, seeking to escape the constraints of her traditional family, the film disrupts the myth of a woman's escape from her Turkish family into a German "happily ever after" that was evident in films such as *Yasemin* and *Auf Eigenen Füssen*, or even *40 Quadratmeter Deutschland*, discussed in Chapter 2. The film thus addresses the conflicts that arise from the reordering of gender and sexuality in a diasporic space.

Some commentators have described the film as being about Sibel's efforts to break away from her family, an interpretation that is symptomatic of the spotlight of Western attention on the oppressed Muslim woman as exotic other. But the film begins and ends with Cahit, the man Sibel marries. The film features a hero who, like the central characters of many films created by filmmakers of Turkish background, struggles to find a viable way of being a man in a modern world in which family ties have dissolved and traditional Turkish mores are hollow and oppressive. At the film's core is a love story that emerges out of the rootlessness of the diasporic hero and the constraints of the heroine's traditional family. When the film opens, Cahit is an alcoholic derelict at the bottom of the social hierarchy, scavenging for old bottles on the streets of Hamburg. After a drunken binge, he attempts suicide by driving head-on into a brick wall. It is eventually revealed that he has sunk to this condition because of the death of his German wife and his inability to connect emotionally with anyone since this tragedy. Sibel meets Cahit as a fellow attempted suicide who has been admitted to the same psychiatric hospital. At first meeting, she asks him to marry her because he is Turkish and thus offers a means of escape from her family. He reluctantly agrees to a sham marriage. Despite her sleeping around with other men, they eventually fall in love, but their future is disrupted by an accidental "jealousy killing" that sends Cahit to prison for several years and Sibel to Istanbul to escape her brother's efforts to kill her for shaming the family.

Sibel's parents stereotypically embody images of the problems of integration that prevail in German public discourse: women are eager to assimilate into German society but are hindered by their men, who refuse to integrate and struggle to maintain traditional Turkish practices—namely, controlling their women to maintain their honor—in order to perpetuate a parallel society. Sibel's father (who looks more like her grandfather) has a long white beard, a signifier of the religiously conservative, rural Turkish man. Sibel's mother, in contrast, is fully European in appearance: her short hair is bleached blond, and she dresses like a stylish German woman. At Sibel and Cahit's wedding, she wears a fitted v-neck knee-length dress. In the script, she is described as being approximately fifty years old—fifteen years younger than her husband—"with a tender face in which can be seen life's experience."[2] The film alludes to the difficulties she has experienced as a Turkish wife and mentions that she was married at age seventeen. There are several indications that she is sympathetic to Sibel's needs but is powerless to resist her husband's authority. Nevertheless, she is subtly subversive and frustrated that Sibel has not learned from her similar strategies of covert resistance. Hence, when she and Sibel are left alone in the cafeteria of the hospital after Sibel's attempted suicide, and after the men in the family have left in annoyance, Sibel pulls out a cigarette, and her mother asks for one, too—presumably something she would not have done in front of her husband. Twice in the film, Sibel's parents quarrel about the causes of their problems with their daughter. When they are discussing whether to approve of Sibel's marriage to Cahit, her father says: "She made mistakes because of how you raised her. From childhood."

Akin goes to great lengths to portray the alienness and hypocrisy of traditional Turkish male honor and gender relations, in ways that set Cahit's character and ethical stance as resistant to this tradition. When Sibel and Cahit pay an obligatory visit to Sibel's brother, Cahit finds himself playing a card game with her brother and two of his male friends. The conversation, tinged with bravado, turns to their experiences in a brothel. When Sibel's brother suggests that Cahit should accompany them the next time they go to the brothel, Cahit asks, "Don't you fuck your wives?" The others are outraged, close to violence, and one of them shouts, "Never again use the word 'fuck' in connection with our wives!" (Akin 2004: 102). This scene emphasizes the disjunction between honor and fidelity to one's wife in Turkish gender practices. In the other room, in stark contrast, the wives are discussing in Turkish details of their husbands' sexual practices. All participate in the exchange:

Hatice: And how is he in bed?

Sibel: Good.

Canan: Does he lick?

Sibel: Like a cat.

Murcan: God be praised. Mine licks like an ox and moos at the same time!

The women laugh.

Audiences are likely to interpret this scene to mean that Turkish women are more modern and thus ready to assimilate fully into German society than are their more honor-obsessed and violence-prone husbands, thereby reinforcing negative stereotypes about Turkish men.[3] The content of the women's remarks also reinforces the image of the black Turk, who is crude in his desires and bodily habits.

The pivotal incident in the film, an accidental killing, reconfigures the issue of honor. Niko, an acquaintance of Cahit's whom Sibel has slept with, taunts Cahit after he learns that they are actually married: "What kind of fucked up husband are you? Your wife whores around all over and you don't even give a shit. Do you even fuck her? Oh, I get it. You're her pimp, right? Does her cunt bring in good money? Tell me, what does it cost to fuck her in the ass? Is 50 euros enough?" At this, Cahit, who has been sitting silently at the bar with his back to Niko, jumps up and takes one swing at him. He hits Niko in the head, and Niko falls to the floor dead. Seeing what he has done, Cahit calls "Niko?" And then, in alarm, "Call a doctor!"

This "murder" is an irruption of the uncanny into a "modern" bar scene, the emergence of "traditional" violence, which has been repudiated and yet is all too familiar. The killing has occurred unintentionally, but it is triggered by the unexpected appearance of rediscovered, seemingly primordial sentiments of love, jealousy, and honor. It echoes the honor-linked violence that Cahit had nearly triggered in the card game by alluding to the sexuality of the men's wives. Ironically, it is a moment that had been triggered by Sibel's earlier rejection of

Niko with her words: "I'm a married Turkish woman. If you try anything, my husband will kill you." Sibel had rejected Niko after falling in love with her husband. In angry reaction, Niko insulted Cahit in terms of this honor.

Akin puts this killing in tension with the traditional honor killing. We see in the film how the event is taken up into the German press with the newspaper headline: "Eifersuchtsdrama auf St. Pauli" (Jealousy Drama in St. Pauli), accompanied by a wedding photo of Sibel and Cahit. Sibel's family is shamed, and her brother sets out to kill her in order to restore the family honor in the traditional way. When Cahit is released from prison several years later, he talks with his brother-in-law before setting out to find Sibel:

Cahit: Where is your sister?

Yilmaz: I have no sister now.

Cahit: You have the same mother. So how is your mother doing?

Yilmaz: We had to save our honor [Ehre]. Don't you see?

Cahit: Did you save it, your honor?

Despite Cahit's rejection of the traditional Turkish contours of manhood, he begins a journey back to his "home" in Turkey. As he is released from prison, he is met by his closest friend Şeref (which means *honorable* in Turkish). This friend, who has himself rejected marriage and entanglement, demonstrates the loyalty of a true friend by persuading Cahit to take the money he has saved up for him. With much suppressed emotion, he says, "For fuck's sake, I am your uncle after all," a reference to the fact that he had pretended to be Cahit's uncle in order to persuade Sibel's parents to agree to the marriage. They are drinking milk instead of the usual beer, a sign that Cahit has begun a new life. Earlier in the film, when others ask why his Turkish is so bad, Cahit asserts, "I threw it away." At the end of the film, he is on a bus, alone, on a journey back to his natal town, fifteen hours from cosmopolitan Istanbul.

Filmmakers' preoccupations are an articulation of issues that lie at the conjunction of their own fantasies, conflicts, and experiences and what will appeal to diverse audiences. These audiences include Germans, who are attracted especially to crime shows with a dash of violence. Just as global audiences imagine what they see in the American films that dominate their theaters as representing American reality, German audiences invest the marginalized subject of the immigrant with a kind of reality, as a literal representation of that which is unfamiliar and other. In this context, directors of Turkish background such as Demirkubuz and Akin have taken up themes that on the one hand simultaneously reproduce and reject stereotypes of Turkish masculinity while on the other hand expose the void that is left when these repudiated sources of honor are gone.

CONTEXTUAL HONOR

I now look at how men talk about honor, reputation, and self-respect in conversations with anthropologists. Is there evidence of renegotiations of honor and sources of respect that reflect the effects of stigmatization?

An example of the flexibility and contextuality of the practice of honor can be seen in Paul Magnarella's study of men before and after their migration to Germany from Anatolia in 1965. Whereas their honor had initially rested on being able to keep their women safely in the village, it quickly shifted to a new foundation that encompassed being successful in Germany and encouraging their wives to hold jobs there. Magnarella described the rapid changes in attitudes of men from one village in northwestern Anatolia between the time a first contingent migrated from the village to Germany in 1965 and Magnarella's subsequent research in 1976. The first group of men were encouraged to bring their wives with them to Germany but typically responded: "What business do our wives have there among infidels? Isn't it enough that we go away to work? Our wives will stay at home where they belong." According to Magnarella, "for them, preserving their women at home was a matter of honor. To do otherwise would have meant a loss of prestige and status according to their village system of sociocultural values" (Magnarella 1998: 165). But the men's perspectives shifted quickly: "Within a year, they began sending for their wives. By 1976, almost two-thirds of [the village's] 93 emigrant workers . . . had their wives with them in West Germany, and most of these women were working" (Magnarella 1998: 165). When these families returned to the village for their summer vacations, they reported positively on the Germans they lived among: "They described Germans as industrious, ingenious, honest and 'clean people who knew neither lies nor curses.' Because of these outstanding qualities, the workers credited Germans with being more Muslim than some fellow Turks" (Magnarella 1998: 166). Many learned some German, rose to supervisory positions, and, though some were critical of the freedom and openness of German women, adopted a wide range of German cultural practices, including the consumption of pork and alcohol, which Islam prohibits.

Tracing these migrants from the perspective of their village of origin, a picture of integration emerges that is very different from those that focus on lack of integration, retention of traditional attitudes, and the problem of parallel societies. Much of this difference stems from the fact that migrants who successfully integrate tend to disappear from the view of those who are worried about integration failure. But this does not mean that these men and their families have stopped caring about their honor. They were surprised to see Germans acting in ways that they interpreted as "Muslim," which encompassed principles of honor and respectability that they had brought with them from their village and recognized as operative in their new home. Yet even those successfully integrating to the extent that they disappear may think about what it means to be modern in ways that do not involve a rupture with their past and its sources of self-esteem, respect, and honor. They did not stress a sense of being caught "between" cultures.

An example of how variable and negotiable paths to honor can be even within one family can be found in Werner Schiffauer's long-term study of the lives of several migrants from one Turkish village (Schiffauer 1991). Schiffauer identified striking differences between Asiz and his elder brother Bayram, which he attributed, not to the fact that Asiz had migrated to Germany (since Bayram had also migrated within Turkey, from the village to cosmopolitan Istanbul), but to personal styles that were evident even when they were adolescents in the village. As a young man, Asiz had been a rebellious and ironic taunter of others, a position that can be a source of prestige in the eyes of other youth. This was an image that, according to Schiffauer, later evolved into that of the liberal (though not educated) intellectual as he grew older and settled into his marriage and job.

Schiffauer had observed that as a young man Asiz did not live up to the village ideal of honor, which requires the demonstration of strength, decisiveness, and force. Later, during one particularly tense period when Asiz was back in the village during a vacation from his work in Germany and Schiffauer was also present, Bayram explicitly insulted him and accused him of lacking honor. At that point in his life, early in his marriage, Asiz was openly defying village norms: refusing to fast, having an affair back in Germany, being irregularly employed, and dealing drugs. Villagers accused him of not showing his wife respect (Turkish: *izzet*) because he had neglected her for three years, though he had wanted her to move to Germany. But even during this time, when he was criticized by his brother and other villagers, and his mother and wife were allied against him, he maintained an ironic distance and reduced conflict by asking for forgiveness whenever he offended anyone too much (Schiffauer 1991: 328–330).

Bayram, the eldest brother of the family, had migrated to Istanbul as a young man. He was successful in business, "a hard man with principles," who imposed restrictions on his wife. Asiz drew the contrast between himself and his brother in terms of how they treated their wives: Bayram expected that

> she should remain a woman, not talk too much, not get involved in affairs. Even if she has an idea, she is not allowed to help. . . . If he drinks something, for example, and then she says, "Don't drink," then he is very strict and criticizes. That's how he is. But if my wife says to me, "Drink less, you drink too much!" then I say, "My soul wants it, I drink." It's not necessary to answer in a very strict way. (Schiffauer 1991: 330)

Asiz's actions were consistent with this statement: Schiffauer saw him and his wife laughing together in the village, an unusual sight (Schiffauer 1991: 330). Bayram's wife, in contrast, left Bayram to return to the village instead of tolerating his treatment of her.

Asiz's ability to act in defiance of village expectations with apparent confidence suggests that he had used alternative tactics to gain respect, ultimately seeking honor through his ability to support his family, raise successful children, and prosper in Germany. As an adult he emphasized the idea that everyone, including his wife and children, should have their own political opinions and religious orientations and not be subjected to force. Speaking of his son, he said, "In terms of freedom, he should do what he wants. I can't make him choose my way. . . . That would be forceful" (Schiffauer 1991: 335). This statement is an explicit self-positioning vis-à-vis the alternatives of maintaining family honor through force and its opposite, a respect for the freedom of others. Schiffauer noted that Asiz manifests this identity even in his appearance: in 1985, he had the same haircut and beard as his political role model Bülent Ecevit, the leftist Turkish politician and former prime minister who had been incarcerated following the 1980 military coup (Schiffauer 1991: 335). Asiz and other men from the same Turkish village have differing orientations to and success at performing masculinity[4] and draw on alternative models of respect or honor. To impose the categories of "modern" and "traditional" on this array of strategies and models would distort the identities and practices of these men and force them into stereotypes of honor and masculinity.

ISLAM AND THE REJECTION OF "VILLAGE HONOR"

For Muslims in Germany, the association of Islam with violence and terrorism has been a source of negative stereotyping—as in the rhetoric surrounding
honor killing. The perceived backwardness of immigrants is often attributed to
their Islamic beliefs and practices. But a growing minority of Turkish Muslims
in both Turkey and Germany have contested such denigration of Islam, turning
to Islamic practice with renewed attention and explicitly resisting the hege-
mony of secularism and its claim to be the only possible foundation of a modern and just society. Some youth of Turkish background in Germany cultivate
an Islamic identity and, through this identity, actively distance themselves from
other Turkish youth and their status negotiations, a trend that has been increasing since 2001. Though even in village settings, Turks often draw on Islam as
an alternative source of principles for negotiating honor and respect, many of
these diasporic Muslims reject what they know of "village Islam."

Ibrahim and his family are among those who, though they maintain ties
to the family village in Turkey, reject most local customs as being un-Islamic.
I have known this family for many years. Ibrahim has dedicated considerable
resources and time to supporting Islam in Berlin. In his factory job, he works
hard and performs well, but the job is stressful and exhausting: he often works
night shifts, and the threat of being laid off has hung heavily over him for the
past several years. Though we have had many conversations, he has said very
little to me of the specifics of his work, or of how he interacts with colleagues,
even when I ask directly about it, suggesting that his work is a source of frustration, even embarrassment, rather than self-esteem or respect. Like many of his
friends, he had planned to return to Turkey after working in Germany for a few
years, but when it became clear that it was too late for his children to become
well-established in Turkey, he and his wife moved their family into a larger
apartment in Berlin and bought attractive furniture that made it possible for
them to entertain visitors with some elegance, thereby maintaining his reputation as a successful and respectable man.

Though unable to attend a mosque for Friday prayers because of the constraints of his factory job, Ibrahim has set up a prayer room in the factory and
leads others in Friday prayer there. He is active in a local mosque and donated
a large sum of money to support an Islamic organization. A lively conversation-
alist, Ibrahim often becomes very animated when speaking of his support of
Islam. I watched one heated discussion in which he argued with the principal
of a Berlin school about the place of Islamic education in the schools. His wife

and daughters all wear headscarves and long skirts in public, and everyone in his family prays regularly, fasts during Ramadan, avoids alcohol, and eats only halal (permissible) foods.

Ibrahim vehemently rejects village Islam, which he considers to be full of un-Islamic practices. Chief among these are authoritarianism and patriarchy. He emphasized that he would not force his daughters to wear a headscarf, and his daughter told me that he would allow her to decide whom to marry. He takes pride in being an intellectual: he had read a chapter of my book on Sufism that had been translated into Turkish and introduced me to his friends by extensively summarizing the chapter. He has encouraged all of his children to complete a university education and has a strikingly cosmopolitan vision of their place in the world, though he himself is not fluent in German. He supported one son's interest in global travel and his daughter's efforts to finish her university studies and become a professional. His self-respect and honor appear to me to rest on being a positive role model in a modern Islamic community and on being a father whom his children respect because of his kindness, wisdom, and concern for their welfare.

Sezai, the gymnasium student described in Chapter 3 who differentiated himself from most Turkish youth, has also made Islam a central element of his identity: "I'm working on an Islamic course of study outside of school, and I'm also very successful there. And after these successes, my father's trust in me has really gotten very strong." Both his emphasis on a positive relationship with his father and his intense criticism of other Turkish youth are consistent with what I have heard from other actively practicing Muslim youth who have been involved in Islamic groups. Sezai articulated an alternative model of masculinity, with an emphasis on professional success, clearly defined and articulated goals, and the importance of family ties as well as a rejection of what he identified as attributes of the Turkish village such as violence and laziness. His harsh rejection of other Turkish youth, including many of those at his gymnasium, can be seen as an instance of this discursive strategy. In conversation, he presented Islam as a source of status and respect that allows him to distance himself from the competitive struggles over status and honor that he felt characterize many young men of Turkish background. As practiced by Ibrahim and Sezai, Islam is a source of respect and honor that these men use to sharply distinguish themselves from negative stereotypes associated with village practices and locate themselves in the modern world as educated men and intellectuals.

FATHERS AND SONS: HONOR AND RESPECT,
CONSUMPTION AND EDUCATION

Stories of village life are replete with images of the strict and honorable father who gains the respect of his sons and asserts his authority over them through firm discipline and physical beating, and these stories are often told as a way of foregrounding very different strategies for maintaining honor and respect in the father-son relationship, as I have described. But a man's honor, as well as his son's respect for him, is also closely associated with the ability of that man to provide for his family. In a world of escalating global consumption, the issue of what children need, and what a father is expected to provide, can become a source of contention within the family. In these struggles between fathers and sons, honor, respect, educational and career strategies, and the consumption of transnational products can become intertwined. Desire and consumption can transform the relationship, changing the practice of honor and the criteria for bestowing respect.[5]

This intertwining has played out in rather dramatic ways in some Turkish families, thanks to the intervention of the German state, which is suspicious of the Turkish family as a locus of oppression and abuse. Governmental policies focused on protecting children from possible abuse have had unintentional effects, shaming some fathers whose children were removed from the family because of apparently unsubstantiated claims of abuse. With young men often being caught in their own struggles over status and prestige and frustrated by their inability to afford stylish clothing and other consumer goods, a new "cultural" practice developed. According to stories told within the Turkish community, some boys would go to German social services and report that their parents had abused them so that they could be placed with a German foster family in order to be able to dress better. One young woman, Fatma, described to my daughter Julia what had happened with her brother, who is now approaching thirty years old:

> When you go out, then you know how other children dress, then you want to be integrated among the other children. At that time, for example, my brother wanted Diesel pants and Nike shoes. My parents couldn't pay for that. And then eventually this caused problems. Because children feel inferior if they are not dressed like the other children, like the German children. And that was a problem. Then this child comes home and says to the parents, I don't want these pants anymore, I want Diesel pants. Or Nike shoes. And the first generation

came here with one goal: they wanted to save. And earn money and then go back [to Turkey]. They had been here for maybe ten years already but they still thought: at the most maybe twelve or fourteen years and then back again. And, I think that some of these youth might have started to steal, maybe. And then because of this, criminality increased. Then they maybe started smoking, started with cigarettes. I don't want to generalize now, but . . . they could have also been individual cases. But in any case, some said to youth services, "My parents beat me." They said this even though it wasn't true at all. They just wanted to go to a German family as a foster child so that they could wear Diesel pants and Nike shoes. . . . These children were then taken from their families and taken care of. . . . The girls were not like this. The girls were always among themselves, had Turkish friends, they dressed exactly alike, they had the same interests, were not allowed to do many things like go outside, and they just accepted it. And because they were at home, they also studied, or read books, and so they developed much more in an educational sense. The boys were always looking outside, they just felt inferior, less worthy.

Nikes, Diesel pants, and other items such as gold chains take on meanings that resonate with the Turkish backgrounds of the youth Fatma described. In this environment, issues of respect and honor play out in manifold ways, including the ability to enact the current style of dress. Fatma's brother had been an adolescent fifteen years earlier, at a time when most families had not yet committed themselves to remaining in Germany for the long term and were focused on sending money back to Turkey. Youth such as Fatma's brother, who did not share their parents' goal of returning to Turkey, felt that their parents neglected them and their concerns—a feeling that fit well into the discursive environment in which German authorities readily characterized some Turkish parents as not caring for their children, and even being abusive. At some level, the Turkish youth bought into the representations of their parents as abusive or at least neglectful. The way Fatma told the story suggested that this had been a painful issue for her family: though she launched into the story by describing her brother's situation, she then shifted to a more generalized description and avoided linking the practice directly with her brother.

In this environment, many first-generation men seem particularly sensitive to the need to keep their children's respect, going to great lengths to ensure that their children see them as generous and loving. The immigrant men whom Werner Schiffauer first interviewed in a Turkish village before their migration remembered that the issue of clothing had often been a source of conflict between fathers and sons. Several sons remembered needing new clothes to travel out of the village, especially for their education, but their fathers would or could not provide the money to buy them. Schiffauer described one young man who said that one of his reasons for not wanting to go to school as a child was the fear of not having good clothing and thus feeling humiliated (Schiffauer 1991: 120). This demand for new clothes was no doubt a new one for many rural families whose sons were leaving the village for school and work for the first time.

Suleyman, a man Schiffauer interviewed, recalled his experiences with his father in the village from the vantage point of his position as an adult immigrant worker with children of his own. He contrasted how he is with his own sons with how his father treated him as a child. When he was young, he felt rejected when his father did not buy him what he thought he needed to go to school even though he had the money (Schiffauer 1991: 65). Clothing and other consumer goods come to stand for the emotional tones of a relationship, as well as honor and status, in ways that can change over time. When interviewed several years earlier, Suleyman had attributed his inability to have the things he needed to the family's financial difficulties, a significance that marks a very different relationship between himself and his father. A new structure of memory and meaning has developed in Germany in which the failure to buy things for a child symbolizes rejection. Suleyman's memories of his own childhood have been recast into a new interpretive frame. Like many first-generation fathers whose sons are growing up in Germany, he strives to maintain a positive relationship with his own son by providing him with clothing and other consumer goods in a way that he recalled his father refusing to do. Consumption has become a vehicle for the maintenance of the reciprocal obligations of love flowing from father to son and respect from son to father.

The young men described here—all of whom were academically successful and career-focused—emphasized how much they respected their parents. These young people expressed respect for their fathers in ways that echo prevailing models of childrearing in Germany today and are very different from the overt expressions of respect that rural Turkish men expected from their sons. Mr. Hacıoğlu, who romanticized old village ways, had bemoaned the fact that his sons did not give him proper respect, even when he beat them. These young people in Germany, in contrast, praise a father for being lenient and providing them with consumer goods. Many first-generation fathers, too, seek to gain the respect of their children by being successful, flexible, and generous, while allowing children to make their own decisions about the direction of their lives.

Sezai expresses close ties to his family and speaks highly of his father. His description of his father is cast in terms that echo attributes of the modern man, who is child-centered and feels a responsibility to provide consumer goods and education, a stance that is placed in implicit contrast to stereotypes of the authoritarian Turkish patriarch:

> My father has always allowed us lots of freedom, lots of room. My father also had a very difficult childhood, not only because of his family's living conditions. His father didn't attend to his children very much. So now my father tries his best to create the best possible life for his children. Never, when any of us needed anything—when we said, "papa, I need this," he always said, "Okay. When I get my wages, you'll get that." I can remember he bought me a [unclear] for 200 DM. So he is a relaxed guy.

Sezai thus talked of his positive relationship with his father. Key evidence of this positive relationship is the fact that his father bought him things. The characterization of his father as a "relaxed guy" stands in opposition to popular and media images of the Turkish man who demands respect and is ready to defend his honor with violence.

At one point, Sezai was talking about how supportive his father has been, allowing him a lot of freedom and the opportunity to make his own decisions—a form of autonomy—while at the same time being willing to support him financially as long as he is in school, even if he studies after marriage. He emphasized that once he achieves his goals, he will also help his father:

> After marriage, if he [the son] studies, it's usually the case that the father still pays for everything. To be honest, for me this will last a long time. I'll be at least twenty-six when I'm finished. I think twenty-three or twenty-four is a good age to marry. But I have to think about all of this, if I'm really ready for it [marriage]. In addition to my studies, to be able to take up the position of the man of the house. If yes, then I'll go ahead and do it. If not, then I'll wait a bit longer. The problem is only at first. After I finish my studies and get a job as a professor, once I have my own income, then it's not a problem any more. Then I can even help my father. And I'd get paid pretty well. So, if I were to manage all of that, it really would be worthwhile for my dad.

Sezai attributes the earlier lack of money for consumption and disregard for education with the family's orientation toward a return to Turkey. He alludes to it as a general orientation that was shared in the Turkish community: "Until the 1990s people still had the same dream, but then in the 1990s they realized that it wasn't working. They weren't going back home." He credits his own focus on education to his father's emotional and financial support:

> Since then [when the family committed to staying in Germany] there's been a little bit more consideration of the children. It's said, "you've got to study [at a university]." In my case, my parents have always tried to convince us, not in a negative sense but in a positive one, "study, study, study. We couldn't do it, so now it's up to you." My father always says, "look at me. I work as a laborer for a man who doesn't even guarantee me my payment. You should become a man who earns his money with his pen." And it is true that when you look at the family, there are certainly higher goals. It's that way for us. For the Germans, I don't think this would be anything new. But for us it's really something new. And it is finally time that someone went to university!

Sezai articulated an identity framed in opposition to the typical young man of Turkish background in Germany. This identity is cosmopolitan and focused on a career. In conversation with an American researcher, he seeks respect and recognition through his success. His goal after completing the *Abitur* is to attend a university and become a professor of political science. He envisions his future in these terms: "With the goal that I've set for myself, if I were to reach it, then I would have everything. But of course, it requires a great deal of work, time, and patience. But if I were to manage it, then I would have the respect of the entire world." This respect that he seeks can be linked to the concept of honor understood as reputation and includes components of honor that are continuous with the past, including generosity and competitive success.

For a seventeen-year-old, Sezai has remarkably clear life plans that are articulated explicitly in terms of his identity vis-à-vis his father. In this plan, achieving his educational goals takes priority over marriage, and both of these take precedence over achieving financial independence. Sezai does not envision total independence, but rather a reciprocal relationship in which he moves into a position to help his father financially.

We can also see in Sezai's depiction of his father a manifestation of a masculinity explicitly recast in contrast to that of the traditional villager:

the modern Muslim man who values intellectual labor over manual labor and supports this by paying for years of his children's education well into adulthood, is attentive to the needs of those children, can provide them with consumer goods that mark them as middle class, and teaches them to be independent by encouraging their own decision-making. In Sezai's case, these decisions include whether to choose Turkish or German citizenship when he turns eighteen: "I have a Turkish passport. I spoke to my father about it recently, and he said, 'I won't force you to do anything. Think about it yourself. I don't ever want you to say to me, You were the reason why I took German citizenship, and now I'm having problems.'" Sezai is clearly proud of his father and appreciates his efforts to do the best he can for his children. What he says about his father would seem to be an instance of a more broadly emerging discourse on the diasporic Turkish father: after Sezai provided the description of his father, the young woman who also participated in the interview felt at each point that these characterizations described her father as well: "Exactly. Just like my dad."

Bulent, the university student in Kiel, is similarly accepting of his father, but he foregrounded a shift of perspective in his move from a rebellious adolescence in which he felt that his father had not provided the goods that Bulent wanted, into a more positive relationship with his father. He described having been critical of his father's choices when he was young, "But at some point I said, 'my father did a good job.'" Nevertheless, he, too, envisions himself giving his children more than his father gave him, which will be possible because he will complete higher education: "In two and a half years I will be finished, and then I will want to give my children more than I would have wanted from my father. I want to give my children that."

Bulent is also concerned about the respect that a child owes a parent. After discussing how his parents would accept his marrying a German woman, he continued:

> But my wife would also have to respect my parents. That is important to me. I don't want . . . my father is sixty-six years old. And my father is from Turkey. And I don't want anyone to say, "Your parents are farmers, they don't know anything." I respect my parents. My father has done the best with his life that he could. He could have also gone to school, he could have learned German. I always used to say, "Papa, if you had done this or that, things would have been better for us." But at some point I said, "My father did a good job" . . . That's why

I'm going to university, I want, that's why I'm studying, so that later I—for me, I'm not doing it for my parents, I'm not doing it for my brother, I'm doing it for myself because I want more. So that I—I always said to my father, "If my father had studied." After that he said, "Why don't you study?"

Like most of the other young people of Turkish background I knew, Bulent spoke of respecting his parents. He remembers not respecting his father, articulating a complex process of identity negotiation in which he had rejected his father before coming to a new stance. He can now appreciate his father for being nonauthoritarian and can follow his guidance rather than simply taking him as a negative role model. Given Bulent's personal history of dropping out of school and joining the military before returning to school as an older student, he has rearticulated the meaning of honor for himself, away from the status hierarchy prevalent in the groups of Turkish young men among whom he grew up. For Bulent, to be honorable now means to distinguish himself from other Turks by being modern, nonviolent, cultured, and successful in his education; getting a good job; and providing for his children by giving them more things than his father was able to give him.

In the stories of these young men, honor, consumption, education, and respect are inextricably intertwined. The Muslim woman's headscarf has been identified with the issue of maintaining family honor, but clothing also plays an important role in the lives of young men as a means of marking one's identity and garnering the respect of others. Many young men express a sense of shame if they feel that they cannot afford to wear what they regard as appropriate clothing, indicating that one's clothes are closely associated with the maintenance of honor and respect. The ability and willingness of parents, and especially fathers, to buy what the sons feel is appropriate clothing—which in today's globalized economy often means items such as the "right" running shoes or bomber jacket—often play an important symbolic role in the relationship between father and son. This issue takes on specific contours in the diasporic setting in this era of global fashion and consumption, but it is one that also has its roots in Turkish villages and first-generation men's memories of conflicts in their relationships with their own fathers. These memories seem to play a powerful role in shaping men's strategies for handling their sons in Germany. It is one aspect of a broader concern with how fathers should properly care for their children as an index of their love for them. The ability to provide for one's children in terms of consumer goods is, in the long run, linked to the importance of education.

Now that these families are focused on Germany as their new homeland, they see honor and respect to be closely tied to educational success and the ability to sustain a middle-class lifestyle.

HONOR AND SEXUALITY: NEGOTIATING MODERNITY

The young men presented here were all successfully negotiating the German educational system and would be considered well-integrated into German society. Their ways of talking about their fathers echo values that many German youth also articulate. Given this common ground, one might assume that they share other orientations with German youth and that concerns about honor, especially surrounding women's sexuality, have also been supplanted by German/Western ideas of sexual freedom and gender equality. But what can be seen in these young men's conversations with young American women in the context of research suggests uneasy efforts to accommodate these two dichotomized modes of gender organization and their own relationships to principles of honor and reputation.

Mustafa's discussion of the honor killing of Hatun Sürücü (see Chapter 5) revealed some of the contours of his own sense of honor, which he cast in terms of a Muslim identity and his role in the family. He utterly rejected the idea of carrying out an honor killing:

Mustafa: What my parents said was that the whole thing was totally incomprehensible, unimaginable. When I think about what I would do, for instance, if my sister married a German, that doesn't even come into the question. OK, so she decided to marry a German, but I still wouldn't shoot her! That is not normal, it's totally unrealistic for me, for my entire family. It's madness.

Margo: So it wouldn't matter to you—

Mustafa: No, of course it matters to me. But I still wouldn't shoot her! I would try to convince her, and OK maybe it wouldn't work, but I would try. And if she still decides to marry a German, then that's that.

Margo: Why would you try to convince your sister not to marry a German?

Mustafa: It has to do with religion. I am a Turk, the religion is Islam. You're a Christian, you have a different religion. That's why I would try to convince her.

This interchange, like his earlier discussion of difficulties facing Turkish youth, suggests that Mustafa does not sharply differentiate himself from other young men of Turkish background and their orientations to culture and religion. He, like other youth of Turkish background, is concerned with the actions of his sister. He contradicted Margo's assumption that it wouldn't matter to him whom his sister married, thereby indicating that he was not presenting himself in terms of a strictly "modern" discourse cast in terms of total personal autonomy and independence. Rather, he sees himself as responsible for guiding his sister. He created a social boundary that he justified in terms of religious identity as Muslim versus Christian, rather than in ethnic terms as Turk versus German. Though he repudiated the violence of honor killing, his emphasis on trying to persuade his sister is not simply an expression of the complete independence of each person in the family, but is rather consistent with a sense of family honor that is his responsibility to maintain.

In his conversation with my daughter Julia, Bulent enacted a highly ambivalent relationship to principles of honor that are linked to a woman's sexuality and stand in tension with his efforts to present a modern cosmopolitan identity. Bulent was speaking to a young American woman—an embodiment of the modern and foreign other—close to his own age, alone in his own apartment. In another setting, or with another person such as me, the "mother" as well as the scholar, the recurring themes of the conversation would no doubt have been different. The consequence of this particular context was that he began the conversation speaking to me through my daughter. He took a distanced, scholarly stance on his family, even showing Julia a book that he thought would be useful for my research. He talked about stereotypes that he took to be the subject of my research. Nevertheless, he quickly turned to issues of sexuality and returned to them repeatedly, to the extent that he made Julia quite uncomfortable.

Fairly early in the conversation, he talked of the double life that many Turkish girls in Germany live:

> At home the good, sweet, with headscarf, yes Mama . . . then they go out, see their boyfriends. The parents must never know that she has a boyfriend. Yes, I also have friends who . . . A Turkish girl is always complicated. Yes, always complicated. If I had a girlfriend and I said, sweetie, stay with me tonight . . . that is unthinkable! There are also Turkish girls who say, OK that works. OK, my God. Or: Mama, I'm at a friend's house, Ayse, Fatma, whatever, and then go to their boyfriend. And some have sex and then have the skin sewed closed again. Yes, that happens too!

He brought up this procedure of repairing the hymen several more times during the course of the interview. It was part of his rather graphic sexual talk, which Julia eventually experienced as an effort at seduction. But it also seemed to be a part of a meditation on the fact that it is impossible to tell whether a girl is really a virgin.

Bulent explicitly alluded to the tensions in his self-representations as they emerged in his conversation with Julia about sexuality and honor: "I think very differently from many. I also couldn't have this discussion . . . if there were five Turkish men here—I couldn't have this discussion. Because everyone says, 'You don't have any honor, you want your wife to have had sex with him and him and him, and you are stupid, and your wife should only be for you.'" He appeared to distance himself from this opinion, yet if we look at the structure of the conversation, during which he talked for long periods of time only occasionally punctuated with a question or comment from Julia, it is apparent that he was conflicted about this issue, returning to it obsessively, even after interrupting himself at one point to say, "And I've already said enough about virginity."

He also knew other young people whose parents were more liberal than prevailing stereotypes:

> What I'm saying, you can't generalize it. I also know Turkish parents . . . a friend of mine, she, a Turkish girl, she said, "I had a boyfriend in Germany. And at the dinner table I said to my father, 'Papa?' 'Yes, daughter?' 'I want to tell you something. I have a boyfriend.' And then they ate, 'So who is he?' 'Yes, Hans. . . . Yes, he's a good boy. Bring him to dinner.'"

Bulent's discussion moved explicitly toward family honor as something he personally feels. But he also sought to detach this notion of honor from its negative Turkish stereotype by universalizing it to all men, including modern Western men:

> But I don't let someone insult my parents. And there—in that way I'm a Turk. If someone says, "You son of a horse's ass" or I don't know, "You son of an oxen," then I say, "Hello. If you want to insult me, call me an asshole, or an ass, whatever." My father, my mother, my people, leave them out of it. That's clear. So in that way I'm also a Turk. But not if someone says something little. And there have also been times for me when someone said, "You Turks, you're all . . . goat's asses." OK, fine. Not with every little thing, but . . . I think people can understand that. It doesn't have anything to do with being Turkish, it doesn't have anything to do with being American, European. It's about your family. If you meet someone from America, there is a strong tie, a strong connection between him and his family. He also

won't let someone say, hey your mother is this and your father is this and that. He would also say, hey, watch out. It doesn't have anything to do with being Turkish. I think I have a healthy relationship with my parents. And that's why, because I love my parents, I wouldn't let anyone say anything about them. And if someone says, "You bastard," I'm not. . . I know who my father is, I know who my mother is. But you wanted to go back to the subject of honor killings . . .

Despite Bulent's effort to universalize this threat to family honor, his hypothetical depiction of a verbal duel that could actually impel him to respond with violence echoes images of violence that are often associated in German discourse with the problem of Turkish youth, who lash out with violence at any attack on their family's honor. After just hinting at his own willingness to respond with violence, he quickly changed the subject.

The subject he returned to again was virginity and Turkish girls, an issue on which his own sense of masculinity and honor turned. Considering the sequence of his utterances (and he spoke for long periods of time without interruption), it is clear that violence, family honor, virginity, and sexuality were closely linked for Bulent. The specific contextual elements of this interview with a foreign young woman brought this linkage to the fore.

His openness about sexuality in a conversation with a foreign young woman is actually consistent with Turkish gender practices, in relationship to reputation and honor. In the interview, he began with a discussion of his family and himself that established him as thoroughly modern in orientation. But fairly quickly, the interview situation itself brought to the fore a set of tensions about masculinity, honor, and sexuality that were enacted in his conversation, despite his assertions of a modern attitude that distinguished him from other Turkish-German men. In the most graphic passages, though they retained the frame of analytical description, the content was clearly driven by the fact that he was speaking to an available young woman who, if she had been a "traditional" Turkish girl, would not have allowed herself to be in this situation. He was thus acting like a "typical Turkish man," as a young woman of Turkish background later told Julia when they talked of this aspect of the interview. German or other foreign women are considered potentially available sexually, in contrast to Turkish women, who are seen as unavailable. Kaya has described the perspective of Turkish boys in Berlin: "the Turkish women have their own place in the private sphere of the Turkish boys, whereas the German women belong to the public space that is easily accessible" (Kaya 2001: 132). An American student falls within the realm of public space and public sexuality. Yet Bulent was well-integrated into German society, with German friends, and a cosmopolitan orientation far from that of the stereotypical Turkish man.

In Bulent's evident expressions of conflict over how to present himself in the interview, he enacted a struggle over issues of honor and respect and how to maintain them while at the same time negotiating an identity as a modern, upwardly mobile young man who seeks to integrate fully into German society. He cannot ignore the judgments of his Turkish friends, yet he also described seeing himself through German eyes. He was worried about maintaining his honor by enforcing the principle that people speak respectfully of his parents and of his imagined future wife. He presented his parents as worthy of respect because of their modern concern with his education and the contrast between their tolerance and the rigidity of most Turkish immigrant parents. He wants equality for women, but he overtly expressed difficulty reconciling this with his need to maintain his reputation and self-respect in front of his Turkish friends. At the same time, he was obviously (at least to Julia) trying to interest an available young woman, which put him into the category of "typical Turkish man," according to the young women of Turkish background who judged his actions from a discourse of gender equality. Bulent's conversation with Julia produced a complex performance of masculinity, sexuality, and honor cast in terms of a balance between tradition and modernity.

Young men continue to be concerned with their honor and, like previous generations growing up in rural Turkey, enact competing, often inconsistent strategies for negotiating honor and status. Seduction is still an element of this process, a practice that was fraught with risk in rural communities, where seducing a woman could lead to an attack from her brothers concerned with defending their family's honor. In Germany, young men can gain status among their peers by getting sexually involved with German women or other outsiders. Those who view themselves as modern are pulled between an ideology of gender equality and this competitive calculus.[6]

CONCLUSION

Here is one young woman's reflection on the meaning of honor in diaspora:

> Honor . . . People interpret honor very differently. For example, honor of the family could be that a woman or a girl is a virgin when she gets married. That is one concept of honor. Or honor is when children are raised well. If a child does

not steal, if a child never turns to crime, that is also honor. Honor is also when a child has studied, then you feel good, you are clearly proud of this child.

Instead of rejecting the concept of honor as a relic of Turkish village life, she foregrounded the ways that honor continues to be relevant for Turks in Germany. Most of the men I talked with would have agreed with her, particularly with the emphasis on honor resting above all on success in German society, including the success of one's children, and the maintenance of a positive relationship between father and son, based on a father's care, the provision of necessities, and love reciprocated by a son's hard work and respect.

In tension with this principle of honor based on respect from one's children is the ever-present possibility that a son will rebel against his father. Some first-generation men recalled struggles with their own fathers in which, sometimes after years of resistance and conflict, they ultimately submitted to the will and wisdom of their fathers within the context of village life. They contrasted this outcome with the ability of sons to simply reject their fathers because they have so many other options, even within Turkey, where sons go off to serve in the military, go to school, or move to the city and become financially independent. In Germany, this potential loss of authority over one's children is exacerbated by children's misperceptions of their own parents due to the stigmatizations that they are exposed to growing up in German society.

Most of the men described here have responded to this possibility by building relationships with their sons (or imagining relationships with their future sons) that are based on a model of care and love that is different from one based on authoritarian discipline. While first-generation men originally moved to Germany in order to provide more adequately for their families, their understandings of adequate provision have changed over time so that for many it includes providing their children with popular consumer goods so that their children can maintain self-respect in the adolescent world of status competition, urging them to perform well academically so that they can succeed professionally in Germany, and allowing them to make their own decisions. When fathers succeed in this role, they maintain the respect of their sons and their own honor and reputation in relationship to their peers. The stories of these men demonstrate that their sense of themselves as men cannot be separated from honor, but that the basis of that honor is subject to negotiation.

In European public discourse the concept of honor is seen as the key point that keeps Muslim men from integrating into democratically based Western societies. It is because of their honor that Muslim men are thought to maintain a parallel society in which they oppress their wives, sisters, and daughters, denying them autonomy and equality, even murdering them in the most extreme cases. However, when we look at how first- and second-generation men of Turkish background talk about honor and position themselves with respect to stereotypical notions of traditional honor, we see that honor is a fluid concept. Rarely is the effort to be identified as modern associated with a total rejection of the principle of honor. Even men who view themselves as well-integrated into German society are concerned with issues of honor and are struggling to negotiate identities in which honor continues to be an important component.

Part 2

STIGMATIZED MASCULINITY
AND THE GERMAN NATIONAL IMAGINARY

5 THE HONOR KILLING

ON FEBRUARY 7, 2005, Hatun Sürücü, a young woman of Turkish background, was murdered in Berlin, allegedly by her brothers. After several weeks of the local police and media attention that a murder usually draws, this particular one suddenly received a flurry of media coverage. Labeled an honor killing (*Ehrenmord*), news of it even reached international audiences in simultaneous radio reports on NPR and the BBC on March 29. According to most of the stories surrounding this murder, it had become the most recent, dramatic evidence that the integration of Turks—even third-generation Turks—into German society had "failed."

Significantly, it was not the murder itself that triggered international media attention, but the comments of several fourteen-year-old boys of Turkish background during a school discussion several days later. At the Thomas-Morus Oberschule in the Berlin district of Neukölln, near the site of the murder, these boys blamed Hatun for her own death. One boy was quoted (in many newspapers over several weeks) as saying, "She deserved what she got—the whore lived like a German" (Phalnikar 2005; *Frankfurter Allgemeine*, March 18, 2005). Another said, "She had only herself to blame." Turks were portrayed as unassimilable because of the way that Turkish men treat their women. The comments of the schoolboys were evidence that Hatun's murderous brothers were typical of young Turkish men. This honor killing was therefore readable as an enactment of Turkish Muslim culture.

It is rather extraordinary that the informal comments of these boys were taken so seriously. It is even more extraordinary that the world even heard of these statements, which had been made in the relative privacy of the class-room or schoolyard. This came about because the director of the school was so outraged when he was informed of these comments that he sent a letter to parents and students, as well as to teachers across Germany, castigating the students and warning that the school would not tolerate "incitement against freedom" (Phalnikar 2005). He clearly felt that he was alerting teachers of the real and dangerous attitudes of young Turkish men throughout the country. It was this letter that triggered the ensuing media attention, which extended to a meeting held at the school to discuss the issue on March 9, one month after Hatun's death. At that time, the school principal reported that he had received fifty-seven press inquiries after publicizing the boys' comments (Bauer 2005).[1] Eventually, the boys were punished rather severely for their comments (one was reportedly forced to leave the school; another received a written reprimand; and a third was required to participate in a discussion with victims of domes-tic violence [Bauer 2005]), though some people declared that it was the boys' parents who should be punished; and others, including a spokesperson for the Turkish Union of Berlin and Brandenburg, said that the boys were just trying to provoke their teachers and draw attention to themselves (Vieth-Entus, von Törne, and Keller 2005).

These schoolboys came to stand in for Turkish men and their unassimilable masculinity. Furthermore, the public call to punish their parents was an asser-tion that the boys' statements were evidence that virtually the whole Turkish community subscribes to the principle of honor killing. The school principal had characterized their remarks as an incitement against freedom, framing the issue in terms of a constitutional principle and placing their attitudes in stark contrast to those of the proper national subject, the true German citizen.

The publicity surrounding Hatun Sürücü's murder generated a sense of cri-sis that was fed by the fact that some journalists designated her murder as the sixth honor killing in Berlin within only four or five months—a dramatic in-crease in a practice that had been thought to be on the decline. Human rights organizations, activists, and organizations for the protection of Turkish women estimated that there had been forty-five honor killings in Germany since 1996 (Fleishman 2005), a frequency that is considerably lower than the rate reported in the press for Berlin in the five months preceding Hatun's death. Karl Mol-lenhauer, the head psychologist for the Berlin police, maintained that this high incidence of honor killings in Berlin over a short time could well be a statistical anomaly, a coincidence (Lau 2005: 1); nevertheless, many Germans took this perceived increase, along with the infamous comments of the three Turkish schoolboys, as a sign that Turks continue to cling to their traditional, patriarchal ways despite their residence in Germany for two or three generations. The concern reverberated through the press that Turks are actually becoming less integrated and more isolated in their ghettos within German society, creating a parallel society operating on principles inconsistent with German values.

The spate of honor killings in Berlin was not likely even a statistical anomaly, as Mollenhauer had suggested, but rather an artifact of classification, in which a range of murders under various circumstances retrospectively came to be labeled honor killings. Most of the murders in Berlin were actually cases of husbands attacking their wives, a pattern that could at least partially be explained by the common phenomenon of jealousy. Mollenhauer, attempting to downplay the emerging media sensationalism, emphasized that "it is generally known that German men commit murder out of jealousy as well" (Lau 2005: 1). Feminist activists throughout the West have worked for decades to bring cases of spousal abuse to light and have found it in all communities. That the motives for the outcry against honor killings were culturally biased and not feminist is clear from the fact that the articles that appeared in the wake of Hatun's murder made no mention of how many women may have been killed by their husbands of German background during an equivalent period of time.

There is quite a disconnect between the spousal murders that had been retrospectively classified as honor killings and much of the rhetoric surrounding the paradigmatic honor killing, in which a blood relative—typically either the woman's father or brother—commits the murder. In contrast to Berlin's previous five murders that were retroactively dubbed honor killings, the murder of Hatun Sürücü is something of an "ideal type" in the Weberian sense. It is a paradigmatic act of a brother killing a sister, an act that is unambiguously *not* considered German or Christian or Western. It confirms the cultural distinctiveness of the Turkish Muslim community. Hatun's murder marks the Turkish man as an alien other. Only after her death had crystallized in public discourse were the other murders recast as suspected honor killings, defined by one reporter as "slayings arranged by families who believe that their reputations have been stained" (Fleishman 2005), though this definition does not comfortably fit the earlier murders. Faced with this suddenly recognized string of honor killings, Germans began to chastise both themselves and the Muslim community for failing to take notice of these earlier murders or to publicize the names of the women who had died.

This particular flurry of media production—a paroxysm in a discourse in which immigrants serve as a focal point for the country's ills and a threat to the democratic principles that are the foundation of the German state—is the sort of event that periodically constitutes the Turkish minority vis-à-vis the German nation and crystallizes public understandings of Germany's Turkish and Muslim minorities. The discussion of honor killing in public arenas and in the press displays facets of German self-understanding that draw on the concepts of equality, freedom, and human rights. At the heart of these discussions is a juxtaposition of an idealized, hegemonic German masculinity and the stigmatized masculinity of the Turk who refuses to integrate. However, the deployment of these concepts and ideals reveals the complex, emotionally charged relationship with the past that continues to plague German collective memory and identity. This resonance with the past has direct consequences for the integration of minorities such as Turks and Muslims into German society.

This process of reclassification of a series of murders as honor killings raises the question: why such an intense focus on honor killing at that time? In this chapter I examine how Hatun's murder was one of a conjunction of events that congealed an image of the Turkish Muslim man as dangerous other and generated a state of moral panic at the threat to social order. I identify how Turkish Muslim masculinity is constructed through the discourse that emerged at this moment and consider what effects this discursive environment may have on Germany's Muslim minority, particularly on young men of Turkish background. What are the implications for how these young men understand their own honor and self-respect within the context of an honor killing committed by a Berlin youth?

MEDIA REPORTS AND THEIR DISCURSIVE CONTOURS

Twenty-three-year-old Hatun Sürücü was killed by several gunshots at a bus stop around 11 p.m. The police immediately suspected that she knew the assailant because she was not robbed during the act. Some of the earliest articles in local newspapers reproduced the tone of police reports, laying out what had been learned at the crime scene and requesting more information from the public (for example, Laninger 2005). From the beginning, even before Hatun's assailant had been identified, the tabloids marked her murder as "other." According to a short article in the newspaper *Tageszeitung* that was itself not sensationalist, the police had denounced as "cheap propaganda" early speculation that this was a "headscarf murder," as one tabloid had claimed (*Tageszeitung*, February 10, 2005).[2] This early *Tageszeitung* article did little more than describe the progress of the investigation, though it did allude to cultural difference by concluding with a report based on the comments of employees of a crisis center that "fear among girls of Turkish and Kurdish origin of resisting an arranged marriage was rising."

Another article published on the same day also reported the police's caution in attributing a motive: "The police suspected either injured honor or jealousy, and considered many men as suspects, including 'numerous male acquaintances'" (Bakirdögen and Laninger 2005). According to other sources, many of these acquaintances were German. Nevertheless, this article was more heavily tinged with innuendo and was titled "Did Hatun Sürücü Live Too Modern? The criminal investigation department speculates that the 23-year-old murder victim's love for life may have provoked the perpetrators." It noted that one of Hatun's brothers had threatened her in the past, "presumably because of her modern way of living," though the head of the murder commission had stressed that reports against this brother were nearly a year old. The reporters wrote: "Hatun Sürücü was not like other Turkish women. She wore modern clothing, was fun-loving, and sociable. She went to clubs and flirted. Someone seems to have been so offended by her that he killed her. Was it that she had turned away from orthodox Muslim values, did not wear a headscarf, had boyfriends?" This question echoed the tabloid headlines. But the term *honor killing* had not yet been used in this early coverage. The focus was, rather, on the absence of a headscarf and Hatun's modern lifestyle, which stood in explicit contrast to a stereotypical generalization about "other Turkish women." It also associated the concerns of her murderer with "orthodox" Muslim values, thereby implicitly linking Islam with violence.

The European edition of the Islam-oriented Turkish-language newspaper *Zaman* was particularly critical of the German press's quick and unsubstantiated association of the headscarf with murder and published the first of several articles about Hatun's case on February 11, two days before the assailants were identified. The article extensively quoted Hatun's elder brother Mutlu and was titled "Mutlu Sürücü: My sister uncovered her head 5 years ago."[3] Its main thrust was to highlight and contest the distortions that *Zaman* felt were being propagated in the German and secular Turkish press. For instance, it criticized the German tabloid *Bild* for immediately linking the murder with the issue of the headscarf: "While the 23-year-old Sürücü's murder remains shrouded in mystery, in the February 9 edition of the newspaper *Bild* the event was given the following shape: 'She was killed for taking off her headscarf.'" The quotations from

Mutlu focused on the fact that the German reporters who came to the family's home for rather short interviews never asked about the headscarf issue, and it was never discussed during the conversation. The title quotation from Mutlu continues: "Why would she be killed now for not wearing a headscarf?" He also pointed out that the wife of one of his uncles also did not wear a headscarf. This is the only source I saw in those early days that actually represented the point of view of one of the men in Hatun's family, and it was not in the German language.[4]

Three of Hatun's brothers, including Mutlu, were arrested a few days later on a tip from the youngest brother's girlfriend, who had indicated knowledge of the plot to murder Hatun. In statements to *Zaman*, Mutlu suggested what the core issue leading to the murder likely was the fact that "she began to fight with mother, father, and us."

> Once she even called the police because she was supposedly under pressure. After this she went to a home and lived there for a time. Meanwhile I maintained our contact and extended the offer of returning to our family. But I never received a positive answer. I broke contact three years ago. At that time, my sister had begun living like a foreigner. She had created a new friend circle for herself. She said that she wanted to find a partner herself. We know that she was with three or four people that we knew of for four or five months. During that time, it is possible that the number of people that she had met was even greater. It was after that point that we were confronted with the fact of her murder. (*Zaman*, February 11, 2005; my translation)

Though from a German perspective, there may be very little difference between murdering a woman for abandoning the headscarf and murdering her for promiscuous behavior, emphasizing the former exoticized the murder and her brothers, making their actions incomprehensible and alien. (If a German husband had murdered his wife for promiscuity, the act would have been at least comprehensible to a German audience.)

Approximately three weeks after the murder, the intensity of media coverage and the harshness of the rhetoric began to increase. An article published at the end of February in the German weekly news journal *Die Zeit* noted that "the horror has increased with distance from the event" as "the horror over the act itself has become mixed with the horror over the moral brutality of the young men who approved of the act and thus feel themselves as consistent with the values of their community" (Lau 2005).

On February 22, a "solemn vigil" was held at the bus stop where Hatun was murdered. It was called "not by the city's Muslim community but a gay and lesbian organization" (Phalnikar 2005), an indication that the German public was mobilizing around a cause that Hatun Sürücü represented. This vigil received considerable press coverage, and in the media it became a sign that the Turkish Muslim community was not mobilizing with the German community to express its horror at this honor killing (by this time the label *honor killing* had become firmly attached): "At a memorial vigil held a few weeks after Hatin's [sic] death, a mere 120 people showed up. Almost none were Turkish. In fact most were from a lesbian and gay organization that—outraged by the crime—organized the makeshift ceremony" (Biehl 2005: 2). Jody Biehl,[5] along with a number of German journalists and the international press, took this as a sign that the Muslim community could not be counted on to work for the reduction of honor killings: "It is often not the Muslim community that expresses outrage over how its women live, but those on the outside" (Biehl 2005: 2). The Turkish community was also accused of taking three weeks to mobilize against honor killing, although German press coverage had only just begun to escalate around this time.

These press interpretations of the vigil were an instance of how Muslim and German discourses about gender are pitted against one another with little sensitivity to the possibility that members of the Turkish community might be operating on different terms and that the Turkish community's failure to appear at a vigil staged by a gay rights group might have had little to do with their attitudes toward honor killing. Just as the press equated removing the headscarf and sexual promiscuity, glossing over what is a crucial distinction for many Turkish families, the rhetoric surrounding the vigil created an equivalence between rejecting honor killing and expressing solidarity with a gay rights organization. The press was demanding that the Turkish Muslim community "prove" itself to be against honor killing by participating in a public action that had other, very different political implications.

In a newspaper report two days after the vigil, titled "When Freedom Gets the Death Sentence," the circumstances of the murder were summarized in a manner similar to the many articles that began to emerge around this time, creating a crystallized story of the Turkish woman as victim:

> All Hatin [sic] was doing was leading her life the way she wanted.
> But it was a choice she paid for with her life. On Feb. 7, 23-year-old Hatin Sürücü was gunned down at the aforementioned bus stop. She died on the

spot. Shortly afterwards, three of her brothers—who reportedly had long been threatening her—were arrested.

Investigators suspect it was a so-called "honor killing," given the fact that Sürücü's ultra-conservative Turkish-Kurdish family strongly disapproved of her modern and "un-Islamic" life.

Sürücü grew up in Berlin and was married off at 16 to a cousin in Istanbul. After a few years, she returned to the German capital with her young son, moved into a home for single mothers, completed school and began to train as an electrician. She stopped wearing a headscarf and was said to be outgoing and vivacious. (Phalnikar 2005)

The elements of Hatun's life that were repeatedly stressed were the conservatism of her family, including her threatening brothers; her "forced" marriage at a young age to a cousin in Turkey; her rejection of this traditional life, including the headscarf, in favor of free choice, a career, and independence as a single mother; and an outgoing personality. In the earliest reports, there were hints that her social life may have been *too* outgoing: "'Rarely do we have such a broad environment,' one observer says sighing. What he probably meant, according to the head of the department of the murder commission, André Rauhut, was: 'Ms. Sürücü had not only a large circle of friends, but also numerous male acquaintances'" (Bakirdögen and Laninger 2005). In a lengthy article in *Die Zeit*, Hatun's love life was mentioned but soft-pedaled: "she had many friends, liked to go out, and had a few love stories, also with German men" (Lau 2005: 2). As the image of Hatun Sürücü crystallized into a symbol for a cause, any hint that she might have been *too* fun-loving for some tastes disappeared.

The murder remained in the public eye for many months. At least two TV documentaries, including "Mord im Namen der Ehre? Der Tod von Hatun Sürücü" (Murder in the Name of Honor: The Death of Hatun Sürücü) by Gert Monheim (2005); TV interviews with her acquaintances; other TV programs; a play; and countless newspaper and magazine articles were produced. In Monheim's documentary, Hatun's life was presented through interviews with some members of her family, a couple of female friends, teachers from her old high school, a woman she had worked with, and her boyfriend, with whom she had shared an apartment during the summer before the murder. No mention was made of other boyfriends. Scenes of the site of her training as an electrician, as well as images of her holding her son, were presented, but not sites where she may have socialized. Though such a murder is never justifiable under any circumstances, the depictions of the victim created an image of virtue that had the effect of making the actions of her brothers incomprehensible and alien. This one-sided portrait created by silences may reflect the principle "speak no ill of the dead," but it prevents the audience from even trying to step into the shoes of the brothers in order to empathize with or imagine their concerns. If they are utterly evil, they are to be simply castigated and abjected.

Public interest was rekindled when Hatun's brothers were put on trial for the murder. The trial began in early March 2006 and concluded on April 26 with the sentencing of Ayhan, the youngest of the three accused brothers, as a juvenile because he was eighteen at the time of the murder. The sentence of nine years and three months was close to the juvenile maximum of ten years, reduced in consideration of the duration of Ayhan's pretrial confinement and the fact that before the start of the trial he had confessed to shooting his sister at close range (*Deutsche Welle* 2006c). The two older brothers, ages twenty-five and twenty-six, were acquitted because their complicity in the murder could not be sufficiently proved, though both had been accused of planning and supporting the crime.[6]

Immediately after the sentencing, pronouncements of variously positioned spokespeople for the "German-Turkish community" were summarized in a Spiegel Online headline: "Reactions to Honor Killing Sentence: 'Not the Signal We Need.'" The story continued: "The sentence in the so-called honor killing trial has split the German-Turkish community. The acquittal of two of the accused has caused outrage. Some see the strict punishment of the perpetrator as a positive signal" (Doeleke and Schröder 2006). Despite the so-called split, the concern of all of the quoted spokespeople was whether the sentence was adequate to send a message to the "community" that the German government would not tolerate such honor killings.

A few days later, the news that Hatun's younger sister Arzu was planning to apply for custody of Hatun's young son prompted yet more public uproar, as manifested in headlines such as this one, published by a major German news source (*Deutsche Welle* 2006b): "German Politicians Outraged by Custody Demands," and the subheading, "Politicians have condemned the idea that the boy grow up in the family responsible for his mother's death." Though the judgment had explicitly found the youngest brother Ayhan solely responsible for the murder and the older brothers not guilty, it appeared that there was near-consensus among the German public (including both liberal and conservative politicians) that the entire family, as the bearer of Turkish culture, was to blame for the murder and that Hatun's son must be rescued from this family. Both liberal and conservative politicians, church leaders, and other public figures spoke out. A spokesman for the Social Democrats stated to the press that it was impossible that turning the boy over to the family could be considered, while a Christian Democrat legal expert said, "That would be like putting a fox in charge of the henhouse" (*Deutsche Welle* 2006b).

The word *clan* (German: *Klan*) appeared in newspaper articles within the context of this custody furor, as in a statement by Berlin's youth senator Klaus Böger: "it can't be in the interest of this child's well-being to grant the family clan custody" (*Deutsche Welle* 2006b). This word, which often appears in the work of anthropologists writing about non-Western, premodern societies, clearly marked the Turkish family as alien. The clan was understood to be a patriarchy in which women had few rights.[7]

ANOTHER CONTROVERSIAL MURDER

One likely trigger of the intensity of public sentiment surrounding the murder of Hatun Sürücü was the dramatic murder in the Netherlands of the filmmaker Theo van Gogh by a Muslim Dutch national of Moroccan descent on November 2, 2004, three months before her murder. Van Gogh's murder occurred in response to his controversial film *Submission*, which had been critical of the treatment of women within Islam.[8] The film set the stage for a renewed polarization of sentiment around the symbol of the Muslim woman. Many Muslims found van Gogh's characterization of Islam and of Muslim immigrants highly insulting: "Some called him a champion of free speech. Others, referencing inflammatory terms such as 'goat-fuckers' (his preferred moniker for Muslim immigrants), found his irreverence for all things religious to be utterly repellent" (Ifilm Short Videos 2005). Shortly after Van Gogh's murder, *Der Spiegel* published an article, "Muslim Integration: Germany's Lost Daughters" (Spiegel Online 2004), and produced a television program (Spiegel TV 2004) that were indicative of the direction of German public discourse in the murder's wake: harshly negative rhetoric focused on the issue of forced marriage, the issue that had been raised so dramatically in the film. The article was particularly extreme in its representations of the situation of Turkish women, epitomized by its opening, which was a vivid rhetorical assault on the Turkish man: "Thousands of Turkish women live like slaves in Germany. They are locked into apartments, beaten and kept deliberately ignorant. Their men don't want them integrated and—until now—neither did Germany. That, say women's rights workers, politicians and social workers, has to change" (Spiegel Online 2004). The article proposed a list of policy suggestions that might be taken to prevent Muslims in Germany from "sink[ing] into their own world":

1. Requiring immigrants to take classes on human rights and women's rights beginning as early as grade school.

2. Strengthening the laws regarding women brought from Turkey and Muslim countries as young brides. For instance, say some, the women should be at least nineteen. And they should be forced to take language classes upon arrival.

3. Forbidding arranged marriages and including a means to prosecute parents who force their children to marry against their will.

4. Breaking up the Turkish-Muslim "ghettos."

5. Creating more programs for Turkish youth.

6. Creating a larger network for women in need.

7. Controlling what gets taught in Qur'an schools.

8. Aggressively campaigning against violence in Muslim families.

9. Creating job training programs and job opportunities for Turkish women. (Spiegel Online 2004)

Thus, well before the murder of Hatun Sürücü, drastic proposals were being made to insert the power of the state more directly into Turkish neighborhoods and families.

THE ROLE OF FEMINIST ACTIVISTS IN THE SYMBOLIC VIOLENCE

In this particular historical moment, following the murder of Theo van Gogh in a post–September 11 political climate, German public discourse was also being shaped by another, more local force that further facilitated the demonization of Muslim men. The contours of the discourse that crystallized out of this honor killing were largely shaped by several prominent activists/authors who have written about the oppression of Muslim women through forced marriages and confinement. The most prominent of these activists are women of Turkish background who have played a role in organizations set up to offer practical assistance to women seeking to escape their families. Three feminist activists of Turkish background—Seyran Ateş, Necla Kelek, and Serap Çileli—have used the murder of Hatun Sürücü as a platform for urging policy changes and new legislation and to force closer public and political scrutiny of the lives of Muslim immigrants. Their activism echoed feminist activism in Turkey, which since the 1980s has had as a primary focus the abuse of women within the family and has in recent years focused on honor killings in Turkey. During the honor killing controversy in Germany these three women were frequently quoted in newspaper reports and made numerous TV appearances to argue that the German government needed to make policy changes in order to protect such women.

All three of these activists are extremely negative in their depictions of the Turkish family. Çileli, who describes in her book *Wir Sind eure Töchter, nicht eure Ehre!* (We Are Your Daughters, Not Your Honor, 2002) how she was herself forced to marry at age fifteen, is involved in hiding women from their families. Her criticism of both German authorities and the Turkish media is harsh, and she has claimed that the police do not take seriously the danger that Turkish women face. Çileli attributed her inability to find a publisher for her work for several years to publishers' fear of appearing racist but stated that after September 11, "suddenly the hidden lives of Muslims became a hot topic" (Biehl 2005: 2). She has appeared in numerous TV interviews promoting her views, contributing with other activists to this growing clamor to expose the situation of the Turkish woman who is at the mercy of the Turkish man.

Seyran Ateş is a lawyer based in Berlin and a civil rights activist who wrote an autobiographical book, *Grosse Reise ins Feuer* (Big Journey into Fire, 2003). She has argued that multiculturalism has contributed to the "slavery" of Muslim women and has criticized the German government's "fake tolerance" of Muslim conservative radicalism. Like Çileli, she links this tolerance to a post-Holocaust fear of appearing racist. She calls honor killings a "cancer brought from the East" (Fleishman 2005). Ateş argues that Germany's efforts to spread social equality and its "oversensitivity" toward minorities have allowed a conservative radicalism to flourish in some Muslim neighborhoods. She links current attitudes to fears associated with Nazism. Since the Holocaust, German governments have been careful not to single out religious or ethnic groups, an approach some critics say spawned an atmosphere that aided several September 11 hijackers who had studied in Hamburg. "This false dream of tolerance and Germany's fear of being called racist are helping fundamentalists," Ateş said (Fleishman 2005). Immediately after Hatun Sürücü's brother was sentenced, Spiegel Online presented Ateş's reaction, which focused on the acquittal of the other two brothers: "'It is terrible'. . . . Seen objectively, the decision of the judges may have been a 'fair legal decision.' However, Ateş fears that the acquittal of the two older brothers could have negative consequences for her clients—for women who accuse their own families of violence" (Doeleke and Schröder 2006).

Sociologist Necla Kelek has deployed the metaphor of German "sleep," asking, "How many more women have to die before this society wakes up?" This question and the image of a "wake-up call" were picked up and repeated in a number of articles (for example, Lau 2005, Paterson 2005). Her book *Die fremde Braut* (The Foreign Bride, 2005), which criticizes arranged marriages, has been controversial for its unsympathetic depiction of Turkish families and the lack of rights for women in those families: she claims that half of these women and many of the men are forced with great pressure into marriage. Kelek told journalists that the reports from Hatun Sürücü's burial "turn my stomach. . . . The exhibition of Islamic piety by the family [is] a 'mockery' of the young woman who had separated herself from the family and religious tradition. Not even in death is the right of self-determination accepted. The German public has long ignored the fact that in many Turkish families, the right of girls and women to a self-determined life is trampled" (Lau 2005).

Members of the Turkish community have not always responded sympathetically to the harsh critiques of Turkish family life by these activists of Turkish background, and the newspaper *Hürriyet*, the Turkish-language newspaper with the largest circulation in Germany (Rasche 2005), has reflected some of this sentiment. *Hürriyet*'s position has, in turn, been criticized in the German media. In an extensive "background report," Uta Rasche, a reporter for the German newspaper *Frankfurter Allgemeine*, accused *Hürriyet* of conducting a smear campaign against Ateş, Kelek, and Çileli, beginning at the end of February 2005, just as the media attention on Hatun's murder was heating up. The article is a harsh attack on the newspaper, indicating (but not specifying) other slanders the newspaper made against prominent German politicians such as Chancellor Gerhard Schröder and Cem Özdemir (former Green Party representative to the Bundestag—the lower chamber of the German Parliament—who is of Turkish background) when they took positions that were unpopular with the Turkish government. Rasche then went into a more detailed account of what she argues were *Hürriyet*'s unjustified attacks against the activist women, from which I draw several quotations:

—"At the end of February 'Hürriyet' reported on new books by Çileli and Kelek, with headlines to the effect that the two authors had denounced Turkish men as violent brutes."

—"The author [Çileli] was accused of telling stories in order to sell a few more books. 'I feel personally threatened. If anything happens to me or the others, "Hürriyet" is responsible. The way in which they dealt with my biography leads to other girls and women becoming discouraged.'"

—"Author Seyran Ateş . . . has also felt the wrath of 'Hürriyet.' According to her, Turks in Turkey are more progressive than most Turks in Germany . . . 'Hürriyet' exploits this 'not particularly literate or education-oriented group' [of backward Turks in Germany], she says. The newspaper accuses her of insulting Turkish women, making the Turkish community look bad, and reconfirming German prejudices against Turks by making generalizations. In particular it was Ateş' statement in an interview with 'Tageszeitung' that women who are forced to marry are 'slaves on the Muslim marriage market' that drew protests from 'Hürriyet.'"

—"The Hamburg sociologist Necla Kelek explains 'Hürriyet''s reaction: 'Turks are not allowed to say anything bad about the Turks, and especially not to a German.'"

In the article Rasche suggests that the Turkish newspaper operates with the market strategy of catering to "the tastes of the conservative immigrant community." She reports that "Terre des Femmes," an organization that shelters Muslim women, was reluctant to participate in *Hürriyet*'s April campaign against domestic violence (begun in Turkey but carried to Germany in the wake of Hatun Sürücü's case) because it found the newspaper's articles "irritating and counterproductive" (Rasche 2005).

This article is an example of the kind of convergence of interests that has formed between these activists for women's rights and proponents of anti-immigrant sentiment. Rasche's perspective is harshly critical of the Turkish community. The activists are passionately involved in projects to protect Turkish women; they have ready access to the press and speak from the authority of personal experience. In the process, they have cast the Turkish community, family, and especially the Turkish Muslim man in negative terms in order to strategically protect women. But these public statements also reproduce the Orientalist divide between East and West, perpetuate stereotypes of Turkish families, and play into the hands of conservative anti-immigrant politicians.

The murder of Hatun Sürücü has become ammunition for arguments about policy changes that have serious implications for Muslims in Germany. In the context of the anti–honor killing rhetoric, there was a proposal in Germany to follow France's and Turkey's lead in banning headscarves in public classrooms, even for students—a big step beyond the current controversy surrounding banning from the classroom public schoolteachers who wear the headscarf. But the debate goes well beyond the public sphere into a concern with the details of Turkish Muslim gender relations within the family and the home. A new bill barring forced marriage was proposed by the Berlin representative to the upper house of the German parliament in the wake of Hatun's murder and adopted by that house in February 2006. As an article in *Die Welt* stated, "Until now there were misgivings about changing the rights of foreigners" (Schomaker 2005). The bill was intended to deter families by making forced marriage a criminal offense and raising the costs to families involved in such marriages. Provisions of the bill include a punishment of up to five years for forced marriage. Victims would be allowed to annul their marriages within three years, thereby lengthening the time for application for annulment from the current one-year deadline; and relations who supported the forced marriage would be excluded from inheritance in the event of the deaths of the parties forced to marry. The law would also apply to "export brides"—young women who live in Germany but are sent by their families to marry in Turkey. These victims would be allowed to return to Germany (see Europäisches Forum für Migrationsstudien 2006a).[9] The liberal Social Democratic Party (SPD) and the Green Party have pushed this initiative (Schomaker 2005). The assertion of the need to protect the human rights of young women is one that no one can legitimately protest; nevertheless, the language of the bill is grounded in a set of understandings about the nature of traditional Turkish gender relations that takes for granted their inhumanity.

Right-wing groups also picked up the rhetoric surrounding the honor killing controversy for their own purposes. As a reporter for the *Los Angeles Times* noted:

> Conservative German groups and right-wing websites say Sürücü's slaying is another indication the Muslim immigrant community ignores Western values and is growing increasingly volatile. "Along with Hatun Sürücü, so has the dream of multiculturalism died," states the website run by the far-right Republikaner political party. "The death of this young woman must convince the last multiculti romantic that the dream of a peaceful coexistence of different cultures and religions is over. Islam is and stays incompatible with the values of our constitution." (Fleishman 2005).

In this right-wing rhetoric, honor killing is equated with Islam. Multiculturalism is equated with a tolerance for undemocratic practices and, by extension, with policies that violate the spirit of the postwar German Constitution.
There has been a call to replace multiculturalism as an administrative policy
with other principles—most notably the demand for Turks and other Muslims
to assimilate to German culture. These demands have taken the form of the
so-called Muslim Test and the idea of enforcing a German *Leitkultur*, both of
which have also generated intense controversy (see Chapters 6 and 7).

In response to the push for legislation to prevent forced marriage, some
scholars accused activists who were pushing for this legislation, such as Necla
Kelek, Seyran Ates, and Ayyan Hirsi Ali, of producing inflammatory publications and statements unsupported by scientific evidence. An open letter directed against these activists was published by scholars Yasemin Karakasoglu
and Mark Terkessidis in the news weekly *Die Zeit* (Terkessidis and Karakasoglu 2006) and signed by fifty-eight scientists. (See Europäisches Forum für
Migrationsstudien 2006b.)

Following the sentencing of Hatun's brother Ayhan Sürücü, Edmund Stoiber,
chairman of the conservative Christian Social Union (CSU) (the state-level party
associated with the national Christian Democratic Union [CDU]) and Bavarian
minister-president, used the judgment as a platform for reiterating his demand
that immigrants accept German culture, stating in a magazine interview that immigrants must learn the German language, acknowledge the state's monopoly on
power, and accept the equality of men and women (Focus Online 2006). When
the family requested custody of Hatun's young son, one headline read: "Stoiber
Has Demanded the Expulsion of the 'Honor Killing' Family" (RP Online 2006).
He was clearly using the controversy to further his party's immigration policies,
by stressing that the whole family had been responsible for the murder.

ALTERNATIVE EXPLANATIONS AND PERSPECTIVES

The reporting on the trial of Hatun's brothers in the mainstream German media
showed remarkable conformity, with one quote from Ayhan's testimony being
reproduced in most trial coverage:

> Ayhan Sürücü told prosecutors he was appalled by her [Hatun's] Western
> lifestyle and concerned about his nephew. As a result, he had visited his sister
> at home before walking with her to the nearby bus-stop. When she defended
> her way of life, he pulled out the gun he said he had bought off a Russian

seller and killed her. "It was too much for me," he told the court. "I grabbed the pistol and pulled the trigger. I don't even understand what I did anymore." (*Deutsche Welle* 2006b)

Whatever Ayhan may have understood as "her way of life," the public had its own understanding that was based on months of media reports that had emphasized Hatun's efforts to build an independent life for herself as an employed single mother. This particular quotation emphasized the blind rage of a Turkish man overcome by the need to defend the family's honor, which had been threatened by Hatun's efforts to live a normal German life.

Other perspectives emerge from reporters and commentators outside of the media mainstream. For example, Justus Leicht, a regular contributor to the World Socialist Web Site, reported on the trial through the lens of his socialist agenda of working to overcome ethnic divisions in order to unite the working class (Leicht 2006). He sought to disrupt the discourse that was shaping the mainstream press: "The murder of a young mother by her juvenile brother is a terrible act, which raises complex questions about the social, cultural and political background of the case. However, neither the media nor official politics have shown any interest in clarifying these questions." Leicht described Ayhan in terms that suggested a motivation that was not simply due to his culture, which is what the mainstream press stressed, but was a result of his personal circumstances, transnational cultural influences, and immediate social environment, thereby downplaying ethnicity: "He had abandoned his commercial apprenticeship and sought recognition in Islamic circles, and affected a ridiculous macho persona modeled on Hollywood mafia films. His brothers and the court report certify that the now 20-year-old is very immature." Leicht sought to explain how Ayhan could have acted without the knowledge of his family, arguing that acts such as this murder can be attributed to the increasing social and economic exclusion of these young men and their increasing consciousness of difference due to their having been born and raised in Germany.[10] Ayhan, therefore, looked for self-respect "in the barbaric ideology of 'blood and honour.'" (Leicht 2006). In his effort to rescue Turks from the prevailing media discourse, Leicht reported on the association of Ayhan's masculine identity with models drawn from Hollywood. Yet he, too, reproduced the stereotype of the Turkish male—a barbarian who turns to violence in the name of honor—rather than questioning its simplicity. Nevertheless, he raised the possibility of thinking about the murder, not merely as an inevitable manifestation of tradition, but as an effect of institutions specific to Germany that lead to an invention of tradition among such young men.

The Militant Islam Monitor, a website not particularly sympathetic to Muslims or Islam whose agenda is to document the activities and identities of Islamist individuals and groups, stressed the cultural argument, equating Islam with the cultural practice of honor killing (Militant Islam Monitor 2006). It emphasized that the whole family was involved and that the youngest son had become a hero in his community. This site also reported that "according to witnesses the victim had been the victim of sexual abuse within the family by one of the brothers," and it speculated that the murder may have been to save the brother from prosecution: "A friend revealed that one of her brothers had sexually abused her, and that the killing was more to rescue his 'honor' than that of the family." This argument was probably based on an interview conducted by Stern TV with one of Hatun's close friends, which was headlined, "Her Brother Had Sexually Harassed Her" (Beseke 2006). In the interview, Hatun's friend had said, "Her family had repudiated her when she had told her mother that her brother had sexually harassed her." Though the intention of the Militant Islam Monitor was to locate this family as an instance of the danger of Islam and Islamic culture, this possibility of inappropriate sexual conduct on the part of the brother puts a somewhat different light on the issue of a family closing ranks to protect its honor and reputation. A public accusation of incest is shameful for most families, even within German circles. Hatun had earlier gone to the police about her brother's threatening behavior, which, if connected to issues of incest, makes his reaction all too comprehensible and far less exotic.

Publications and spokespeople representing Turkish and Islamic groups responded with considerable concern about the German media campaign in the wake of Hatun's murder. Eren Unsal, a spokesman for the Turkish Union in Berlin-Brandenburg (TBB), was quoted as saying: "Something like this happens, and suddenly all Turks in Germany get recognized through Hatun . . . This is not fair or accurate" (Fleishman 2005). Unsal also stated that he assumed

> students who express themselves so menacingly in favor of honor killing want to provoke above all. "They do this to draw attention to themselves." Often this is the students with the narrowest chances of a career: "Those who are difficult to place look for stability in presumably traditional concepts of values." They are particularly at risk from the influence of Islamic fundamentalist organizations or falling into a life of crime. (Vieth-Entus, von Törne, and Keller 2005)

Unsal thus offered an explanation that stressed the marginalization of these youth and avoided the cliché of timeless tradition even though such explanations for honor killing are common in Turkey itself, where among the urban elite, the traditional other is located in villages, most often in marginalized areas, especially in the southeast where the Kurdish minority dominates. Unsal was acutely aware that in the German context, Turks of all social classes are essentialized as traditional and readily marginalized as other and sought to disrupt this stereotyping. TBB responded to the publicity surrounding the statements of the boys from the Thomas-Morus Oberschule by working with the media and setting up a planning meeting that brought together the principal of the school, the district mayor of Neukölln, the Turkish parents union, and Muslim imams. A TBB board member asserted: "Unions that call themselves Islamic must also clearly commit themselves to a stance against violence. . . . It cannot be the case that these organizations remain silent on certain subjects, even though they claim to be democratic" (*Die Welt* 2005). Some spokespeople emphasized the actions being taken within the Turkish community to change people's cultural orientations. The German edition of the Turkish-language newspaper *Hürriyet*, for example, began a campaign against domestic violence: "A flyer by *Hürriyet* on the campaign can be found at the newspaper itself or at many Turkish organizations and institutions in Germany" (Wali 2005). This approach was consistent with the Turkish nationalist orientation of modernizing its citizens.

Islamic groups were particularly concerned with repudiating the practice of honor killing and distancing it from Islam. Ali Kizilkaya, the president of the Islamic Council, which is made up of thirty-two Muslim organizations, stated: "When students approve of self-administered justice, it is very disturbing, but not a religious problem, rather a problem of education." He was quoted in an article from February 22, 2005, which was one of the few that included statements from prominent members of Muslim organizations (Vieth-Entus, von Törne, and Keller 2005). But the media controversy did catch Islamic organizations off guard: "The Islamic Federation of Berlin, which teaches classes on Islam in 37 elementary schools, saw no reason in the past few days to discuss 'honor killing' in class and what the students think about this subject. 'That is too recent,' says Burhan Kesici, board member of the federation. However, a class presentation is already being conceptualized for this" (Vieth-Entus, von Törne, and Keller 2005).

Spokespeople for Islamic groups were concerned with disentangling the phenomenon of honor killing from mainstream Muslim practices, including,

above all, the headscarf issue. Islamic groups sharply distinguish Islamic practices, such as the headscarf, from local cultural traditions, such as honor killings,
that they characterize as customs that violate Islam. This linkage is a particularly
sensitive issue for Islamic groups, many of which are strong advocates of the
headscarf for women, which is a focus of intense political controversy in Turkey,
where secularist governments have prohibited headscarves in all government
buildings. A commentary on Hatun's murder by an Iraqi resident of Berlin in the
Arab newspaper *Al-Hayat* attributed the practice of honor killing to "Anatolian
family law," marking it as a distinctively Turkish—not Islamic—custom (Wali
2005). This writer argued that many Muslims view the headscarf, in contrast,
as an important part of a woman's practice as a Muslim. Women themselves
choose to wear it, and wearing it must not be construed as a sign of male abuse
of women. Most Muslims argue that the abuse of women is against Islam, and
the leaders of many Islamic organizations assert that gender relations as they are
prescribed in Islamic law are entirely consistent with the principles of human
rights that are embedded in Western constitutional democracies.

Islamic groups stressed that youth and families must be educated that Islam
forbids murder in the name of honor, consistent with the teachings and social
programs of these groups. Islamist groups such as IGMG stress that one of their
basic goals is to improve the situation of women. The organization has engaged
in an educational campaign that discourages parents from arranging marriages
between their children and relatives in Turkey because they find that such marriages often fail or are unhappy.

In the heavy media coverage surrounding Hatun Sürücü's death, *Zaman*
printed four articles that touched on either her death or the honor killing issue.
The first, discussed earlier in the chapter, quoted Hatun's brother extensively
and sought to disentangle the headscarf issue from the murder. It also criticized
the secular Turkish newspapers *Cumhuriyet* and *Hürriyet* for their coverage,
which, like the German media, linked the murder with the headscarf issue.

The second *Zaman* article, on February 23, "Islam dini, namus cinayetlerini
reddeder" (The Islamic Faith Repudiates Honor Killings), sought to distance
the idea of honor killings from the teachings of Islam, countering their conflation in the German media, which was being heavily influenced by the activists
Çileli, Ateş, Kelek, and others. This theme was echoed in a commentary in the
German-language *Islamische Zeitung*, published in Berlin, which complained
that a whole page of the daily *Tageszeitung* (Berlin) had been devoted to the
comments of one of these activists, with no counterbalance from other per-

spectives. Writers in the Muslim press were upset by the uncritical quotation of the perspectives of "human rights activists" and feminists.

In order to counter the media campaign against Islam, the Islamic press sought to present explanations other than "Islam" for the practice of honor killings. To do this, they often drew on the work of German scholars and other writers who had closely analyzed the social pressures on Turkish families and youth in Germany. Two of the four articles in *Zaman* drew on the statements of German experts to reinforce the point that Islam does not condone honor killings. One, a lengthy article based on interviews with Berlin senator for internal affairs Ehrhart Körting, appeared on March 3 under the title, "Dr. Körting: Sürücü olayının Islam dini ile bir ilgisi yok" (Dr. Körting: There Is No Connection between the Sürücü Incident and the Islamic Faith) (*Zaman* 2005). Another *Zaman* article, "Alman Etnolog Schiffauer: Islam namus cinayetine izin vermez aksine önler" (German Ethnologist Schiffauer: Islam Does Not Give Permission for Honor Killing; on the Contrary, It Forbids It) (Semiz 2005), was a brief report on an article by German anthropologist Werner Schiffauer that had appeared in the German newspaper *Süddeutsche Zeitung* (Schiffauer 2005). *Islamische Zeitung* also drew on an alternative German perspective, reprinting in full an article by Theo Wentzke, a member of the editorial staff of the Marxist journal *Gegenstandpunkt* (Counter-viewpoint), who in this article was critical of the emerging discourse in the mainstream press (Wentzke 2005).

What were these alternative explanations and how do they differ from those that dominated the mainstream media? Wentzke's article began with the murders of van Gogh and Sürücü and focused on the preoccupation among reporters with the "Islamic immigrant milieu" of the perpetrators. Wentzke saw this as a sign of the expansion of the war on terror into an emerging culture war in which "politics declares 'multi-kulti' [multiculturalism] a failure" (a part of the article's original title). Wentzke expressed a concern that the civil liberties of immigrants are increasingly being breached, a move that he saw politicians and the mainstream press justifying by playing on fears of a hidden parallel society. These are precisely the concerns that a number of spokespeople for Muslim communities had expressed.

Schiffauer's arguments provided a perspective that a range of people, from socialists to Muslims, found useful for critiquing mainstream press coverage in the effort to disrupt a growing popular consensus about the problems with the developing parallel society. Schiffauer's basic argument was that Turkish youth are drawing on symbols of Turkish culture and Islam as they self-segregate from German society in gangs because of discrimination. He suggested that honor killing is a manifestation of these gang practices, which are influenced by transnational popular culture, and is not something encouraged by elders or by the teachings of Islamic leaders.

Writing in the newspaper *Süddeutsche Zeitung* after the murder in the article that was quoted extensively in *Zaman*, Schiffauer identified a dramatic increase in the incidence of honor killings, reversing a trend of decline in Germany over the previous several years. Though the basis for asserting such an increase could be questioned, Schiffauer analyzed the reasons for this increase in a way that challenged the explanation that was dominant in the media and in political discourse: that Turks refuse to become more fully integrated into German society and cling to their traditional group- and family-oriented concept of honor. Schiffauer stressed that these murders were not simply an indicator of the failure of migrant families to give up their traditional notion of honor located in the purity of its women. He argued instead that with the rise of street gangs self-consciously identified as ethnic Turkish, "the idea of family honor was carried over to the gang" (Schiffauer 2005: 2). According to Schiffauer, boys in these gangs categorize women into "street girls" and "family girls." Schiffauer himself served as court evaluator in a case in which a murder attempt was triggered by bragging within a gang vis-à-vis one of the sisters of a gang member. He thus suggested that the initiative for honor killings in these circumstances is less likely to come from the patriarch, but from the youth themselves.

Schiffauer stressed disentangling an orientation to Islam from this form of honor killing. Though these youth do engage Islamic symbols, he argued, the symbols function more as markers of resistance from the dominant society, as in the battle cry "Scheiss-Jesus" (shit-Jesus). He suggested that access to these youth (presumably by social workers and other governmental services) might best be established by using Islam to create a bridge between the youth and the dominant society, since most Islamic communities emphasize avoiding violence. Muslims appreciated this argument, as evidenced by the February 26 *Zaman* article that reproduced much of Schiffauer's article.

Both Schiffauer and Wentzke stressed the marginalization of Turks and their constitution as an ethnic underclass, thus emphasizing a perspective on Muslim men that echoed an earlier public concern with the exploitation of guestworkers and social discrimination against them. Honor "is excellently suited as a marker of boundaries between them and the dominant society" (Schiffauer 2005: 3). This understanding of honor killing moves away from an essentialist characterization of it being "tradition" that is difficult to eradicate, and rather sees it in the Barthian sense of a signifier that is newly deployed to mark ethnic boundaries, just as other objects, images, and practices might be taken up as gang insignia.

I suggest that at this particular historical conjunction, "honor killing" is a signifier that is imbued with additional significance by the events of September 11 and the van Gogh murder. This does not mean that these youth have any direct connection with al-Qaeda or any Islamist movement, whether or not it advocates violence. Nor would most of those who might assert with bravado that someone like Hatun Sürücü deserves to be killed actually participate in such an act of violence. Rather, honor killing can be seen as a fluid signifier that (1) has a very different significance for the German press and public than it does for the Turkish-identified youth associated with it, and (2) acquires its significance partially in relation to media representations. The succession of media images, including characterizations of van Gogh's murderer, have coalesced with a set of other forces, including these youths' sense that Islam is under siege from the Western-Christian powers because of the United States' war on terror (which many Muslims, even moderate ones, interpret as a war on Islam); their own marginalized position in German society; and the prestige hierarchy within youth gangs. This hierarchy is based on the ability to act with violence to produce a milieu in which an overdetermined act of violence can be construed as a traditional honor killing by the media, representations of which in turn may become a model or script for these young men.[11]

In this process, it is important to stress that Islamic groups in Germany are not themselves advocating honor killings. Rather, some youth, especially some of those in gangs, are linking specific symbols that they interpret as "Islamic" with their identity and sources of status vis-à-vis their social groups / gangs. Schiffauer suggests that these youth are "self-segregating" from mainstream German society and that their anger at that society is targeted against their women who appear to betray the group by taking up German practices.

The logic of taking on a mark of stigmatization and using it as an identity claim is a common strategy of resistance to social discrimination. Jenny White (1997) has described how the significance of the term *Barbaren*, used as a derogatory term by some Germans against foreigners, was inverted and used as a source of power and pride by a Turkish street gang, who selected it as the name of their gang. This logic has also entered a more literary popular culture. The Turkish-born writer Feridun Zamioğlu, who has become a well-known author in Germany, has similarly promoted the cultural label *Kanak*, adopting this derogatory term for Turks and transmuting it into a political category to be taken up by all minorities. His strategy has been to disrupt racism and subvert a multicultural discourse of identity by aggressively overfulfilling stereotypical expectations, self-consciously assuming the identity of the dangerous alien (Cheesman 2002: 187). This dangerous alien is overwhelmingly male. In his book *Kanak Sprak*, Zamioğlu deployed a slang spoken by young Turkish men that signified a kind of authentic, tough, and subversive power. The book presents twenty-four life-story interviews, which in his subtitle he calls "discordant notes from the margins." By using this format, Zamioğlu "provocatively reworked a non-fiction genre which had become commonplace in Germany in the 1980's: books explaining Turkish life in Germany, framed by German natives, based on life-story interviews, variously produced by journalists, sociologists and ethnographers," a part of what might be called *sympathy literature* (*Betroffenheitsliteratur*) (Cheesman 2002: 183). This literature is replete with stereotypes of Turkish masculinity that are presented as authoritatively authentic representations of otherness. By subverting this genre, Zamioğlu sought to disrupt the naturalness of the discourse out of which such life stories are produced.

One of Zamioğlu's recurring themes is "the majority culture's division of the figure of the young male Turk into two stereotypes: the welcome, submissive 'lieb-alilein' [loveable one] who conforms to bourgeois norms; or the feared, violent criminal—'gefährlich fremd' [dangerous foreign one]" (Cheesman 2002: 185). This sort of dichotomy is common in depictions of alien masculinities. It echoes, for example, racist representations of the male African American under slavery that portrayed him as being submissive and childish on the one hand and unrestrained and dangerously animal-like on the other (see Herd 1991); colonial characterizations of the Indian male, who was by turns viewed as subordinate and feminized (Sinha 1995) and threatening (as in the image of the tribal Pathan); and representations of Turkish men in nineteenth-century German travel narratives (see Chapter 1).

MORAL PANIC AND ITS LINKS TO
A GERMAN SOCIAL FANTASY

The intensity of increasing media coverage in the weeks immediately after Hatun Sürücü's murder suggests that Germany was in the grip of a spiraling moral panic.[12] Although some journalists and scholars presented alternative perspectives that sought to defuse the panic and its distortions by suggesting structural

and institutional causes for the marginalization of Turkish youth and their en-
dorsement of violence, on the whole the media themselves played a major role
in fostering the panic.[13]

One theme that developed as coverage escalated was the sense that the
media and the public were coming together to create a deliberate transformation in public discourse, expressed in the tropes that this honor killing was a
"wake-up call" to the German community and that taboo issues were being
discussed at last (for example, *Die Welt* 2005). It was asserted in the media that
as a result of Hatun's murder, Germany had "turned its attention to previously
taboo subjects, such as forced marriage and violence against women in Turkish
homes" (*Frankfurter Allgemeine Zeitung* 2005). A headline in the newspaper *Die
Welt* (2005) read "Türkischer Bund will Tabuthemen in die Diskussion bringen"
(The Turkish Federation Wants to Bring Taboo Subjects into the Discussion),
referring to violence against women. These two images of "taboo" and "wake-
up call" were used to signal the emergence of a basic shift in public discourse,
founded on the idea that there was a festering social problem that the public
had been ignoring and that the media and social activists needed to create pressure for a change in social policy. Why the talk of a "taboo"? What is the slum-
ber from which Germans must awaken? Why a "wake-up call" at this particular
time? What are the contours of the conflict that these images are a sign of? Why
did they have such a powerful effect on the media and the public?

Criticism of the plight of Muslim women and Muslim cultural difference
had already been quite visible in the German media. Public consciousness had
been focused on the threatening emergence of a parallel society, in which Muslims "sink into their own hidden world" such that "most Germans never get
a look inside of the life of their friendly Turkish baker, butcher or green grocer" (Spiegel Online 2004). This suggested a sinister underside to the public
presentations of the Turkish men that Germans encountered in their everyday lives. The subject of women as victims of their men and their culture had
been particularly visible in German media over the years, appearing not only in
newspaper articles well before the murder but also in both an extensive social
work literature seeking to alleviate the plight of the Muslim woman and cinema
depictions of Turks (see Chapter 2). Yet the idea of taboo came up repeatedly.
This articulation of a sense of taboos being lifted or even violated therefore calls
for interrogation.

Among those who have most vocally deployed the idea of disrupting taboos
have been the three feminists of Turkish background, Çileli, Ateş, and Serap.

These women have powerful voices in the media, and one or all of them are interviewed as experts whenever an issue related to headscarves, honor killings, and other aspects of the situation of Muslim women in Germany emerges into public attention. These activists frequently and explicitly use imagery that evokes the German public's relationship to Nazism and draws an analogy with it. According to an interview with Çileli, for example, "People were afraid they would be called Nazis if they dared to bring up issues of human rights in the Turkish community" (Biehl 2005: 2). Erich Goode and Nachman Ben-Yehuda have argued that the leaders of movements seeking to bring about social change often try to capture media attention and shape public opinion by framing their target issue in exaggerated terms, fostering moral panic. They draw on a language of moral indignation, focusing on the worst aspects of the condition they are denouncing as if these were typical (Goode and Ben-Yehuda 1994: 120). The campaign to rescue Muslim and Turkish women from their families certainly bears many of the features Goode and Ben-Yehuda identify, emphasizing as it does the "enslavement" of thousands of Muslim women by their husbands and, in the case of honor killing, foregrounding an extreme but very rare practice. By implicitly linking their cause and the fate of Muslim women with the victims of the Holocaust, spokespeople such as Çileli have drawn on one of the most powerful images available in German national discourse to elicit support for their cause.

The concept of taboo is associated with deep silences surrounding the memory of the Nazi period, and this invokes ongoing sensitivities that shape German historical memory. It also shapes the contours of political argument, as we will see in Chapter 7 in the controversy that developed when the topic of *Leitkultur* (leading culture), also considered taboo, was articulated in public by a conservative CDU politician. The establishment and maintenance of the modern German nation as a free and civilized society on the ashes of its Nazi past have been accomplished in part through the mechanism of silences enforced by taboos.

This idea of taboo has been taken up by the public. It was expressed, for example, at a teacher-parent meeting held at the Thomas-Morus Oberschule, the school where the boys who had expressed their controversial opinions about Hatun Sürücü were students. Participants in the discussion, which was held after the controversy surrounding these students erupted, expressed a sense of relief in being able to voice outrage over Turkish traditional values. This is the relief and even pleasure associated with breaking a taboo. A journalist described the scene, which opens with a German speaking: "'We have let our cultural values be pushed away for too long, we have become too little aware of ourselves.' He strikes a nerve in the teachers present. 'Yes! That is it!' one cries out, relieved. As though a weight were falling from her, as though someone had finally pushed open the school gates behind which she had despaired for years" (Bauer 2005). The pleasure of venting is palpable in this snippet of public dialogue. Another article presented a similar sentiment: "If the reason were not so tragic, one could feel relieved that the beating around the bush finally has an end" (Lau 2005). In report after report, there is a sense of the floodgates of outrage opening and the articulation of a determination to root out and expose to the scrutiny of the press and the reformers of social policy a secret world of horrific practices, generating a rallying cry that the Muslim woman be freed from her slavery and from the brutality of the Muslim man. The relief that people expressed suggests that they were experiencing a social fantasy that involved an enactment of transgressive pleasure made acceptable through a sense of moral outrage and panic.

The result was an eruption of rage against the Turkish community for its failure to respect German law and the basic organizing principles of German society. As is often the case, it focused on the Muslim woman as the victim of the Muslim man. This rage was considered justified because of the comments of the Turkish schoolboys who condoned the killing. In the heat of the rage, the rhetoric in mainstream media sources was fierce: a journalist, for example, wrote of "murderous macho patriotism" in families where "women are treated little better than slaves" (Biehl 2005: 1). This one killing was portrayed as only the tip of the iceberg, a hint of the situation of "thousands—perhaps even tens of thousands" of Turkish women who live in virtual enslavement in a "hidden world" in ghettos at the heart of German cities (Spiegel Online 2004). The media identified a huge potential for similar violence across the country. These are some of the fantasies associated with the idea of breaking or overcoming a taboo. The trope of the "wake-up call" operated in tandem with the taboo to create a justification for the intense rhetoric that developed even in mainstream journalism, fueling the sense of moral panic.

These images display the contours of a social fantasy of hidden violence and contagion that have emerged from a state of moral panic that has been rising among the German public and media. Journalists, activists, and politicians vehemently defended the victimized Turkish woman against the indifference of Turkish and Muslim organizations, which were portrayed by Çileli and others in the media and the public as analogous to those who stood by and watched the Nazis exterminate the Jews. It is Turkish men who are the perpetrators of violence. German symbolic violence against the Turkish man is thus safely displaced onto the threatening presence of the other that is hidden within German society behind the face of the friendly Turkish grocer or baker who in reality lives a secret life in which he abuses and even enslaves the women in his family. In a twist of logic, this discourse suggests that the German who stands by and allows practices such as honor killings and forced marriages to continue is like the German public during the Nazi era, who stood by and did nothing while the events of the Holocaust unfolded around them.

Uli Linke (1997, 2002) has traced a logic of German national fantasy and argued that echoes of the race-based violence of the Holocaust have continued to play out in postwar Germany and continue to organize German political thought today, shaping the ways Germans perceive immigrants. Linke has described how antifascist slogans of the New Left advocate tolerance of ethnic diversity yet covertly reproduce assumptions of a "pure" nation and a demonized, threatening other that echo Nazi rhetoric. In a symbolic inversion, the neo-Nazi is now the demon that threatens the purity of Germany as a democratic state (Linke 2002: 255).[14] The metaphors and images that appear in depictions of honor killings reveal similar fantastic images associated with violence and racial difference. Like the neo-Nazi, the Turkish man is accused of threatening democratic principles. With this equivalence, the parallel between the demonization of the Turk and the Jew is disguised. The resemblance of this fierce rhetoric about the threat to the German social order posed by the character of the Turkish man with an analogous abjection of the Jew during the National Socialist era generally goes unnoticed. Furthermore, public distance from xenophobia is actually reinforced by neo-Nazi activities: over the past two decades, neo-Nazis have brutally attacked several Turkish immigrant families. The German public responded by staging demonstrations denouncing the attacks and asserting support for the recognition of Germany as a tolerant, multicultural society. I develop this argument further in Chapter 7.

CONCLUSION

Moral panic emerged and escalated in the wake of Hatun Sürücü's murder, which was seen as a manifestation of a growing problem with Turkish Muslim men and their refusal to integrate into German society. This moral panic was stoked by the media and by activists who were seeking to protect women from the violence of the men. Though situations exist in which young women are in desperate need of protection and shelter, the claim that such violence is the results from traditional Turkish culture and the teachings or practices of Islam is inaccurate and results in the further marginalization of Turkish immigrants and intense stigmatization of Turkish men. This reasoning ignores the extent to which the actions of young men like Hatun's brother are shaped by the institutions and discriminatory practices they confront in their everyday lives, including scripts constructed by media accounts. As I argue in Chapters 6 and 7, Hatun's murder was linked to a broader threat of the Turkish man that forms an important component of the German national imaginary, the ground on which current ambivalent notions of "Germanness" rest.

6 NATIONAL CONTROVERSIES AND SOCIAL FANTASIES OF THE OTHER

AS THE HONOR KILLING controversy demonstrates, German public discourse creates specific flashpoints where recurrent conflicts arise as Turkish Muslim immigrants confront barriers to integration into German society. Some issues and their resolution—such as the policing of borders, possibilities of formal citizenship, and opportunities for bringing family members to Germany to settle permanently—affect all immigrants and have overt, direct, and widespread implications for the nature of German citizenship and for what it means to be German in a modern nation-state founded on the principles of liberal democracy. Over the years, immigration and citizenship laws have been significantly liberalized, moving Germany away from a notion of citizenship rooted in blood to one based primarily on residence within German territory. Though controversial, the idea of Germany as a country of immigration in which multiculturalism is celebrated, accepted, and widespread. It is taught in public schools and espoused by many of the middle class who regard themselves as educated and cosmopolitan. It is consistent with the principles of liberal democracy articulated in Germany's Constitution, since it emphasizes equal treatment and respect for all. Incidents of overt intolerance are typically denounced as manifestations of continuing provincialism among conservative working-class and rural populations, which are sometimes provoked and exploited for political advantage by conservative politicians. Despite this deeply held commitment to tolerance and despite the liberalization of immigration and citizenship laws, other issues constrain the possibility of full cultural citizenship, especially for Muslims, whose practice of Islam marks them as other.

In this chapter I explore three controversies that have been political and media flashpoints over the past decade: the "Muslim Test" for citizenship, the wearing of the headscarf, and the related issue of excusing Muslim children from mandatory gym and swimming classes. In the next chapter, I focus on the *Leitkultur* debate. Some of these issues, such as the headscarf controversy, have close parallels in several other European countries and in Turkey itself, where the headscarf is banned from classrooms and government buildings. Others, especially the *Leitkultur* debate, are more specifically German and resonate with Germany's past in evocative and sometimes disturbing ways. However, even the headscarf issue has taken on a distinctively German cast and manifests specific contours not only of German institutional arguments, but of the national imaginary and its ties to social fantasy. Though some of the issues I discuss focus on women or on gender relations more broadly, together they form the discursive underpinnings of the pervasive stigmatization of Muslim masculinity that affects the possibility of full cultural citizenship. Furthermore, as I demonstrate, this stigmatization is part of the foundation of the German national imaginary and its constitution of discursive subjects as gendered citizens through the process of abjection of an other.

THE MUSLIM TEST

Some of the parameters of German concerns and the stereotyping associated with them are officially embodied in what has come to be called the Muslim Test, a controversial list of thirty questions implemented on January 1, 2006, by the southern state government of Baden-Württemberg as "discussion guidelines" to be used in questioning applicants for German citizenship. The interior minister of Baden-Württemberg, a member of the conservative CDU, claimed to have established these guidelines "because he wanted would-be citizens to defend the Constitution and accept Germany's democratic values" (Dempsey 2006). Ironically, however, others such as Josef Winkler, a Bundestag representative for the Green Party, called the test unconstitutional, arguing that it violates the constitutionally protected freedom of opinion (Hawley 2006). Immediately after information about the test was leaked to the German media and became public, debates ensued about whether to use such a questionnaire at the federal level; but within a month, a motion had been introduced in the Bundestag to ban Baden-Württemberg from implementing the test. Though most politicians and public officials condemned the test, the motion to ban it failed (Hawley 2006).

In addition to political questions that probe attitudes toward Israel, Jews, and terrorist acts, a number of the questions focus on the private domain of gender and family relations. For example:

—One hears repeatedly of cases in which parents forbid their adult daughters from entering a certain career or marrying the man of her choice. What would you do if your daughter wanted to marry a man of a different religion or wanted to enter a career you didn't approve of?

—Do you think that forced marriages are consistent with human dignity?

Some questions are even less subtle:

—Should a man be allowed to lock his wife or daughter in the house in order to prevent her from disgracing him in public?

—Do you agree with the statement that a woman should obey her husband and that he can beat her when she doesn't follow his orders?

These questions reflect controversies regarding the integration of Germany's large Turkish Muslim population and focus on the oppression of women by their fathers and husbands. The media have tended to take up particularly extreme cases of such practices and use them as typical of Turkish family relations, as representing a form of "cultural practice." Thus in the question about marriage, the practice of arranged marriage is labeled "forced marriage" (*Zwangsheirat*) though most arranged marriages are freely accepted by the parties to the marriage and are not in any sense forced. This question, unlike the other three, is, on its face, gender neutral, since sons as well as daughters are often parties to arranged marriages (there are cases of men being forced to marry against their will, as happens in the film *Düğün / Die Heirat* (The Marriage, 1991), by the director Ismat Elçi, who was brought by his father to Germany as a teenager). Media representations emphasize the bride as victim, especially in the highly publicized books by the activists Seyran Ateş (2003), Serap Çileli (2002), and Necla Kelek (2005) (see Chapter 5).

The act of a man locking up his wife or daughter is also used as a cultural marker. Though this situation was publicized in the film *40 Quadratmeter Deutschland* (Başer 1986) (see Chapter 2), it is not typical. The questions on the Muslim Test emerged in the wake of the dramatic media coverage surrounding Hatun Sürücü's murder and the associated concern that Muslim women were increasingly trapped in a parallel society from which they could not escape.

Each of these questions foregrounds gender relationships in which the rights of women are violated, focusing on the point of maximum incompatibility between the most extreme manifestations of Turkish practice taken as normative, juxtaposed with the ideals of a democratic society, also read as normative.

Other questions on the test address the issue of women's bodies and their exposure to public gaze, also within the context of men's oppressive control over their women, which has been established by this entire line of questioning:

> —Your adult daughter or your wife wants to dress like other German women. Would you try to prevent it?

> —In Germany, everyone can decide for himself or herself whether they want to be treated by a male or female doctor. In some situations, however— emergencies, or during a hospital shift change—this isn't possible. In such a situation, would you allow yourself to be treated by a woman doctor (male citizenship applicant) or a male doctor (female citizenship applicant)?

The first question addresses the controversial subject of the headscarf and whether a man would allow his wife or daughter to discard it—again, emphasizing the issue of whether parents would try to control the activities of their daughter. The second question is rather peculiar; it attempts to uncover in a contorted hypothetical situation something that distinguishes the Muslim who will not integrate successfully into German society from the "real" German: if you were in a situation in which you were forced to expose your body to a member of the opposite sex (despite the freedoms normally granted to members of German society to avoid such situations of coercion), would you do it? It is the only question that addresses the body of the Muslim man, as well as that of the woman.

Finally, there is a question about the gym class, this one framed solely in terms of the woman's body:

> —In Germany, sport and swim classes are part of the normal school curriculum. Would you allow your daughter to participate? If no, why not?

Der Spiegel, in an online spoof of the test, suggested two possible responses to this last question: (1) "Of course; swimming is a vital part of integration in Germany." The hypothetical German bureaucrat's reaction to this answer is: "That's right. If you can't swim, you're not German. In fact, that's not a bad idea for a new citizenship test." The alternative response was, (2) "Could you tell me which article of the Constitution requires participation in swim classes?" and the bureaucrat's reaction: "Work with us here. We just want to make sure we're not letting any terrorists into the country."

This question about swimming and gym classes reflects another controversy that has periodically waxed and waned in the German media and the courts since the early 1990s: whether a Muslim schoolgirl should be exempted from a coeducational gym class in order to preserve her modesty (discussed later in this chapter). There were several cases of Muslim girls and their families requesting such exemptions, resulting in a definitive court ruling in 1993 in favor of the girls and their families. Nevertheless, the issue continues to simmer in public debate and the media. Ironically, given *Der Spiegel*'s spoof of the bureaucrat, some media sources have suggested that the gym class *is* a legal requirement stated in the Constitution—specifically in article 7, paragraph 1, though this paragraph (not surprisingly) actually says nothing about gym classes. Rather, it states the broad principle that "the entire school system shall be under the supervision of the state." The spoof, I suggest, taps into something that resonates with a distinctive way of constituting the German citizen vis-à-vis the state that has less to do with the "democratic values" that are enshrined in a constitution that was designed by the Allies after World War II than it does with a distinctively German way of inscribing German citizenship through a particular bodily discipline, which I will discuss below.

THE HEADSCARF CONTROVERSY

Paradoxically, the Muslim woman who "covers" is acutely visible to the Western eye, which is inexorably drawn to the piece of cloth that is intended to preserve her purity and protect her from the inappropriate male gaze. Seeing the headscarf, the European imagination is focused not on the potentially inappropriate gaze of the strange male (including the European) but on precisely those men before whom the Muslim woman need not cover—her husband, father, and brothers. What is "recognized" in the headscarf is a pattern of oppressive gender relations that in turn reflects the practices of the Muslim man. But the structure of this European gaze on the Muslim woman is more complicated than this: as in the multiple, not-quite-reciprocal gazes depicted in Diego Velázquez's painting *Las Meninas* (in which the viewer is partially conflated with some of the figures in the background), what is being painted on the canvas that is just out of sight of the viewer is the European's own national pride in a progressive social order based on gender equality.[1] And imperfectly reflected off of this pride is a side of the European subject and discursive order that has been disavowed, and in the case of Germany, pushed into the past. This side encompasses the culturally particular aspects of bodily practice and gender organization that masquerade as universal prerequisites for life in a modern, democratic society. In the struggle over integrating Muslims into European societies, cultural particularities and national idiosyncrasies are rhetorically confounded with the universalized Enlightenment values of the liberal democracy. Exploring moments when the prescriptions of Islam confront everyday practices in German schools points us to aspects of Germanness that I suggest are confounded with the "democratic values" that are articulated in the Constitution—gender equality and religious freedom—but that actually have quite different roots linked to ideas of German national culture and the cultivation of the body. I argue that German ideas of the relationship of bodily exposure and purity form the interpretive framework for judging Muslim concerns with bodily covering.

In the German national imaginary, the health of the state has historically been linked to the cultivation of bodily purity, and the ideas of purity have been based on exposure of the body. Though controversies surrounding the headscarf and gym classes have not been framed explicitly in terms of the positive value of bodily exposure, but rather in terms of constitutional principles such as religious neutrality and gender equality, specific court rulings and public discourse emphasize the right of the state, in effect, to force bodily exposure and the right of children to experience this exposure. The relationships among freedom, the body, and purity thus take on a configuration that is directly challenged by Islamic understandings of bodily purity and character development, which rest on modesty and the covering of the body.

Clashes between German and Muslim bodily practices have played out in the courts around the issues of whether a public schoolteacher should be permitted to wear a headscarf in the classroom and whether Muslim girls should be allowed exemption from required gym and swimming classes. The distinctively German contours of the gym class debate, as well as the struggle over whether university-educated Muslim women who have grown up in Germany are to be prohibited from teaching in the public schools if they wear a headscarf, are particularly visible against the background of a similar yet significantly different headscarf controversy in France, where even schoolgirls have been forbidden to wear the headscarf.[2] In each case, multiple layers of justification and contestation juxtapose ideological concerns about the nation articulated in terms of the principles of equality, human rights, national security, and the constitutional foundation of the state, with more implicit anxieties over the organization of gender and the enculturation of the individual as a "German" or "French" national subject. At this implicit level, culturally particular practices are conflated with universal principles. In the background lurks the Muslim man as an other who is unassimilable because he refuses to accept these supposedly universal principles of modern gender organization and allow the liberation of his women from the constraint of bodily covering.

In France, secularism is the common ground on which cultural citizenship rests. State institutions such as public schools are to be rigorously secular, even if this means constraints on the freedom of religious practice. With respect to Muslims, the French government has endorsed the principle that the absolute separation of church and state means that individuals and groups are forbidden to manifest their religious practices and beliefs in government settings such as public schools. The result has been controversy over the permissibility of headscarves for Muslim girls while in school. Protecting the rights of women by banning the headscarf was equated with protecting the republic itself. Joan Scott (2005) has argued that the intensity of the political fracas over the headscarf can be explained by a displaced enactment of French anxiety regarding a basic contradiction in the principle of French citizenship: French national identity is based on the abstract principle that equality depends on sameness, but sexual difference is not susceptible to this abstraction because sexual difference violates the basic criterion of sameness or indistinguishability. The French "solution" is complementarity of the sexes, in which the couple is the unit of citizenship and female sexuality is flaunted. This culturally specific French way of "doing sex" has been rhetorically linked to the Enlightenment principle of equality, though it has no necessary connection with it. The Islamic organization of gender, with its covering of sexuality in public, is a challenge to this French conflation of a universalized principle of equality and a culturally French mode of gender organization.

Germany has had its own culturally distinctive ways of responding to the challenge of Muslim gender relations that analogously reveal the tensions and contradictions on which German national identity is built. In contrast to France, where the legal challenges have been presented by students who sought to wear the headscarf, in Germany, Muslim schoolgirls have been generally free to wear it, though the French controversy has led some German politicians to propose a similar ban in Germany. Furthermore, the strict separation of church and state in the French sense does not exist in Germany. Rather, the Constitution, or

Basic Law (*Grundgesetz*), guarantees state "neutrality" with respect to religion. In several German states, religious education takes place in public schools. In this context, neutrality is ensured by the schools offering a range of choices in denominational religious instruction rather than the state keeping religion out of the schools altogether. Nevertheless, this principle of neutrality has been deployed in the arguments against the headscarf in Germany, especially with respect to teachers. As in the French situation, there appears to be a lot of public angst about issues that would seem to have little connection to what has been called the threat of Islamic fundamentalism or even to the success of integration. Could the threat posed by the modesty of Muslim women, girls, and even boys arise instead because that modesty challenges inconsistencies in the discursive constitution of the German citizen vis-à-vis the state?

A lawsuit focused on the permissibility of a teacher wearing a headscarf in the public schools has received considerable attention since it first arose in 1998, when Fereshta Ludin, a young Afghani refugee, was denied a position as a teacher because she refused to remove her headscarf (Hilbk 1998). This case brought the issue to public consciousness. Earlier, during her teacher training, Ludin had been assigned an internship in an elementary school where the parents of some of the children objected to her headscarf in the classroom, triggering a lawsuit that wound its way through the German courts over several years. The Federal Constitutional Court ruled quite narrowly in its 2003 decision: headscarves could not be banned without a legal basis. But the justices also determined that it was possible for state lawmakers to create a legal basis for such a ban and to determine the admissible amount of religious expression in schools. The effect of this decision was to throw the issue back to the individual states, which, as a result, were free to enact laws banning teachers from wearing headscarves in the classroom. By mid-2006, half of Germany's sixteen states had enacted such legislation. Most of Germany's Turkish immigrants live in these states, which include Berlin and other western German states.[3] In Berlin, a law was subsequently passed that went even further, banning all civil servants from wearing the headscarf.

The issue has been framed in terms of a conflict between two constitutional principles: the guarantee of a teacher's freedom of religion on the one hand and the required "neutrality" of a teacher as an employee and representative of the state on the other. The neutrality is not just with respect to religion but also political orientation. The neutrality issue was also accompanied by a constitutional argument about gender equality.

The various strands of reasoning included considerable logical slippage and faulty equivalences, especially when the courts' rulings were transmitted to the public through media reports. With respect to religious neutrality, it was reasoned that exposure to a teacher wearing a headscarf would violate children's religious freedom, that is, the negative freedom not to have any religion imposed on them,[4] since a woman who wears it was considered likely to promote Islam in the classroom simply by being visibly Muslim.[5] The core issue was not religion in the classroom per se, but rather neutrality. In Bavaria, a law requiring the crucifix to hang in every classroom was challenged in the 1990s, but the Federal Constitutional Court allowed the state to retain a version of the law. In light of this background, proponents of the headscarf challenged the notion that the school system is religiously neutral, since the state sponsors courses in religious instruction and allows the wearing of crucifixes in the classroom. In the highest court's ruling on Ludin's case, however, the minority opinion characterized the Bavarian crucifix as a "cultural symbol of openness and tolerance" that therefore did not threaten students' religious freedom; it was distinguished from the headscarf, which, according to the opinion, represented the subservient role of the woman and thus conflicted with the Constitution. In this opinion, the issue of gender equality was linked with neutrality.

In Germany, teachers at all levels, including the university, are civil servants, so they are not permitted to express their political views to students[6] but rather have a constitutional duty to act as a neutral and objective representative of the state. Parents entrust their children to the state in sending them to school, where they are perceived to be especially vulnerable to the influence of their teachers. The argument was made that since the headscarf is contested among Muslims and is associated with Islamic fundamentalism, which involves active proselytization, it is not simply a religious symbol but a political symbol. Furthermore, a policy tolerating the headscarf in the German civil service would send a political message that the state was "supporting a side linked in the public mind with cultural exclusivism, the repression of women, and intolerance" (Barbieri 1999: 922).

Many groups also felt that banning the headscarf would promote the integration of Muslim youth because it was assumed that wearing a headscarf prevented a girl from fully interacting with her classmates and that it was likely that she was being forced to wear it. Some officials argued, however, that barring the headscarf was likely to disadvantage Muslim women rather than promote their integration. The education and children's minister of the state of North Rhine–Westphalia, Ute Schäfer (SPD), warned of the effects that a law concerning Muslim headscarves in schools would have on the Muslim population and its consequences for integration policy. One report quoted Schäfer saying, "we should carefully consider whether or not such a law might lead to an effect opposite of what we wanted," and then went on to explain: "That desired effect is to put a stop to fundamentalist Islamic forces. Muslims could understand a headscarf law as being against Islam in general" (*Deutsche Welle* 2003). This state finally voted for a ban in June 2006 under conservative CDU leadership (*Deutsche Welle* 2006a).[7]

Not surprisingly, young Muslim women with teaching credentials were dismayed at the federal court ruling. The ban has forced some Muslim women who wear headscarves out of the teaching profession. The immediate effect of the Constitutional Court's ruling was to trigger efforts to establish new Islamic private schools where these women would be able to teach. Muslim groups responded to the ban in North Rhine–Westphalia in the following terms:

> The Central Council of Muslims in Germany, which represents 3 million Muslims, called the new law unconstitutional because it does not treat all religions as equal, banning only the headscarf and not the Christian cross or any other religious symbols. They argue that the measure practically bans Muslim women who wear traditional headscarves from working as teachers. Furthermore, young women students who adhere to Muslim traditions are now practically expelled from the workplace. (*Deutsche Welle* 2006a)

The courts ruled in terms of rationalized arguments about religious and political neutrality associated with the principle of free and autonomous subjects of a democracy, yet they kept returning to the point that the headscarf symbolizes the oppression of women and that women who wear headscarves do not have the kinds of equal opportunities that the German Constitution guarantees. This argument ignores the hardships that the ban itself would impose on covered women, a hardship that can now be overcome only by forcing the covered woman to expose herself to public view by removing her headscarf. This association of the headscarf with women's oppression was explicit in the 2003 *Der Spiegel* article discussed in Chapter 2, which juxtaposed the situation of an uncle raping his niece with the oppression of being forced to wear a headscarf. Similarly, press coverage of Hatun Sürücü's murder (see Chapter 5) suggested that her honor killing had been motivated by her removal of her headscarf. The headscarf is closely associated with the issue of male violence and even the possibility of honor killing, as articles about Hatun Sürücü's murder demonstrate.

Women who wear headscarves are still under the sway of the oppressive Muslim man. The oppression argument is closely tied to the protection of the principle of gender equality enshrined in Germany's Constitution. But why this powerful reaction to a piece of cloth that hides a woman's hair but does not otherwise hamper her activities?

THE GYM CLASS

Other layers of significance emerge in a slightly different but related controversy surrounding the desire of some Muslim parents to have their children exempted from mandatory gym and swimming classes. Several lawsuits have been filed by Muslim girls and their parents over this issue because they believe it is impossible to maintain proper modesty in gender-mixed classes, where many of the activities preclude the wearing of the headscarf and required gym clothes typically expose the legs and arms. The parents of an eleven-year-old Muslim boy also filed a lawsuit requesting exemption from coeducational swimming classes so that he would not be exposed to girls in bathing suits (*Deutsche Welle* 2005).

In response to a complaint first brought by the father of a twelve-year-old Muslim girl in 1989, the Federal Administrative Court ruled in 1993 that schools are obligated to make all reasonable efforts to offer gender-segregated gym classes for girls. If this is not possible, then the conflict between the state mission of education and upbringing as specified in the Constitution and the right to freedom of religion is to be resolved in favor of the freedom of religion, so that girls must be exempted from gym and swimming classes for religious reasons when they and their parents wish it. When the father first applied to the school for his daughter's exemption from coeducational gym classes because her Islamic beliefs forbade her from playing sports with boys, the school rejected the exemption on the grounds that it would be in accordance with the clothing regulations of the Qur'an if she were to participate in gym class wearing widely cut clothing. With this decision, the school took the interpretation of the Qur'an into its own hands. The appeals court subsequently rejected the father's appeal, but the Federal Constitutional Court overturned the appeals court ruling, thereby supporting the girl's right to exemption.

But public commentary continues around this issue. According to a 2003 *Der Spiegel* article, for instance, the 1993 federal court decision

> shows how lightly German courts deal with the oppression of women by their
> parents in the name of religious freedom: A Muslim girl can be released from

sports and swimming classes if they are not strictly segregated by gender . . . In the name of religious freedom, orthodox parents may also have the chance to confine and control Muslim girls with the blessing of the German courts—this is what the headscarf symbolizes. (Cziesche et al. 2003)

In the case of the Muslim boy, the parents lost the suit they had filed against school officials. The court, in what the media represented as a "landmark case," ruled that religious beliefs are not a reason to prevent children from attending swimming classes (*Deutsche Welle* 2005). Although the press usually presents these lawsuits as one of the signs that Turks are refusing to integrate, the issue of gym class has touched a deeper nerve in the public imagination.

The specific way that German concerns were articulated suggests that gym class is felt to be an important part of a child's enculturation and, that by requesting exemption from gym, Muslim children and especially girls can never become fully German. Why is gym class—a nonacademic subject that many children in, for example, the United States regard as something of a joke—so important in Germany? One argument is simply that gym class is mandated by law. By being excused from this class, Muslim children are thus not subject to the same legal requirements as other German citizens and residents. Many Germans in casual conversations said that people feel it is important to draw a line so that European society never succumbs to Islamic law. Allowing Muslim children to follow Islamic law instead of German law vis-à-vis gym classes would seem to be one step in that direction. A similar sentiment is expressed in the 2005 *Annual Report of the Office for the Protection of the Constitution* when describing the activities of Islamist groups, including IGMG:

> They are at the same time endeavouring by legal means to create enclaves for their supporters in Germany so that they can lead their lives according to sharia law [Islamic law]. In their view sharia law constitutes an Islamic legal system which regulates all spheres of life, and implementing such a system in Germany is a precondition for practising "true" Islam. . . . These "legalistic" Islamist groups represent an especial threat to the internal cohesion of our society. Among other things, their wide range of Islamist-oriented educational and support activities, especially for children and adolescents from immigrant families, are used to promote the creation and proliferation of an Islamist milieu in Germany. (Federal Ministry of the Interior 2005: 189–190)

In 2005, the Berlin senator for youth, education, and sports, Klaus Böger, created a minor stir when he publicly linked poor gym class attendance with Muslim society, pointing out that "in some mosques, pre-printed materials circulate on how to officially excuse girls from physical education, along with addresses of sympathetic doctors who are prepared to write official excuses" (Ritter 2006). Böger vowed that he would "no longer play that game" and sent a letter to schools indicating that religion and ideology were not sufficient reasons for missing gym class. But why draw the line protecting German society against Islamic law at the gym class? Is this line arbitrary?

The gym class is intended to educate and discipline the body. It is considered so important to the shaping of the young German that it is mandated by law. A few Germans I talked with even said that it was a part of the German Constitution, though when I studied the wording of the Constitution, I didn't see anything about physical education classes specifically mentioned. In his campaign to prevent Muslim girls from cutting gym classes, Böger gave several reasons for the importance of physical education: "'Sports classes are not just about physical conditioning. Fitness is certainly important, but PE is an elementary part of education and child rearing,' Böger said. 'In physical education classes, they [children] can learn very important attitudes and virtues. Developing self worth, a sense of fair play . . . and now we know that sports help develop the ability to concentrate'" (Ritter 2006). Physical education is seen as an important part of the push to integrate Muslims into German society, not primarily as a venue for students to interact with each other across ethnic and religious barriers, but because it is linked with the cultivation of the whole person as a German.

This German preoccupation with physical fitness has a politically charged history. The significance of gym classes can be traced to the body culture (*Korperkultur*) movement that originated in the nineteenth century when Friedrich Ludwig Jahn established the first gymnastics clubs (see Dencker 2002). During the Weimar Republic in the interwar period, the body culture and "life reform" (*Lebensreform*) movements sought to restore the body to natural health in the wake of the devastation of World War I. The idea of a natural, yet disciplined and hygienic body appealed to a wide spectrum of political movements, ranging from anarchists to German nationalists (Mosse 1975). For example, it spawned youth organizations such as the *Wandervogel* movement, "a mixed gender youth group that would be subsumed in 1933 by the Hitler youth" (Gordon 2002: 186). There was a hypertrophied emphasis on disciplining and perfecting the Aryan male body, but women were also subject to physical discipline, with the idea of containing their dangerous sexuality and channeling it into service to the nation. Similarly, the discipline of gymnastics and other physical training were important for cultivating the physical and moral hygiene that would enable the German woman to raise a healthy family and contribute to the maintenance of social order.[8]

Though the cultivation of physical discipline was taken up and exaggerated during the Nazi era, it was not thereby contaminated as something to be repudiated after the war. Rather, physical education continued to be an important aspect of the cultivation of the German citizen, especially important to the restoration and disciplining of German character after the devastation and demoralization caused by the war and defeat.[9] When Muslim children are exempted from the physical training associated with gym classes and swimming, they avoid becoming fully German.

In addition to creating a barrier between the Muslim child and the physical disciplining of the German national subject, the issue of bodily covering in the name of modesty, which includes the headscarf controversy, comes into even more direct conflict with a related issue that is, if anything, even more distinctively German: full nudity in public spaces. As one German research team put the matter rather starkly, perhaps with some exaggeration: "Social nudism is the rule in Germany rather than the exception. . . . Secretaries spend their lunch break in the nude in the nearest park in major cities like Munich or Berlin. Complete nakedness is accepted practice for men, women and children" (Krüger, Krüger, and Treptau 2002: 33). The nineteenth-century body culture movement, with its a romantic, countercultural "back-to-nature" reaction to the demands of industrialization, advocated nudism. Other movements converged with it to support the social acceptance of nudism, including the German Youth Movement and the natural healing movement, resulting in the emergence of a large number of nudist organizations of a wide range of political orientations in the early twentieth century. Even Nazism, with its socially conservative ideology based on tight social control, purity, and decency, was shaped by the social force of those who supported the practice of nudity, including the elite paramilitary *Schutzstaffel* (Toepfer 1997). Though nudity was initially outlawed in 1933 as part of the imposition of law and order, this policy was gradually reversed, and nudity came to be redefined as natural. It was linked to hygiene, racial purity, and bodily perfection and was thus closely associated with physical discipline.[10]

Exposure of the human body and even full nudity continue to be associated with openness, purity, and a healthy sexuality in Germany. This logic is manifest in more recent expressions of a national imaginary, as in the symbolic performances of leftists, who have used the naked body as a form of protest against state policies, with nakedness as a symbol of nature and purity (Linke 2002: 251). As an American raised in social spaces where nudity is generally not accepted or permitted, except perhaps in same-sex locker rooms, I was often startled to see magazine covers with frontal nudity openly displayed in street kiosks in Berlin, especially the week when Berlin's entertainment guide displayed a fully naked man on its front cover—something that just would not occur in the United States. What may appear natural to a German eye is culturally quite distinctive.

One young Muslim woman of Turkish background discussed the stark differences between German and Muslim practices of modesty in an interview with Rhea Wessel, a freelance correspondent.[11] This woman wears a headscarf and is hoping to become a public schoolteacher. Wessel wrote:

> My interview partner was born and raised in Germany and carries a German passport, but before she is a German, she's a Muslim and a Muslim of Turkish descent. She remembers feeling awkward when she confronted different habits in Germany as far back as kindergarten. She and the other children used co-ed restrooms and stalls without doors, and she soon realized that the others had a different sense of modesty than her own. When the education student goes swimming, she's still surprised that women shower together or change in a group locker room. She has never been into one of Germany's many co-ed nude saunas, a shocking experience for the uninitiated. Women and men lounge together in the nude in saunas and whirlpools. Couples snuggle up in corners to smooch, and women have no problem swimming breast stroke in the pools, opening up even more to those who are brave enough to stare.
>
> A female friend of my interview partner converted to Islam as an adult and has told my interview partner about visits to the sauna with her adult brother and father. Apparently, this was difficult for the young German to handle and was one reason she sought Islam, with its strictly enforced rules about modesty. (Wessel 2006b).

This passage appears to juxtapose a German comfort with nudity as a natural practice against Muslim concerns with modesty. Surprisingly, it also captures the shock a Muslim might feel upon encountering a nude coed sauna or a toilet stall with no door. The source of this sense of shock may, however, be the fact that Wessel herself is an American journalist based in Germany and may be expressing some of her own reactions to German nudity. As a result, her depiction itself denaturalizes German nudity practices.[12]

Within the context of the modern gym class, children may, in effect, be required by law to be fully nude before others, at least in schools where showers are required and no individual shower stalls are provided. Though the showers are single-sex, even this practice violates the prohibition against nudity in the Qur'an, which prescribes modesty for both men and women:

> Say to the believing men that they should lower their gaze and guard their modesty [or private parts, depending on the translation]: that will make for greater purity for them: And Allah is well acquainted with all that they do. And say to the believing women that they should lower their gaze and guard their modesty [or private parts]; that they should not display their beauty and ornaments except what (must ordinarily) appear thereof; that they should draw their veils over their bosoms and not display their beauty except to their husbands, their fathers, their husband's fathers, their sons, their husbands' sons, their brothers or their brothers' sons, or their sisters' sons, or their women, or the slaves whom their right hands possess, or male servants free of physical needs, or small children who have no sense of the shame of sex. (Yusuf Ali 1991: 873; chapter 24, verses 30–31)

Many Muslims interpret this prescription to avoid nakedness in front of others as applying to both males and females, and before the same sex as well as the opposite sex. According to one Islamic source: "On the matter of nudity the Holy Prophet of Islam . . . has unequivocally forbidden the exposure of one's private parts. He forbade males to show and look upon one another's genitals and also forbade women to look upon one another's private parts" (*Review of Religions* 1988). As an Iranian doctor practicing in Germany said to a reporter for *Deutsche Welle*: "For some men, getting a sponge bath from a nurse is worse than the sickness itself. Therefore, the medical care should, when possible, be provided by doctors and nurses of the same sex" (Esmaili 2005). Though interpretations of the Qur'anic passage vary, and there is a wide range of specific practices among Muslims (as seen in the Roman-influenced Turkish public baths that were popular during the Ottoman period), Islamic reformism in its most visible transnational forms is especially concerned with strategies for maintaining purity that are radically different from the German association of purity with exposure of the body to public gaze. In this Islamic discourse, spiritual purity is closely associated with bodily modesty.

This can apply to boys as well as girls, though there is usually less concern with male exposure. Though one motivation of the parents of the eleven-year-old Muslim boy who filed the suit to keep their son out of swimming classes was to avoid his exposure to girls in bathing suits, the parents were also concerned with protecting their son's modesty, as indicated by a quotation from the judges, who dismissed the case: "as on the street, the youngster can close his eyes to the girls . . . or wear long swimming trunks" (*Deutsche Welle* 2005). The latter alternative is clearly addressed to the boy's own physical exposure. The court rejected the parents' request that girls and boys receive separate swimming lessons for "organizational reasons." Judges instead said that separate changing rooms should suffice. The result has been that the operations of governmentality within the schools require Muslim children to be exposed to what they regard as the partial nudity of members of the opposite sex.

Some Muslim groups in Germany have pushed to have the German state make accommodations for the modesty concerns of Muslims, arguing for freedom of religious practice. The Islamic Forum of Hessen, for example, has suggested that, in the absence of separate shower stalls, curtains could be used (Hessischen Islamforum 2005); but these proposals often meet with German public resistance.

Physical privacy has a very different significance within German and Muslim discourses and is linked to an array of different bodily practices. German and reformist Islamic discourses articulate different ideas of what is pure, clean, and healthy. Abjection marking otherness is often associated with a sense of disgust at that which is different. There is evidence in the rhetoric of some Muslims that evocations of disgust are used to mark the otherness of the Christian. As a rather extreme (though not in my experience typical) example, one imam in Germany stated that "Christians are despicable because they stink and do not shave under their arms."[13] Similarly, the requirement of using water to wash after each use of the toilet may be used to mark difference and evoke disgust by labeling those who use only toilet paper as impure.

Given the German emphasis on public nudity and its link with the cultivation of the body and purity, could there be in the structure of the German national imaginary an analogous potential for the evocation of disgust at its opposite—that which is covered or hidden? I suggest that in German discourse, the cliché of the Muslim woman who is "hidden" behind the headscarf and modest clothing and refuses to participate in the hygienic discipline of the gym class can be deployed to evoke disgust associated with that which is hidden and therefore uncontrolled. This evocation adds emotional charge to German reactions to the headscarf and contributes to the abjection of the Muslim in German public discourse.

One strategy for identifying the process of abjection in public discourse is to identify emotional flashpoints to which people return over and over, especially when their arguments don't quite cohere. In this case, Germans seem to be particularly bothered that Muslims are avoiding gym class, but associated with this is a disturbance over the fact that Muslims seek to avoid even the open locker room, that they will not allow themselves to be seen naked. A hint of this dynamic can be seen in Wessel's interview with the covered woman of Turkish background, mentioned earlier. Wessel had asked her what was underneath her headscarf, a question that made the interviewee uncomfortable: "Although she was uncomfortable describing the hair beneath her wrap, she said most women wear a pony tail below the headband, and long hair is much easier to manage than short hair" (Wessel 2006b). This woman resisted Wessel's attempt to expose her metaphorically.

Overt expressions of horror and disgust in public discourse have most readily focused on the honor killing, as discussed in Chapter 5. Nevertheless, the honor killing is associated with the headscarf and that which is hidden. What is the significance of that which is hidden? Looking back to nineteenth-century travel literature (see Chapter 1), the Ottoman harem, hidden to the male traveler, was a site of Orientalist fantasy. The Turkish man was to be simultaneously envied for his access to his hidden women and abjected for his decadent, unmanly lifestyle. These fantasies of the harem—manifest much later in the 1943 box-office hit *Münchhausen*, with its topless harem women, to name one example drawn from popular culture—have not disappeared and are evoked by the very words *Der Harem*. The ambivalence of these fantasies can be seen in the National Socialist rejection of the Oriental veils common among revue dancers at the time as one of the "degenerate" aspects of Weimar culture (Gordon 2002).

The association of horror and disgust with that which is hidden draws on an ideology that was explicit in the past but, to the extent that it is associated with Nazism, is also disavowed.[14] In today's rhetoric about the fate of Turkish women, the female who is controlled by her husband and family is described as a slave. Ironically, the most horrific figure of the conditions of slavery within the concentration camp, those who walked about in a daze on the edge of death, were called *Muslims*, perhaps because when seen from afar, they moved with a stiffness that resembled Muslims praying (Levi 1986; Agamben 1999: 43). The hidden women of today are also imagined as a festering secret, subject to arbitrary murder by their male family members. The girl hidden under a headscarf, her body a secret to public gaze, evokes imagery reflecting this horror.

CONCLUSION

Though many understand the Islamic organization of gender as manifested in the wearing of the headscarf to challenge gender equality as this is expressed in the German Constitution ("Men and women shall have equal rights. The state shall promote the actual implementation of equal rights for women and men and take steps to eliminate disadvantages that now exist." Article 3, paragraph 2), the emphasis on modesty that many Muslims espouse challenges German ideas of the body in ways that have little to do with equal rights. Though the media have focused on the issue of young women requesting exemption from gym and swimming classes, the tensions between German bodily practices, involving the celebration of public nudity, and the requirements of bodily modesty, especially as understood by many reformist Muslims, also play out vis-à-vis young men, some of whom express discomfort about having to deal with the level of bodily exposure that is taken as natural in many German contexts. Many Germans, and the Ministry of the Interior, understand the protests some Muslim parents initiate against a form of governmentality in which their children are forced to be nude or nearly nude in front of others as an effort to create an enclave of those who follow Islamic instead of German law. However, the intensity with which the public, the media, and public officials have criticized the requests of Muslim children for exemptions from gym class is an instance of the effort to discipline the Muslim subject by instilling a peculiarly German national character associated with the cultivation of a body whose purity is demonstrated through public exposure.

The Netherlands has also instituted a Muslim Test that is analogous to that in Germany. Like the German version, it reveals an idiosyncratically Dutch response to the threat of Muslim difference. In the Dutch version, prospective citizens are obliged to sit through and respond to a video that includes images of gay men kissing and topless women on a beach. Why this rather bizarre display of what to many (and not just to the strict Muslim) would seem to belong behind closed doors? The Dutch take national pride in their tolerance, which includes looking the other way when something seems morally questionable. How this principle of tolerance is enacted in everyday life is embodied in a maxim they often tell of themselves: the Dutch are expected to keep their living room blinds open—to demonstrate that they have nothing to hide—but at the same time passersby are expected to avert their gaze. It is as if the prospective citizen is being tested to determine whether he or she can appropriately walk past an open window in the distinctively Dutch way.

In each of these national cases—the German requirement that a child stand nude before others in a locker room, the Dutch enactment of the tolerant covert gaze, or the French way of "doing sex" discussed earlier—specific cultural practices are entangled and confounded with abstract, universalized "democratic values." The consequence is that the defense of these democratic values becomes, ironically, a demand for sameness. When the Muslim is positioned as a threat to these values, then cultural and religious practices that are simply different ways of organizing gender or managing the body are interpreted as a violation of democratic values—and in the German case, as a threat to the Constitution itself. "Protection of the Constitution" and "protection of the Muslim woman" become rhetorical and institutional mechanisms for enforcing German cultural values. The gym class is an arena in which the German state regulates the disciplining and exposure of the citizen's body in a way that the child is not free to resist. The Muslim body, either male or female, challenges and exposes this particular contradiction. Public rhetoric obscures the contradiction by foregrounding the oppression of the Muslim girl whose parents do not permit her to expose her body. The situation of the Muslim boy, who, according to some interpretations of the Qur'an, is also forced to violate the teachings of Islam and expose himself in order to satisfy German notions of national hygiene, is ignored. But the emotional charge of this public rhetoric—what to the rest of the world may appear to be a tempest in a teapot—points to the deeper challenge for German public culture. In a national imaginary in which the nude body is a pure body and its public exposure is viewed as natural, and as a right to be protected, the man who is believed to force his women to cover is therefore depriving her of this right to be pure, natural, and German.

7 GERMANNESS AND THE *LEITKULTUR* CONTROVERSY

Protecting the Constitution from the Muslim Man

MOST MUSLIM MEN in Germany are of Turkish background and belong to families that migrated to Germany from rural Turkey in search of work as guestworkers. The perceived lack of modernity associated with a Turkish village background makes their integration problematic. But in transnational media coverage of Islamic terrorism, Germany is better known for its hidden "cells" of Islamic terrorists who first moved to Germany in the 1990s as students from Arab countries and flew the planes in al-Qaeda's attacks against the United States on September 11, 2001. The discovery of such terrorists on German soil has generated considerable rhetoric about the dangers of the Muslim man and his ever-potential link to the threat of terrorism. Though Arab students associated with al-Qaeda and men of Turkish background who have grown up in Germany are distinct populations, public anxieties about integration and the threat of terrorism have coincided temporally and even, at certain moments, become intertwined. This has been especially true since 2004 and 2005, when bombings in Madrid and London brought terrorism to European soil and governments became concerned about radical imams influencing second- and third-generation Muslim youth in European countries.

While the United States and the governments of many European countries have faced the very real threat of terrorism, they have each framed the threat in rather different ways, even when some of the measures undertaken to enhance national security have been similar and, to some extent, coordinated. In such a situation of crisis, leaders and spokespeople draw on a range of resources—including existing institutions, everyday understandings of social space, and already existing national imaginings—as they search for solutions. Discovering terrorists in their midst has for each government triggered a crisis, generating responses that, though constrained by these conditions of possibility, momentarily transcended political fault lines, allowing the enactment of measures to ensure the public's security against its worst fears. In some cases, these measures would not have been possible without that sense of threat. The dramatic events of September 11 thus evoked reactions that throw into relief some of the social fantasies through which the state is sustained. Within these social fantasies, the foreigner and the Muslim operate as signifiers in culturally specific ways. I focus here on how the conjunction of perceived threats—a large unassimilated Muslim minority and the ever-possible presence of small numbers of individuals planning violence—foregrounds particularities in the discursive processes that constitute a conflicted German national imaginary; these particularities have roots in Germany's specific institutional structure, historical memories, and social fantasies, just as the responses in other countries are peculiar to those countries.

As in other countries, Germany's response to September 11 led to an intensification of already existing national agendas and concerns. Germany's experience of Islamic terrorist cells evoked a conflictual but familiar response: a fear of the enemy within. In contrast to the United States, the German national imaginary does not allow access to the patriotic fervor associated with World War II, except as manifested among a deviant and publicly excoriated minority in the repudiated form of neo-Nazi extremism. In fact, a key response to September 11 provides a collective defensive wall against the National Socialist period in German history. It involves constant vigilance against neo-Nazism and other forms of extremism within the nation-state: "protection of the Constitution" (*Verfassungschutz*).

A year before the September 11 attacks, uneasiness over the growing Turkish Muslim population and intensifying debates over immigration policy and citizenship laws had erupted into the public arena in the form of a controversy over the word *Leitkultur* (leading or guiding culture), which had been deployed by leaders of the conservative CDU as a way of mobilizing political support for their anti-immigration and assimilationist policies. In using this term, a few politicians advocated a policy that would require immigrants to assimilate by adopting the German *Leitkultur*. It was an unfortunate term that, though a neologism, bore uncomfortable echoes of German nationalistic sentiment from an earlier era. Given that the concerns over integration policy focused

primarily on how to manage Germany's Turkish Muslim population, the ensuing controversy juxtaposed Nazi treatment of the Jews and other minorities
and current treatment of Muslims, especially Turks. This connection between
Nazi ideology and *Leitkultur* was made most vigorously by spokespeople from
both Jewish and Muslim groups, who protested the use of the term because of
its dangerous associations with the German ethnic nationalism of the Nazi era,
thereby linking the reunified Germany of the present with the repudiated Germany of the past. This association echoed in the media and everyday conversations in which I participated. It was also evident in online discussion forums
such as leitkultur.de, which was set up shortly after the controversy began and
was very active, with thousands of postings over several months. For example,
a German student wrote that she had been assigned *Leitkultur* as a paper topic
and wanted to know whether the term had been newly invented or had come
from Hitler's time. Another posting was titled "Nie wieder die Deutsche-NAZI
Leitkultur" (Never Again the German-Nazi Leitkultur").[1]

   In this chapter, I examine these two phenomena, the protection of the Constitution and the *Leitkultur* debate. When they are juxtaposed, it is striking how
the noisy storm around the latter—mostly focused on rejecting the term *Leitkultur*—contrasts with and obscures the comparative silence surrounding the
former. Yet since 2001, legislation that has had a significant effect on immigrant
populations has been enacted in the name of the protection of the Constitution. Examining a discourse that encompasses both foregrounds the current
contours of German citizenship and the place of the Muslim immigrant in this
national imaginary.

THE PROTECTION OF THE CONSTITUTION
AND CONSTITUTIONAL PATRIOTISM

The German Constitution stresses the inviolability of human dignity and human rights. It was promulgated for West Germany in 1949 while the Allied powers still occupied Germany in the wake of the defeat of the Nazi regime during
World War II. It was retained with only minor modifications after the reunification of East and West Germany in 1990. The federal Office for the Protection
of the Constitution (Bundesamt für Verfassungsschutz [BfV]), a branch of the
federal Ministry of the Interior (Bundesministerium des Innern), is charged
with ensuring that no group within Germany subverts the principles of the
Constitution. The office's annual report focuses on several "extremist" groups
that have been under surveillance for many years. It is particularly concerned

with right-wing extremist groups and Islamist groups but also includes sections on left-wing extremist groups, extremist foreigners (of which Islamists
currently receive the most attention), foreign espionage, and the Church of Scientology. Protection of the Constitution operates as the idiom of a collective
conscience that is dedicated to monitoring unruly impulses of violence and
undemocratic tendencies in whatever form they may appear.

In Germany the concern with protecting the Constitution is closely linked
to the idea of constitutional patriotism. Though not, of course, unique to Germany, these related concepts play out in particular ways in Germany that have
implications for the position and treatment of minorities, and especially for
the Muslim man in his position as threatening other. Monitoring in the name
of protection has been associated with increasingly coercive force as a result of
legislation since 2001.

The concept of *constitutional patriotism* is closely associated with Jürgen
Habermas. Habermas had been concerned that conservative historians were attempting to normalize German national identity and return to the idea of German national pride in a way that was too close to the repudiated nationalism
of the National Socialist era (Habermas 1986). He countered this conservative
agenda with his articulation of constitutional patriotism, which he proposed as
a universally applicable alternative to nationalism based on any form of primordial attachments, whether racial, ethnic, or cultural. Habermas stressed universal
democratic principles enacted in a public sphere in which free and equal individuals communicate in a reflexive way based on decentered, post-traditional identities. He argued that "unrestrained freedom of communication in the political
public sphere, a democratic process for settling conflicts, and the constitutional
channeling of political power together provide a basis for checking illegitimate
power and ensuring that administrative power is used in the equal interest of all"
(Habermas 1994: 135). Though Habermas stressed the universal applicability of
his concept of constitutional patriotism, it has been pointed out that the concept
nevertheless relies on "supplements of particularity" within each nation-state
that stand in tension with the goal of universality (Markell 2000). In the German case, some of the affective force of constitutional patriotism, according to
Habermas, would come from a collective memory involving a repudiation of the
German Nazi past that would reinforce universalist norms.

The charge of particularity is perhaps even more applicable to the concept
of constitutional patriotism as it was first deployed, not by Habermas, but by
Dorf Sternberger, in 1979 (Sternberger 1979)[2]. Sternberger's usage "focused

primarily on loyalty to the state and, in a very broad fashion, to the rule of law, rather than on specific civil liberties or the social rights which a constitution might also guarantee" (Müller 2006: 284). He emphasized a "militant democracy," which posited opposing "friends" and "enemies" of the constitution, and justified the restriction of civil liberties of those who oppose the constitution. Jan-Werner Müller has juxtaposed Habermas's and Sternberger's rather different premises: one the one hand, Habermas's purification of the public sphere reinforced by collective memory of a fascism transcended and on the other, Sternberger's vigorous defense of democratic institutions. Müller argued that, though relying on "'supplements of particularity,' to become effective forms of political attachment," constitutional patriotism is nevertheless better suited to constraining antidemocratic forces than the alternative of liberal nationalism (Müller 2006: 294). Yet these historically contingent particularities can play out in distinctly nondemocratic or discriminatory ways. Craig Calhoun, for example, has suggested that Habermas's vision of constitutionalism is weakened by a reliance on a negative image of a nationalism based on essentialized primordial identities as the other to be avoided (Calhoun 2002: 151).

The BfV and the broader concern in Germany with defending the nation-state against enemies of the Constitution are concrete enactments of Sternberger's articulation of constitutional patriotism, supplemented by Habermas's concern with remembering the past in order to avoid repeating it. This office enacts a form of governmentality that stresses Sternberger's focus on "ensuring political stability and social cohesion" (Müller 2006: 285). In the self-representations of the BfV, the link between the protection of the Constitution and the renunciation of Nazism is explicit, though indirect:

> The Constitution of the Federal Republic of Germany, known as the Basic Law (*Grundgesetz*, GG), guarantees German citizens a variety of basic rights, including the right to freedom of expression (Article 5), freedom of assembly (Article 8) and freedom of association (Article 9). These rights are extended even to opponents of our state's free democratic fundamental order. But limits to these rights must be clearly set wherever it becomes obvious that they are being misused for undermining the free and democratic order and thereby destroying the foundation on which these same rights are based. Drawing on the painful lessons learnt from the failure of the Weimar Republic, whose Constitution lacked effective mechanisms for its defence, the principle of a strong democracy

prepared to defend its values has been anchored in the Basic Law.

This principle is characterised by three essential features:

—Commitment to values, i.e. the state recognises its attachment to certain values it considers especially important and which are therefore not negotiable;

—the readiness to defend values, i.e. the state is willing to uphold these most important values against extremist positions; and

—preventive action to protect the constitution, i.e. the state does not wait to react until extremists have violated the law. (Federal Ministry of the Interior 2003: 11)

The reference to the "failure of the Weimar Republic" is in regard to the rise of the Nazi state, a looming presence. Here, as in much public discourse, the modern German state is founded on a recurring act of renunciation, in which Germany as a modern democracy is defined in opposition to the repressive Nazi regime. The Nazi as extremist is abjected, as that which is the modern German is not. Judith Butler's articulation of the experience of abjection captures the ordinary German's relationship to Nazism: "I would rather die than do or be that!" (Butler 1993: 243 n. 2).

The emergence of neo-Nazi groups into visibility is like a manifestation of the uncanny, when the discursively abjected, the archaic, "emerges in the midst of margins of modernity as a result of some psychic ambivalence or intellectual uncertainty" (Bhabha 1994: 143). A central purpose of the BfV is to ward off Nazism's uncanny return in the form of neo-Nazi groups, whose views are explicitly located as the antithesis of the Constitution. In its introduction to the section on right-wing extremist groups, the BfV's annual report explicitly links these groups with the National Socialist era:

Right-wing extremist ideology is characterized by nationalist and racist beliefs and attitudes. It is governed by the idea that ethnic affiliation with a nation or race determines the value of a human being. Because, according to right-wing extremist thinking, human and civil rights are subordinate to this criterion, right-wing extremists fundamentally contradict the Basic Law, which accords these rights special priority and protection. . . . They typically call for an authoritarian political system in which the state and the people—in their view an ethnically homogeneous group—join together as a single unit within a supposedly natural order. In this ideology of *Volksgemeinschaft*, a National Socialist term for a community based on shared racial characteristics, the state's leaders intuitively act in accordance with the supposedly uniform will of the people. (Federal Ministry of the Interior 2003: 22)

In the categorization scheme the BfV uses, however, a wide array of extremist groups under surveillance are made in some sense equivalent, appearing as similar headings in the annual report's table of contents. The Islamist is also associated with extremism and placed alongside the neo-Nazi and skinhead as abjected other. Like the neo-Nazi, the Islamist is linked with authoritarianism, violence, and even anti-Semitism.

Though the goals and methods of the BfV are antithetical to those of the Nazi propaganda machinery, its ideological structure, being founded on an act of repudiation, itself reproduces elements of that machinery, though in attenuated form. The office's articulations of a threatening "other within" that has the potential for corroding the fabric of German society because that other is an enemy of the Constitution are ironically reminiscent of the significance of stigmatized others—Jews, gypsies, and foreigners—during the National Socialist era. This theme is reflected in a statement about Islamist groups in the BfV annual report: "These 'legalistic' Islamist groups represent an especial threat to the internal cohesion of our society" (Federal Ministry of the Interior 2005: 189–190). In the paragraph from which this statement is drawn, "legalistic" groups are explicitly distinguished from groups advocating violence, yet they are nevertheless defined as an "especial threat to the internal cohesion" that the Constitution seeks to preserve. Through the interpretive lens of an enactment of constitutional patriotism, that is, the defense of constitutional principles, Turkish Muslim groups have been linked, sometimes implicitly and sometimes explicitly, with the threat of Islamic terror, despite the absence of any connection between the Hamburg terrorist cell and Muslims of Turkish background. Even those explicitly not associated with terror are linked through the same discourse of constitutional patriotism to a threat to the nation-state.

AL-QAEDA AND THE TURKISH MUSLIM COMMUNITY

The Hamburg cell that played a major role in staging the September 11 attacks was composed of young men from various Arab countries who had moved to Germany between 1992 and 1997 to study. Several attended Hamburg's technical university, as well as a local mosque whose imam was Moroccan and primarily served North African and other Arab Muslims (Associated Press 2002). Some, especially outside Germany, identified the group as members of

Hamburg's "Muslim community of about 130,000" (Online Newshour with Jim Lehrer 2002), though these Arab students had few if any ties with local Muslims of Turkish background. One German resident of Turkish background, Murat Kurnaz, was arrested in 2001 while attending a Qur'an school in Pakistan and was held at Guantanamo Bay before being released in 2006. There was no evidence that he had any connection to al-Qaeda. The United States offered to release him to Germany in 2002, but Germany at that time canceled his right of entry and did everything it could to prevent his return (Leyendecker and Goetz 2007), though he did return after his release.

A year after the attacks, there was a major news story in Germany about another Turkish Muslim, Osman Pekmezci, who was allegedly plotting to attack a U.S. military base near Heidelberg on the anniversary of September 11. The discovery of explosives in his apartment was the first time that someone of Turkish background could be definitely linked to a planned terrorist attack. But it was quickly established that, though he had a picture of Osama bin Laden on his wall, he and his German-American girlfriend were operating independently of any terrorist network and were not even associated with any Turkish-Islamic group. Nevertheless, the German right used this incident to push for the loosening of human rights safeguards. Responding to this event, Edmund Stoiber, the conservative challenger to Chancellor Gerhard Schröder, told his supporters at a political rally that "suspicion of belonging to an illegal organisation should be enough to justify the expulsion of foreigners from the country: 'We absolutely cannot wait until something has happened'" (Hooper 2002). Aside from these isolated events, however, there was a remarkable dearth of concrete news concerning links between any of the major Turkish-Islamic organizations in Germany and al-Qaeda.

German policy responses to September 11 included a generalized and intensified surveillance of all Muslim groups. Through strained associations, the Islamic terrorist and the Turkish immigrant were linked in German public discourse. The result has been increased discrimination against Muslims, not just by the public,[3] but also by the government, manifest in specific policy decisions such as the Muslim Test (see Chapter 6) and legislation that facilitated the deportation of suspected terrorists.

Despite the lack of involvement of those of Turkish background, policies emerged over the next several years, beginning with antiterrorism laws passed soon after September 11 and including the immigration law of 2005, which made it easier to expel "foreigners," including those of Turkish background born and raised in Germany, with little more grounds than suspicion of endangering constitutional democratic structures. In this context, concern about Muslim youth of Turkish background in Germany being influenced by Arab imams proselytizing in local mosques has been increasing. Such naturalized assumptions about the linkages among all Muslims regardless of their differences shape some of the contours of a discourse that constitutes Germany as a part of Europe, and Muslims who have come to Germany as "in" but not "of" Judeo-Christian Europe, as those whose home is not Europe (Asad 2003: 166).

The tightening of antiterrorism laws in the wake of September 11 was used to put pressure on Turkish-Islamic groups about which the Ministry of the Interior had been concerned for many years. Two security packages were passed quickly in the wake of September 11. The first package, which had already been drafted before September 11, eliminated a special provision of the Constitution that had prevented the federal government from banning religious organizations. A ban could now be imposed on any "extremist organization" found to be involved in unconstitutional acts or having dangerous foreign ties. The second package focused on more detailed implementation of security measures. As part of the second security package, an antiterrorism law that expanded the powers of the security agencies, including the BfV, went into effect on January 1, 2002. The controversial Immigration Act that went into effect in January 2005 further tightened security by allowing officials for the first time to deport people if they had evidence to support fears that the suspects might commit a terrorist act in the future (Deggerich and Stark 2005). This led state interior ministers and others responsible for security to construct deportation lists of people who they felt had been troublesome for years. After the implementation of the 2005 immigration law, it became possible to deport people on the authority of a panel within the Federal Administrative Court with no further appeal (Fekete 2005). *Der Spiegel* reported that officials were drawing up lists of hundreds of people to be deported.[4]

The fear of Islamic terrorists is not new in Germany: there has been intensive surveillance of this potential threat for many years. The German gaze, however, has been directed, not primarily at the Arab Muslims who have come to Germany to study or at others with explicit ties to al-Qaeda, but at the much larger Turkish-Islamic groups that have drawn their membership from those who originally moved to Germany as guestworkers and their families. As Walter Wellinghausen, state secretary of Hamburg, one of the city's top officials, said in 2002 of the discovery of the Hamburg cell of al-Qaeda: "It was quite a surprise because when you look in the files today, you don't find even a letter about this situation in Hamburg. Our security officers, our police, our intelligence service, didn't have any information about this group in Hamburg" (Online Newshour with Jim Lehrer 2002). In contrast, two Turkish-Islamic groups had been under surveillance for years. The larger of these is IGMG, but the one perceived as most threatening is the Union of Islamic Communities and Societies (ICCB), widely known as Kaplan's group after its founder, Metin Kaplan. This group had split from IGMG in 1983 (see Schiffauer 2000) and had been connected with violence in the past. Kaplan's group was officially declared illegal and disbanded in December 2001, the first time German authorities used the tougher antiterror laws that had been approved after the September 11 attacks. According to an Associated Press report, "No connection has been established between Kaplan's group and the September 11 attacks. But German investigators have said that some members traveled to Afghanistan to meet with supporters of alleged mastermind Osama bin Laden in 1996 or 1997" (Associated Press 2004).[5] The explicit justification for the disbanding of Kaplan's group was an unrelated incident in Turkey that had occurred in 1998.[6] With the tighter antiterrorist laws, Germany's Ministry of the Interior took a retrospective look at this incident to justify the ban. Intense pressure was also put on the much larger IGMG, but this organization, with its sophisticated legal apparatus and lack of any identifiable ties with al-Qaeda or any acts of violence, managed to avoid the fate of Kaplan's group.

Before 2000, Kaplan's group, also called the Caliphate State, and IGMG were the two leading groups under the category of "extremist foreigners" in BfV annual reports, listed under the subheading "Turkish Islamists." IGMG was given detailed treatment, though the specific wording of the report hardly varied from year to year. Al-Qaeda received less than one line in a passing mention. After the September 11 attacks, however, al-Qaeda and other Arab-based groups were the first listed under the category of "extremist foreigners" and received the most pages of coverage.

The ongoing surveillance of these two Turkish-Islamic organizations by the Ministry of the Interior and the BfV had for many years positioned these organizations as already dangerous in the public imaginary, with very real consequences for the organizations themselves. The circularity of these effects is particularly striking for IGMG because during all the years of surveillance, no evidence of IGMG's involvement in violence has ever been discerned. (By the 2005 BfV annual report, IGMG had been labeled one of the "legalistic" Islamic groups that does not advocate violence.) Despite this, the very act of surveillance and the inclusion of IGMG in BfV reports created real and powerful associations between the group and other extremist organizations, associations that resonate with the German public.

In contrast to the sections in BfV reports on skinheads and other neo-Nazis, for which tallies of specific acts of violence are maintained and published, the section on IGMG contained only the vague warning that it is dangerous to expose youths to Islamist propaganda. These reports have portrayed IGMG as an organization tainted by connections with the Turkish-Islamist political party, the Refah (Welfare) Party, which was represented as having as its basic goal the overthrow of the Turkish government and the implementation of Islamic law.[7] IGMG has also been and continues to be represented as seeking to replace German law with Islamic law for Muslims living in Germany, a goal that German officials argue threatens the security of the constitutional order. German rhetoric surrounding IGMG identifies it as a powerful transnational organization with ties to the revolution in Iran and the Taliban in Afghanistan. In BfV annual reports before 2000, IGMG was also condemned as anti-Semitic because of comments of an IGMG leader criticizing Israel twenty years earlier—an accusation that marks the current German government apparatus as vigilantly protective of Jews.[8] This emphasis on IGMG's anti-Semitism was a standard view of the organization among Germans with whom I talked about the organization.

The language describing IGMG, which had been repeated from year to year and intimated that the organization had hidden links to violence, finally changed in 2000, at least in part because IGMG leaders held meetings with the minister of the interior and used their legal staff to pressure the office to drop references to anti-Semitism and the advocacy of violence.[9] Reports continued, however, to stress a contrast between openly declared goals that were consistent with the democratic principles of the Constitution and a hidden agenda:

> As for the organisation's declared aims, there is an apparent discrepancy between what is proclaimed in public and what members are told. In public the IGMG presents itself as willing to integrate and as promoting dialogue between cultures. . . . Internal statements by IGMG functionaries, however, reveal that integration and communication between "societies and cultures" is not seen as a process of understanding in order to establish a new unified society including both Muslims and non-Muslims. Rather, this is to be restricted, if at all possible,

to a majority and a minority living side by side and equal before the law. Therefore, the IGMG condemns the federal government's integration policy as a policy of assimilation. It also always emphasises the value of the cultural identity of Turkish Muslims. (Federal Ministry of the Interior 2003: 194).

The fear of Islamists, embodied in IGMG mostly because of its size as the largest such organization in Germany, rests on vague images such as the idea that Islamist extremists are operating behind a screen of rhetoric about multiculturalism, human rights, and constitutionality while they amass a following and resources that will allow them to control government decision-making.

The focus on the Islamically oriented Muslim, as represented by IGMG, as a fundamental threat to the German national body is reinforced by the power of this discursive structure and its symbolic displacements. But the parallels with the threat of a Jewish other in the past, which are evoked in a somewhat different way in the *Leitkultur* controversy, are generally misrecognized, especially when the vague, unfounded threat of groups such as IGMG can be attached to the more tangible threat of the Islamic terrorist. As a result, efforts to ban Islamic groups are relatively uncontroversial. By the same token, fears of visibly Muslim men are legitimized and go unexamined. Furthermore, the sense of threat and fear of the Islamist man that is presumed to lurk behind the even more visibly Muslim woman in her headscarf is legitimized in the name of constitutional patriotism.

THE *LEITKULTUR* CONTROVERSY

Though constitutional patriotism has been promoted as the basis for a renewed German national identity and the principles of the Constitution have been a powerful idiom for legitimizing the exclusion of Muslims, the embodiment of Germanness as a cultural practice continues to be an important, if ambivalent, aspect of national identity. The issue of assimilating immigrants, especially practicing Muslims and "traditional Turks," has triggered some of the most explicit debates about the concept of Germanness in recent years. In these often fierce debates, played out in political contests, the media, and Internet sites, very few have dared to give Germanness any specific content, beyond the principles of democracy and human rights as articulated in the Constitution, the idea of multiculturalism, and the expectation that immigrants learn the German language. Others have denounced the very idea of asserting Germanness as an identity because of its associations with Germany's traumatic past.

In 2000, there was a firestorm of controversy in reaction to efforts by the conservative CDU to introduce the concept of *Leitkultur* as a guiding principle for immigrant integration. On October 18, 2000, Friedrich Merz, the leader of the CDU/CSU (the Bavarian sister party of the CDU) parliamentary group in the Bundestag, proposed in a newspaper interview that "immigrants who [want] to live here permanently must adapt to an evolved German *Leitkultur*" (RP Online 2000). He introduced the term *Leitkultur* to characterize German culture (Mrozek 2000). Merz suggested that the CDU might decide to make immigration law an issue in the 2002 elections[10] and that a policy should be developed that required immigrants to adopt the language and the "*Leitkultur von Deutschland.*" Controversy erupted over his use of this word and raged for months. The uproar and angst surrounding the concept (a Google search on the word *Leitkultur* produced 441,000 hits in July 2007) far transcended any specifics of Merz's policy recommendations, which, when put in other terms, many Germans did not object to. These recommendations were articulated in a CDU position paper on November 6, 2000, and consisted of learning the German language, professing loyalty to the German nation, and accepting Germany's legal and political institutions (Spiegel Online 2000).[11] These recommendations were subsequently implemented in the 2005 immigration law,[12] which also retained the 1973 ban on the recruitment of foreign workers. But, as became clear in the reactions that began immediately after Merz used the term *Leitkultur* and that echoed for at least a year, the term resonated with a German past from which most Germans seek to distance themselves. Though Merz's remarks were targeted at Germany's large Turkish Muslim population, they stirred up fears of a relegitimation of Nazi rhetoric that upset other minorities as well, especially Germany's Jewish population, most of whom would have been unaffected by the CDU's specific policy recommendations. In this controversy the contours of what is normally left unspoken were starkly revealed.

Depending on one's political agenda and perspective, *Leitkultur* has been variously translated into English as "leading," "guiding," "defining," "model," "hegemonic," or "dominant" culture. Like many words that appear in German speech and writing, *Leitkultur* does not appear in basic German dictionaries but is a compound created for the occasion from the noun *Kultur* (culture) and the rarely productive prefix *leit-*. *Leit-* is defined in the following way: "Used to express [the idea] that someone or something orients itself to the named person or thing" (*Langenscheidts Grosswörterbuch Deutsch als Fremdsprache* 1998: 620), as in the words *Leitspruch* (motto), *Leitbild* (model), and *Leitmotiv* (central melody or theme in a musical composition). The related verb *leiten* means to lead or direct, according to German-English dictionaries, and the noun *Leiter* is defined as leader, manager, director, or conductor.

In the history of German thought, the concept of *Kultur* is closely tied to Romanticism and the elaboration of the idea of a national culture. It has its roots in the thought of the eighteenth-century philosopher Johann Gottfried von Herder, who developed a pluralistic notion of cultures: "The best culture of a people cannot be expressed through a foreign language; it thrives on the soil of a nation most beautifully, and, I may say, it thrives only by means of the nation's inherited and inheritable dialect" (Herder 1784). The association of culture with German nationalism can be discerned in Herder: "If Germany were only guided by the forces of the age, by the leading strings of her own culture, our intellectual disposition would doubtless be poor and restricted; but it would be true to our own soil, fashioned upon its own model, and not so misshapen and cast down" (Herder 1784). Though links can be made between Herder's concept of culture and the eventual emergence of the idea of the German *Volk* (ethnic people) that was so chauvinistically developed in Nazi propaganda, Herder's approach also underlay the very different emergence of interpretive cultural anthropology.[13] It is precisely this ambiguity of the concept of culture that resonated in the debates surrounding the idea of *Leitkultur*.

In the face of the controversy surrounding his use of the word *Leitkultur*, Merz sought to justify it by arguing that what he called the "liberal German *Leitkultur*" encompasses the rules necessary for living together in Germany, namely, the constitutional tradition, meaning the norms and values of the German Constitution (Merz 2000). Merz was also quoted in a newspaper interview as saying, "We should expect people who want to live here for a long time to be able to speak German and accept our constitution's norms and values" (Finn 2000). Merz thereby appealed to constitutional patriotism and linked it to the idea of culture. The term continued to generate an intense flurry of debate for several months, even though Merz and the CDU dropped it from their vocabularies within three weeks.[14]

During the same round of national debates, the general secretary of the CDU, Laurenz Meyer, asserted that he was proud to be German: "Ich bin stolz, Deutscher zu sein." This created a similar uproar (Finn 2000), in which the two concepts *Deutsch* and *Leitkultur* were often linked, as in the newspaper article "Was ist Deutsch?" (What Is German?) That is the question which runs through the debate on immigration—in which the words "German *Leitkultur*" are especially explosive" (Fuhr 2000). Deployment of the concept *Leitkultur* and direct confrontation with the issue of immigration had reactivated the nagging and recurring question of what can legitimately be the foundation of German identity. And an answer to this question hinges on the seemingly unresolvable problem of "how to transcend [the past] without forgetting it" (Finn 2000), a concern that Habermas and other German intellectuals had expressed.

Ironically, the term was apparently coined by the Muslim scholar Bassam Tibi, a well-known professor of political science who taught at Göttingen University in Germany before moving to Cornell University in the United States. He has written extensively on Islam in the modern world, taking a position that diasporic Muslims should integrate into European societies and emphatically distinguishing Islam from politicized Islamic fundamentalism. In his book *Europa ohne Identität?*, Tibi suggested that for multiculturalism to work in Europe, the approach for people of diverse cultures to live together peacefully should not be ethnic, but rather the binding force of a guiding culture [*Leitkultur*] based on cultural modernity (Tibi 1998: 182). Tibi grounded his concept of the nation in the idea of European *Leitkultur*, contrasting this with the prevailing dichotomous choice of ethnic romanticism or a "false self-denial." Its characteristics would include individual (rather than group) rights, separation of religion and politics, and secular tolerance—the substance of a civil society (Tibi 1998: 183). It is for him "a state operating under the rule of law with a western-secular idea of order not based on ethnic nationality as the Germans understand it. A democratic nation state, civil society and secular democracy are parts of a lawful state, which always has a *Leitkultur*, in which Western values are realized" (Tibi 1998). For Tibi, this *Leitkultur* is not specifically German, but European, and he envisions the continent as a civilized whole that could have overcome all forms of Euro-arrogance as well as the ethnic exclusiveness of Euro-racism (Tibi 1998). Islam, too, he argued, is compatible with democracy and European *Leitkultur* because it is also based on tolerance, compassion, and a respect for human rights.

In the mouths of CDU leaders, the word *Leitkultur*, linked explicitly as it was with the concept of German identity in the phrase "German *Leitkultur*," resonated with a significance rather different from the concept Tibi articulated, despite the fact that the CDU's November 6 position paper opened with a statement that seemed to echo Tibi's emphasis on European culture: "We Germans have developed our national identity and culture on the foundation of European civilization in the course of history, which finds expression in our

language and in arts, in our morals and customs, and in our understanding of
law and democracy, of freedom and civic duty." (Manz 2004: 494).[15]

In the weeks preceding Merz's speech and his introduction of the concept
of *Leitkultur* into German political discourse in 2000, a series of attacks against
Jewish sites had occurred, including a firebombing of the synagogue in Düs-
seldorf on the eve of the tenth anniversary of German reunification (Dietrich
2000b). The reunification itself had been an historic event that forced Germans
to rethink prior understandings of what it means to be German that had developed in quite different ways after World War II in West and East Germany.
On November 9, a demonstration against such extremist attacks, called "We
Stand Up for Humanity and Tolerance," was staged in Berlin and drew a crowd
of two hundred thousand. At the demonstration, Paul Spiegel, president of the
Central Council of Jews in Germany, asked the crowd, "What's all this talk of
Leitkultur? Does German Leitkultur include hunting down foreigners, burning
synagogues and killing the homeless?" (Mrozek 2000). Spiegel thus explicitly
linked *Leitkultur* with both anti-Semitism and anti-immigrant sentiments in
language that recalled Nazi violence.

The Turkish community, at which the concept had been directly targeted,
also responded strongly. Members of IGMG expressed considerable distress in
their monthly magazine (a Turkish-language magazine published in Germany)
over the reintroduction of this concept into political discourse. They drew immediate connections with Nazi ideology.

I suggest that *Leitkultur* is a phantasmic image, embodying a movement
of loss and failed or blocked recovery. In public debates and forums, efforts to
restore a lost Germanness by infusing it with specific content were vigorously
repudiated because of their association with Nazism, though some blame the
loss of cultural content on the overwhelming cultural influence of the United
States. *Leitkultur* is an uncanny signifier that links images of the Jew with the
repudiation of the Holocaust, while at the same time allusively evoking these
images and linking them with the Turkish Muslim as the other within the national body.

REPUDIATED IDENTITY AND HISTORICAL MEMORY

The *Leitkultur* debate exposed public uneasiness about claiming an identity
as German. Manifesting this uneasiness about German identity, many cosmopolitan youth in Berlin, whether of German, Turkish, or other ethnicity, explicitly refuse to claim an identity as German, asserting instead, "Ich bin Berliner

[I am a Berliner]." There is a collective ambivalence surrounding the idea of a national identity. This uneasiness has roots in the approach to rebuilding West Germany that was adopted after World War II, in which the Allied powers sought to break Germany's ties to its Nazi past, leading to a repudiation of Germanness. In the heat of the *Leitkultur* debate, reporter Stefan Dietrich complained that the "rejection of German history started with the darkest chapter of all, namely the Nazi dictatorship, and extended not just years, but centuries into the past. Everything from the Reformation and the medieval migration of Germans to the east has since come to be interpreted as a mere preliminary to the historical cataclysm of the Third Reich" (Dietrich 2000a).

For Germans in the post–World War II period, liberalism represented a radical change from the attitudes and policies that had given rise to the horrors of the Nazi era. The Western powers worked with new German leaders after the war to ensure that liberalism, with its emphases on a freely elected government grounded on a constitution, civil liberties for citizens, and a legal system based on rational adjudication, would be firmly institutionalized in Germany. These principles were to take the place of a nationalism founded on the principles of racial and cultural superiority that had given rise to the Holocaust. Even today in Germany liberalism always stands in sharp, if often implicit, contrast with Nazism as its repudiated but ever-potential opposite, which must be suppressed whenever it erupts—a contrast manifested even in forms of governmentality such as the BfV.

A number of scholars over recent decades have pointed out this uneasiness surrounding German identity and the failure of Germany to "work through" its past, manifest in phenomena such as gaps in public discourse and collective memory that mask unrecognized continuities between prewar and postwar Germany. In the 1950s and 1960s, philosopher Theodor Adorno argued that the collective, narcissistic identifications with German nationalism and Hitler were not destroyed with the collapse of the Nazi state but continued to exist as a powerful, because secret, collective force in the postwar period. He was particularly critical of the postwar "economic miracle" because of what he saw as its fascistic tendencies (Adorno 1986).

The tension between a sense of discontinuity generated through an erasure that celebrates German democratic processes and unrecognized continuities can be seen in contexts that are directly significant for today's immigrants in Germany. The economic miracle was based on the ready availability of labor. Ulrich Herbert and Karin Hunn (2001) have drawn parallels between the extensive use of forced labor brought into Germany from other countries during the National Socialist period and the hiring of foreign guestworkers beginning in 1961. The failure of Germans to recognize any parallel can be partly explained by the fact that the need for foreign labor was masked between 1945 and 1961 by the flood, stopped abruptly by the erection of the Berlin Wall in 1961, of "ethnic Germans" from East Germany and other parts of Eastern Europe. Herbert and Hunn note that "there was no recognition in West Germany that the deployment of foreign slave laborers under the Third Reich was among the specific crimes perpetrated by the National Socialists" (Herbert and Hunn 2001: 188). Despite the silence, there were implicit continuities, such as the fact that foreign workers were designated by the same term, *Fremdarbeiter* (foreign worker), that had been used during the Third Reich. Only in the 1960s was the term replaced by *Gastarbeiter* (guestworker) (Herbert and Hunn 2001: 191). Liberals and conservatives alike failed to recognize such discriminatory practices in their constitutionally based democratic social order, despite its ideological emphasis on equal rights.

This arrival of large numbers of foreign guestworkers in the 1960s and 1970s did not challenge the foundation of German identity based on German descent, coupled with Christian values. The granting of legal citizenship solely on the basis of blood did not change until the beginning of 2000. Until late in 2000, conservative politicians also maintained the position that Germany is not a country of immigration, shifting their position only with the beginning of the *Leitkultur* debate.

Adorno argued in 1959 that during the postwar period, "coming to terms with the past" meant wiping it from memory (Adorno 1986: 115). Like other scholars, he used a psychoanalytic framework to analyze this disavowal process, identifying several discursive strategies that reinforced this erasure of memory: a lack of affect in the face of serious matters; the use of euphemisms, such as *Kristallnacht* to refer to the pogrom of 1938 (Adorno 1986: 116); and, above all, the "atrophy of the consciousness of historical continuity in Germany, a symptom of [the] social weakening of personal autonomy" (Adorno 1986: 117), which he and Horkheimer and others of the Frankfurt School investigated empirically in terms of the loss of history among the younger generation.

Alexander and Margerete Mitscherlich (1975) subsequently argued that German efforts to reconstitute a national identity involved a disavowal of the Nazi past without a sustained emotional confrontation, producing a rupture with the past and a focus instead on German efficiency and ability to create a postwar economic miracle. Drawing on this psychoanalytically oriented work, E. L. Santner argued that since World War II, Germany has struggled with what he has called "the poisoned legacy" of Nazism as the country has sought to articulate a German national identity. Santner asked, "How is it possible to speak of German culture, tradition or *Heimat* [homeland] after Hitler?" (Santner 1990: 29). Through the analysis of Edgar Reitz's sixteen-hour television epic *Heimat* (Reitz 1984), which was broadcast on German television in 1984 and depicts the transformation of a village through the twentieth century, Santner demonstrated a collective amnesia in which the filmmaker participates, bestowing his characters with a peculiar lack of curiosity about the fate of the Jews during the National Socialist period.

Anthropologist Marilyn Ivy developed a similar argument about the nature of collective fantasy and memory and the consequences of a failure of collective mourning in post–World War II Japan. She depicted ethnographically the problem of how echoes of a collectively traumatic past manifest themselves and how fragments of tradition such as peasant practices and folklore become phantasms, powerful objects of fantasy that embody Japaneseness through displacement and deferral. Such objects are, in a double movement, simultaneously inscribed as superfluous (since they have been marginalized by the advent of modernity, on which Japaneseness as national identity is founded) and as essential (since they are the "traditions" that give Japaneseness its essential uniqueness) (Ivy 1995: 25). "Traditions" thus emerge as the background against which progressive history can be situated (Ivy 1995: 5). Ivy argues that such phantasms create rigidities and blind spots in popular imaginings, especially in relation to the management of foreigners in Japan.

In Germany, public gestures toward Judaism reinforce the rupture of the country from its past in a manner analogous to the Japanese traditions Ivy describes. Most salient have been efforts to memorialize victims of the Holocaust and to protect the vestiges of Jewish life in Germany. Given the fact that only a remnant of Germany's Jewish population remains, their presence has been reduced to a symbol, a marker of absence.[16] While these gestures—which extend to monuments for victims of the Holocaust such as the Jewish Museum in Berlin and state vigilance in protecting remaining synagogues—may serve as rituals of atonement to ease the guilt associated with being German in the wake of the Holocaust, they also obscure vestiges of German racism that have been disavowed. These public retrospectives are an important acknowledgment of responsibility for the Holocaust and an apology to the global community of Jews, but they also serve to reinforce the reinvention of Germany as a tolerant liberal democracy and are symptomatic of the gulf that discursively separates Germans from their past, resulting in a constricted national imaginary and unacknowledged continuities in German understandings of ethnicity, race, and religion.

Writing in 1955, just a decade after the establishment of the German Federal Republic, Adorno was more concerned with the continued implicit existence of National Socialism within democracy than with the overt fascist orientation of neo-Nazi groups against democracy (Adorno 1986: 155). More recently, Peter O'Brien has argued that the liberal principles that the Allies promulgated after World War II, embodied in a public that is predominantly liberal in attitude and in the Constitution and current laws, do in fact hold sway in Germany, but that such liberalism is itself responsible for many of the difficulties that immigrants face because it is aggressively assimilationist (O'Brien 1996: 9). He thus disrupts a dichotomy, which pervades German public discourse, that assumes that liberalism is the polar opposite of fascism. Constitutional patriotism, when it focuses on protecting the Constitution from its enemies, can be manifest in illiberal policies and implemented through practices of governmentality that reproduce elements of earlier top-down approaches to social order (Müller 2006: 284).

Looking at the practical implications of a liberal agenda for policy and the management of cultural difference with respect to immigrants in Germany, O'Brien traces the commitment in the 1970s to a liberal immigrant policy:

> The cornerstone of this reformed policy was integration, which ultimately aimed at the realization of fully equal rights and opportunities for migrants in social, economic, legal, and political matters. The program moved West Germany further in the direction of a multicultural society based on liberal rather than nationalist principles and therefore strengthened the Germans' image of themselves as a modern, tolerant, democratic people.
>
> But the reformers did not stop there. They detected in the migrants the same ailment that had once afflicted the Germans: pathological fear of rapid, inevitable change. With the new-found zeal and self-confidence of a recovering alcoholic who, once cured, pledges to save other drunks, Social Democrats structured integration so as to resocialize migrants to the enlightened values of the modern liberal democratic society in which they now lived. The campaign was locally analogous to and profoundly informed by the Germans' own experience of having been integrated into the Western community after the

war. Only now, the Germans were the liberalizers, the migrants the ones to be liberalized. And this helped further to convince leaders that they had made an irreversible conversion to Western liberalism. (O'Brien 1996: 44)

The Turkish Muslim man is closely associated in German public discourse with an ever-present concern with protecting the principles of liberal democracy. The unassimilated Muslim man embodies a threat that is immediately articulated as a threat to the Constitution itself. The Ministry of the Interior and public discourse manifest a hypervigilance surrounding the perception of threat and the need for its active protection.[17]

CONCLUSION

The theme of protecting the German Constitution resonates with calls for constitutional patriotism as the foundation of sociopolitical order. Sternberger and Habermas proposed this concept as a way of imagining social solidarity that escapes recourse to inherited identities with their potential for ethnic violence. However, the use of the theme of protecting the Constitution against the threatening Muslim in German rhetoric demonstrates in practice the limitations of a Habermasian notion of constitutional patriotism. This form of patriotism is not simply based on rational universalism, but rather on a reliance on a negative image of a nationalism based on an essentialized primordial identity as the other to be avoided. Far from weakening constitutional patriotism, this negative sense of the threatening other can be a powerful basis for community and for national fantasy. The Enlightenment language of democracy, citizenship, and respect for difference is taken up into a discursive structure that bends these terms into a nationalistic language of concern for the body politic and the need to protect it from the corrosive forces of a threatening internal other who does not share the essence of a democratic "culture." The Muslim Turk, especially the man who clings to traditional culture with an honor code based on violence and the oppression of women, has become this threatening, abjected other.

Continuities in German experience, especially implicit culturally and historically constituted attitudes and, above all, distinctively German forms of intolerance (as opposed to French, British, U.S., or other nationally distinctive forms of intolerance), go unrecognized because they cannot be linked in public discourse with the intolerances of the past. In the German national imaginary, it is the "enemy within" that constitutes the core threat to the German nation. Historically, the threat of this alien presence took the shape of the Jewish community, which had been fully integrated into German society yet refused to shed its cultural and religious difference. The Arab students who formed terrorist cells and ultimately carried out horrific acts of violence are quite a different phenomenon. They are recent, temporary immigrants who went unnoticed by the authorities charged with protecting the country. Turkish Muslims, in contrast, have been under surveillance by the Ministry of the Interior for years, in the name of protecting the Constitution. It is the Turkish Muslim man who is targeted as a dangerous object, as the other who threatens freedom, democracy, and the Constitution.

The result is that German officials and the public fail to recognize these forms of intolerance, leading to a blindness to complaints of discrimination and unequal treatment, especially in the treatment of Turkish Muslim men. This blindness takes the specific form of the defense of democratic principles in the face of cultural traditionalism, Islamism, or both.

The elusive and conflicted nature of Germanness as an object of national desire was manifested in the *Leitkultur* controversy. Given the word's association with Nazi ideology, it was simply not possible for politicians to give the term any content beyond the practical need to learn the German language and abstract, universalized concepts of freedom, democracy, and equality, which are operationalized as a demand for acceptance of the German Constitution. Yet as an empty signifier, the term evoked an ambivalent patriotism that cannot otherwise be articulated.

The forces of multiculturalism and human rights discourse have displaced the overtly racist principle of Germanness based on blood, resulting in a change in the citizenship laws, finally enabling Turks born in Germany to be German citizens. The circle of who can be included as "us" in German national discourse is slowly extending to include not only Jews but even assimilated Turks. But the phantasmic, abjected other remains as the ground on which Germanness rests. This other is the unassimilated Muslim Turk. This Muslim—whether viewed as traditional villager or Islamist—is seen to have no respect for democratic institutions or religious freedom, no sense of civil society founded on the idea that choice of religion is a private affair, no concept of the individual, and no loyalty to the German Constitution, which has become the object that, according to this discourse, Germans must protect at all costs if Germany is to remain intact.

EPILOGUE

IN BERLIN a murder becomes a focus of escalating media coverage, but only after a local high school principal sends a letter to teachers across Germany calling the nation's attention to the comments of a few Turkish schoolboys, who had said that the victim deserved to die for dishonoring her family. The victim, Hatun Sürücü, is the symbolic focus of media coverage, but the real debate concerns the significance of the boys' utterances: are they perpetuating a culture in which women are forced to submit to male violence in the name of honor, or are these boys expressing frustration at their position in German society?

Two years later at Rütli School, also in Berlin, the teachers write a letter to call media attention to the fact that their school is disintegrating into violence and the teachers are at a loss about what to do. The media descend on the school, and graphic images of student violence are splashed across television screens. A reporter, barred from Rütli, asks a crowd of teenage boys gathered behind a fence at another school: "How integrated do you feel in Germany?" The students, all male and probably Turkish, laugh and shout replies; one pulls out a large knife and briefly holds it at another student's throat.[1] Debates rage over what is to blame for what a former principal of Rütli called the "horror school" (*Bild* 2007): is it the social conditions that these immigrants find themselves in? or their cultural background? Media coverage intensifies when it is learned that a reporter paid students to create a riot for the camera.

The media had been caught in the act of stimulating a moral panic. The media play a central role shaping popular imagination. Newspaper stories and TV images resonate with desires and fears that shape the possibilities for being and becoming a national subject, a German. Though the significance of these images is contested, often bitterly, the contestations themselves are structured in familiar ways. It is the contours of these contestations—the recurring terms of debate—that characterize a national imaginary.

This national imaginary comes into public view under the spotlight of national debates that obscure some points through the intense focus on others. This play of highlight and shadow marks a national imaginary's distinctiveness. The most visible controversies surrounding Turks in Germany and the failure of integration concern the oppression of Muslim women—whether it be expressed as the presence of headscarves in a school or gym class, the "rising incidence" of honor killings, or the problem of "forced" marriage. On these topics, moral outrage against a set of cultural practices can be articulated without ambivalence. Modern German society, founded on constitutional principles such as gender equality and the free autonomous subject, must be defended against the incursions of an alternative way of life that threatens those principles.

For more than a century, the covered Muslim woman has been a symbol of cultural difference. The need to "save" Muslim women has been a marker of the superiority of Western civilization that has served a series of political and social ends, obscuring the ethical questionability of policies ranging from Western colonial expansion to the war against the Taliban. This recurring pattern in many Western countries suggests that in Germany, too, the spotlight on the covered woman obscures other, more ambivalently charged issues.

What is obscured may sometimes become visible with a shift of focus. In this book I have turned attention away from the Muslim woman to the source of her oppression: the Muslim man, and specifically, the Turkish Muslim man. This shift allows important ambivalences and contradictions surrounding German national identity and the basis for cultural citizenship in Germany to emerge from the shadows. The obvious plight of the Muslim woman allows unselfconscious stigmatization of the traditional Muslim man and his cultural practices, while calling no attention to problematic elements of mainstream German culture itself. In other contexts, however, German culture is surrounded by ambivalence. Many Germans experience considerable difficulty in directly asserting a German identity or positively asserting German cultural traits (Borneman 1991). The stigmatization of the Turkish Muslim man opens a space in the German national imaginary for a positive cultural identity as German that nevertheless remains implicit. This is the process of abjection. Yet the violence associated with the defense of honor is also an object of fantasy and desire; the

Ottoman warrior with his harem is reminiscent of the German romantic hero, each the echo of a lost masculinity that has no place in the modern world of middle-class citizens who shape public discourse.

The young man we see on camera holding a knife to the throat of his classmate is not clinging to tradition by acting out age-old patterns of honor and violence. Nor is he simply protesting his poor school and the lack of opportunities he is confronted with. Rather, he is reacting to the camera. In this case, he is enacting a script provided (and paid for) by the media, playing the part of the abjected other. The viewer sees fantasies of disintegration and "horror" enacted before the camera, while boys like these devise tactics to distance themselves from this abjection.

Before the evolution of gender studies to include masculinity, "man" was the unmarked category. To talk about the practices of men was to talk about a society and vice versa. It is still difficult to focus on men as men. The problem of school violence at Rütli School, for example, is primarily a problem with young men at the school. The television report described above included only boys. But, in contrast to explanations for problems associated with Muslim women, the explanations for violence at minority schools like Rütli do not focus exclusively on culturally specific practices of masculinity or even on the boys' identities as men, but on their position as socially disadvantaged minorities and their lack of interest in learning. The Turkish Muslim schoolboy rarely stands in explicit contrast to the German schoolboy. Rather, students at the lowest tier of the educational system, who often fail to qualify for apprenticeships when they graduate, are contrasted with more successful, less violent students at better schools. They are abjected, in part for their class position as social failures and in part for their culture, the macho violence they perform before the camera. They are a visible sign of an uncontrollable chaos in the heart of German cities. But it is easier to talk about this troublesome masculinity and label it as culturally other when it is imagined in the hidden oppression of their women. In this context, it is not necessary to draw explicit contrasts with German masculinity and thus to articulate cultural characteristics associated with Germanness.

The ambivalence surrounding a German cultural identity emerged clearly in the vociferous debate that developed when conservative politicians proposed the concept of *Leitkultur* as a way of articulating a new integration policy. These conservative politicians tried to equate the specifics of *Leitkultur* with constitutional patriotism grounded in principles of democracy and freedom. But the effort backfired when the term instead evoked the repudiated idea of a German culture that is to be imposed on others. This phantasmic image creates allusive links between the treatment of the Jews as the threatening internal other during the Nazi era and the position of Muslims, Turks, and other stigmatized minorities in Germany today.

Aside from fluency in the German language, the one basis for German national identity that can be asserted without triggering controversy is constitutional patriotism. It is an ideology, a national myth, that, as philosophers like Adorno and Habermas have stressed, must be protected from any return of nationalistic cultural chauvinism—and its link with the past—through constant vigilance. The Constitution, which was not written by Germans but by an alliance of Western governments during the post–World War II occupation, is an exposition of universal principles based on Enlightenment values. A particularistic German culture must not be imposed on others, but campaigns for social reform gain legitimacy when expressed in the name of the principles of the Constitution. In this context, the past may be evoked as a renewed act of repudiation of Nazi racial policies. Thus, when the former Rütli school principal called it the "horror school" as part of a campaign for social reform, she not only presented school conditions to the public in images of utter chaos but also used a term that is often used to allude to the Holocaust. Misguided governmental policies are blamed because, reminiscent of the past, they throw the most abject minorities together and segregate them from the rest of German society. The horrors of the past are indirectly evoked in the name of change and the protection of minorities.

It is unfortunately only a small step from evoking the Constitution to protect minorities to evoking the Constitution to repudiate the cultural practices of others. One may be ambivalent about talking about one's own origins as German, but not about the origins of others (Schneider 2002). When the oppression of the Turkish Muslim woman is foregrounded, the rights of the individual are placed in opposition to the rights of a group to practice its own culture. The Turkish Muslim man is cast as clinging to a form of masculinity based on patriarchal cultural values centered on traditional ideas of honor and shame, which he feels compelled to defend through violence and the protection of women. Within this discursive context, the modern German man, in contrast, is cast as the middle-class family man, who in most cases at least is an embodiment of modern constitutional values.

Studies of colonial masculinity have highlighted a discursive process in which European men embodied a racialized white supremacy through their hypermasculinity, which was set in contrast to the demasculinization of men whose societies had been colonized (Stoler 1995: 56). Germany participated in this discourse, to the point at which the process of separating out racialized bodies was carried to its logical extreme in the abjection of Jewish and other minority masculinities and the glorification of the Aryan militarized body. The postwar period was marked by urgent efforts to recuperate and recast German masculinity in the face of military defeat, the loss of so many men during the war, and the presence of the victorious Allies on German soil for many years. The moral recuperation of German masculinity occurred in a number of ways, including the publicly celebrated practice of German men becoming adoptive fathers to the interracial children born of German women and African American soldiers during the Allied occupation (Fehrenbach 1998: 107). This was one way of repudiating the association of masculinity with racism. German masculinity has become an embodiment of constitutional patriotism, grounded on a repudiation of the militarism and hypermasculinity of the Nazi era.

The end of World War II marked a turning point in global discourse, when racism as a practice of governmentality linked with eugenics and nationalism was supplanted by a doctrine of universal human rights that was set out in the United Nations charter. Though race continued to serve as the basis for citizenship in Germany and many other countries, through the principle of *jus sanguinis* (meaning, in practice, the citizenship of one's parents)—to which the principle of birthplace was added only in 2000—Germany, too, had renounced racism in public discourse. As Balibar and Wallerstein (1991) and others have argued, talk of cultural difference has become a screen for race, and discrimination on the basis of culture has become the new racism.

Germans, however, have a highly ambivalent attachment to the particularities of German culture, as the *Leitkultur* controversy highlighted. Some have argued against the incorporation of large numbers of Muslims into German society or any accommodation to Muslim practices on religious grounds, with the argument that Germany is a Christian or even Judeo-Christian country; but the argument to protect German culture is more difficult to voice. Constitutional patriotism must stand in for culture. The headscarf is not rejected for being culturally alien. It is not asserted that the gym class is essential because it inculcates German cultural values associated with the discipline of the body. Rather, the constitutional rights of the Muslim woman must be protected. Only in this context can the culturally shaped masculinity of the Muslim man be stigmatized without generating a repudiation of the act of stigmatization itself.

The problem of Turkish men in Germany plays out with stage sets derived from the particular historical and cultural context of that nation, but the deeper themes of this drama have a broader historical logic that is common to Western societies both in Europe and in North America. Western culture universalizes its inherent values and practices, and in the process it challenges non-Western cultures as illegitimate to the extent that these cultures reject the universalizing logic of the West, whether in the great issues of the appropriate role of religion in politics or in the more day-to-day issues of relations between the sexes. Even counterhegemonic discourses that aim to disrupt dominant structures of inequality often rest on this Western universalizing logic. Thus, for example, certain global feminisms, though foregrounding moments of oppression linked with the abuse of women, may inadvertently reproduce other inequalities, such as the stigmatization of a minority, thereby reinforcing a conservative, xenophobic political stance. A correlate of this logic is the tendency for Western societies to equate successful assimilation with an acceptance of Western practice. The West has embraced pluralism as a principle, though in practice pluralism is most comfortably tolerated when the differences in question are different flavors of Western civilization. Muslim immigrants, and Muslim male immigrants in particular, illuminate a disjuncture between Western principles and Western practices whose ramifications go far beyond the particular case of Turkish male immigrants in Germany. Their real challenge is not to Western values, but rather to Western discomfort with the deeper and even contradictory implications of Western values. Recognition of this point is an important step toward eventual reconciliation with the Muslim other as a full member of the Western societies that many now consider their home.

NOTES

Introduction

1. The best seller *Burned Alive*, for example, which was translated into multiple languages from the original French and received considerable attention in international newspapers such as the *New York Times* and *le Monde*, includes on the cover a quotation from the *Washington Post*: "Sounds an alarm on the international stage. . . . Her tale is so shocking . . . [and] nothing less than a miracle" (Souad 2004). Térèse Taylor has argued that this best seller by Souad, the Palestinian victim of an attempted honor killing, was actually fabricated (Taylor 2005).

2. Benedict Anderson, in his articulation of the idea of the nation as "imagined community," addressed this issue of emotional plausibility (1991: 51–52).

3. The concept of cultural citizenship, as framed by Renato Rosaldo (1994) and taken up by Aihwa Ong (1996) and other anthropologists within the context of diasporic and minority communities, refers to "the right to be different and to belong in a participatory democratic sense," with a stress on specifying the conditions that make individuals and groups feel like first- or second-class citizens (Rosaldo 1994: 402), be they equal access to goods and services, appropriate representation in the political process and in school curricula, or treatment with dignity and respect in all contexts.

4. Developed by Julia Kristeva, the concept of abjection refers to a state of being cast off, with an emphasis on the emotionally charged reaction—often of horror—to objects that are ambiguously self and not-self, such as blood that has escaped the body (see Kristeva 1982). Judith Butler also elaborates the concept of abjection in her theory of subject formation, distinguishing it from the psychoanalytic concept of foreclosure elaborated by Lacan and Žižek by emphasizing the historical specificity and contingency of that which is abjected: "I want to propose that certain abject zones within sociality also deliver this threat, constituting zones of uninhabitability which a subject fantasizes

as threatening its own integrity with the prospect of a psychotic dissolution" (Butler 1993: 243, n. 2)

5. Thus, for example, according to Samuel Huntington's model of a "Clash of Civilizations" (1993), the current global "war on terror" is the result of a thousand-year conflict between "Islamic civilization" and the West. Huntington, however, did recognize that this civilizational conflict is aggravated by the presumptiveness of Western universalism. The currently popular concept of cosmopolitanism (for example, see Appiah 2006) also tends to be defined in a way that reproduces a dichotomy analogous to the Orientalist West–East divide, confounding Western liberalism and its discourse of human rights with a universalized ethical ideal of cosmopolitanism that nevertheless manages to abject an other as the intolerable / intolerant in a way that places many Muslims on the other side of the dichotomy between the cosmopolitan and its antithesis.

6. Sociologist Wilhelm Heitmeyer is credited with coining the term in 1996 (Hiscott 2005). Heitmeyer was concerned that Islamic fundamentalist groups on the fringes of society would produce social disintegration through voluntary cultural segregation (Heitmeyer 1996).

7. In the late 1970s, Philip Abrams (1977) recognized the state, not as a thing, but as a public reification, a mask or ideological project.

8. Foucault argued that since the eighteenth century the focus of government has been on the care and welfare of its population, in contrast to the concerns of rulers in an earlier discursive order.

9. Studies of the relationship between state power and subject formation include Hansen and Stepputat (2001) and Friedman (2005).

10. A number of scholars have shown how disempowered groups, especially minorities and women, are often denied recognition for their choices in intimate relationships (for example, Povinelli 2002; Berlant 1998; Wiegman 2002) and are thus constituted as marginal subjects. Sara L. Friedman (2005), for example, discussed how socialist state policies actively sought to cultivate certain feelings among women in what was considered a "backward" area of China, where local marriage practices did not conform to the dominant pattern, persistently "cajoling" women into identifying with these dominant practices and cultivating new "feelings of intimacy" with their husbands.

11. As Bourdieu has observed, "From its inception, social science itself has been part and parcel of this work of construction of the representation of the state which makes up part of the reality of the state itself" (Bourdieu 1999: 55).

12. Arjun Appadurai, in his discussion of "mediascapes," has suggested that the images projected by the media "tend to be image-centered, narrative-based accounts of strips of reality," which "offer to those who experience and transform them . . . a series of elements (such as characters, plots, and textual forms) out of which scripts can be formed of imagined lives, their own as well as those of others living in other places" (Appadurai 1996: 35). Stuart Hall has characterized identity as constituted within repre-

sentation. He views cinema "not as a second-order mirror held up to reflect what already exists, but as that form of representation which is able to constitute us as new kinds of subjects, and thereby enable us to discover places from which to speak" (Hall 2000: 32). Less optimistically, it is also possible to see media images as being so powerful that they constrain not only the ability to imagine who one may become but even who one has been, along the lines of the views of scholars of the Frankfurt School such as T. W. Adorno and Herbert Marcuse, who were concerned with power of the economy and the totalitarian state to shape consciousness.

13. Given that the German government has been a major source of funding for films in which diasporic Turkish characters and situations are portrayed, many of the concerns of social policy makers have been translated directly into guidelines for subsidies to filmmakers (Elsaesser 1989). In the 1970s and 1980s, many films suggested "that state-funded cinema is primarily a force for social work" (Elsaesser 1989: 53). More recently, Germany's federal minister of culture has increasingly tilted subsidy programs to favor filmmakers who have had box-office successes.

14. Judith Butler has problematized the reproducibility of a hegemonic order as theorized by Foucault, given the existence of agentive subjects. Although influenced by Foucault's understanding of the subject as an effect of prior discourses, she has criticized his failure to consider what has to be excluded from "economies of discursive intelligibility" for those economies to "function as self-sustaining systems" (Butler 1993: 35). In this respect, Butler follows Slavoj Žižek, who has also criticized a Foucauldian approach to the discursive constitution of the subject. Žižek, arguing that the subject is formed through an act of foreclosure, emphasized that what has been repudiated continues to decenter the subject (Žižek 1989).

15. See Roland Barthes's *Mythologies* (1972) for one of the founding studies of popular culture as myths that circulate in everyday life and construct the world around us, making that which is socially constructed appear natural. In his analysis of diverse modern phenomena such as wrestling, magazine photos, and film, Barthes identifies myth as a type of speech in which a sign (signifier plus concept) becomes a signifier in a kind of metalanguage that naturalizes and freezes meaning into stereotypes.

16. Such as the "stranded objects" that Eric Santner (1990) describes in his account of German historical memory.

17. Building on a Lacanian interpretation of Freud, Žižek locates the emotional charge of political symbols in their ability to evoke basic, unconscious desires and fears in ways that constitute social fantasies.

18. However, such imagined fulfillments are pleasurable only if they are consistent with the fantasizer's sense of self (*ego syntonic* in Freud's terms). Otherwise, they may provoke intense anxiety, which may be managed through displacement of the aim and object of the fantasy.

19. See Connell (1995) for an overview of the field of masculinity studies.

20. As Connell has argued, however, "changing masculinity in these terms may be therapeutic and comforting but does nothing about equality" (Connell 1987: 4).

21. A Puerto Rican poet born in Brooklyn wrote: "The behavior we collectively refer to as 'macho' has deep historical roots, but the trigger is often a profound insecurity, a sense of being threatened" (Espada 1996: 84).

22. As Leila Ahmed (1992) has argued, the British colonial administrators in Egypt drew on arguments that were being made by feminist advocates of equal rights for women in Britain to justify their policies in the name of rescuing Egyptian women from oppression while at the same time arguing against women's rights back home. Within the context of studies of the treatment of colonized populations under the European powers, Gayatri Spivak pointed out the presumptuousness of a colonial feminism that justified domination in terms of "white men . . . saving brown women from brown men" (Spivak 1993: 92).

23. The concept of constitutional patriotism has been most fully elaborated by Jurgen Habermas (1986, 1994), as I discuss in Chapter 7. Habermas emphasizes a vigilance against the subtlest return of ethnic nationalism.

24. According to a 2006 trend analysis of data from the German Socio-Economic Panel (GSOEP), not only is secularization of Turks in Germany increasing from the first to the second generation, but even in 1992, a majority (more than 60 percent) of first-generation Turks were classified as "secular" in orientation (Diehl and Schnell 2006: 807–808) because they claimed that they did not attend a religious institution or participate in religious events. Diehl and Schnell, however, underestimate the number of observant Muslims. Their figure for secular orientation does not take into account the fact that women often do not attend mosques even if they are religiously observant at home and thus would be counted as "secular" in their analysis. When the GSOEP responses are broken down by gender, it can be seen that more than twice as many men as women participate in a religious event weekly (in 2005, 35 percent of men and 15 percent of women), while only 30 percent of men and 45 percent of women never participate. In 1990, 24 percent of men and 16 percent of women participated weekly, while 45 percent of men and 59 percent of women never did. In any case, a trend toward increasing secularization is not apparent. On the contrary, before 2001, there is no consistent trend, and since then, GSOEP responses indicate a significant increase in mosque attendance. (I thank Markus Gangl for providing me with these tabulations in a private correspondence.)

25. However, they were reopened in 1934 in order to fill the ongoing need for imams.

26. Men were forbidden to wear the fez, and women were not allowed to wear the headscarf in state-run institutions such as schools, hospitals, and the courts.

27. This group of leftists was not limited to urban intellectual elites. Thanks in part to governmental programs such as the Turkish Village Institutes, which during the 1940s

sought to inculcate Turkish nationalism in the rural population by creating "peasant intellectuals," a generation of rural institute graduates emerged with leftist, extremely secularist views and contributed to Turkey's intellectual and political life in the 1960s and beyond (Karaömerlioğlu 1998: 70).

28. Dr. Hans-Peter Uhl, member of the Federal Parliament, Christian Social Union, speaking to the Fulbright German Studies Seminar, Berlin, June 13, 2002.

29. Despite vocal public concern about the failure of integration, little empirical research has actually been done on the question of the integration of migrants into German society, and even less has been done on their children born in Germany, the "so-called second generation" (Fertig 2004). Much of the available research is based on the German Socio-Economic Panel. Virtually no research has been done on the "third generation," which is still quite young.

30. Though by some measures the second generation has continued to have significant difficulties in school and in vocational training, Friedrich Heckmann argues that to interpret this as evidence of failure is basically a static view and does not focus on the fact that integration is a process and that there has been "continuous improvement in school attendance, finishing of basic education, secondary school attendance and completion and success in vocational training" (Heckmann 1997: 1).

31. These contrasting modes of explanation have parallels in the United States in debates surrounding the politically charged "culture of poverty" argument first articulated by Oscar Lewis (1959) and picked up by Charles Murray (1984) (of *Bell Curve* fame), who argued that welfare created incentives that undermined families. This argument was contested by William Wilson (1987), who asserted that the failure of African Americans to assimilate to middle-class culture was caused by structural factors such as the lack of jobs in inner cities.

32. See Akhil Gupta for a concise critique of an "empiricist epistemology" that overstresses the "experience of being in spatial proximity to 'the other,'" as the ultimate ground for the judgment of the authenticity of "data" and interpretation. According to Gupta, this face-to-face methodology, which is at the heart of participant observation, "is unable to comprehend how the state is discursively constituted" (Gupta 1995: 377).

33. This included research in Germany, primarily in Berlin, between 1999 and 2005, including six months in 1999 and regular summer trips. I had conversations and conducted interviews with a wide range of people of Turkish background, teachers, government officials responsible for the administration of social services for migrants, imams at a range of mosques in Berlin, and a number of people associated with Islamic organizations, including those who work at the headquarters of Islamische Gemeinschaft Milli Görüş (IGMG) near Cologne. Participant observation included living with families in Berlin and near Cologne "shadowing" people as they went about their daily lives, and attending meetings and other events. Research was also conducted by my daughter Julia DiPrete while she was in Kiel in northern Germany on a teaching Fulbright during

2005–2006 and by Marguerite Hoyler, who worked in Berlin as my research assistant during the summers of 2006 and 2007. Several of the interviews that I closely analyze in Chapters 3 and 4 were conducted by Julia DiPrete and Marguerite Hoyler. These interviews were unstructured and focused on eliciting narratives of the personal experiences of young men who were close in age to their interviewers.

Chapter 1

1. Said himself skirted the issue of German scholarship in *Orientalism* (1979: 18–19), but scholars have recently addressed the distinctive characteristics of German Orientalism (see Jenkins 2004). As Jenkins has pointed out, Said stressed the connections between Orientalism and European empire building, but a focus on German Orientalism brings to the fore a different dynamic, especially linkages among Orientalism, nationalism, and imperialism (Jenkins 2004: 98).

2. See, for example, Paul Stirling (1965), who used the Turkish village as a site for documenting aspects of social structure that had survived westernization; Carol Delaney's cultural analysis of village gender relations (1991) also presented change in terms of a struggle between the villagers with their static Islamic worldview and the encroachments of a modernizing Western elite (see Nükhet Sirman's insightful book review [1993: 508]). Werner Schiffauer's ethnographies (1987 and 1991) focused on the worldview of villagers and the effects of migration to Europe. Recent anthropological studies have sought to disrupt this dichotomizing by focusing on state processes and national imaginaries. Among them are Michael Meeker's *A Nation of Empire* (2002), which closely examines the active role of a provincial oligarchy in the formation of the state; Yael Navaro-Yashin's *Faces of the State* (2002); and Ayse Gul Altinay's *The Myth of the Military Nation* (2004).

3. Meeker suggests that the Spanish community analyzed by Julian Pitt-Rivers (1966) makes a similar distinction, but that in this case *sharaf*-like honor is about precedence and social status such that high-status people have the power to ignore or flaunt honor based on sexual morality; whereas in Turkey the relationship between these categories is quite different, such that even the most powerful were not exempt from elaborate displays of sexual honor (*namus* in Turkish) through the highly visible protection of the sexual purity of their women (Meeker 1976 I: 263, 266).

4. Other terms include *Izzet*, a form of honor that is linked to honesty and the ability to show generosity and respect to others. It can be embodied by both men and women. *Sevap* (a meritorious action) is associated with moral decency, honesty, and generosity and can also be a source of prestige (see Stirling 1965: 231; Magnarella 1998: 167).

5. For example, according to Paul Stirling, "Although a man can send a woman home whenever he likes, to do so without a good reason is both shameful, ayıp, and a sin, günah" (Stirling 1965: 217). Stirling's field research in central Turkey was carried

out in the 1950s, before the publication of the Péristiany volume, and Stirling notes: "Péristiany and Pitt-Rivers have pursued these concepts of honour in other parts of the Mediterranean seaboard far more thoroughly than I have. Both point out that virility and a man's honour are closely connected. This holds for Turkey too." Yet he also notes, "on the whole, virility seems to be no more than one element in the concept of male honour" (Stirling 1965: 232).

6. Scholars have tended to downplay possible continuities in the process of nego-tiating honor or reputation. Paul Magnarella, fore example, identified among migrants to Germany a rapid transition to new sources of status and prestige in terms of a "new, evolving system, whose basic components were adopted from reference sets and models outside the village" (Magnarella 1998: 165).

7. These efforts include a blurring of the boundaries between Ottomans and other Europeans by stressing the sustained connections and mutual influence between Europe and the Ottomans (for example, Goffman 2002; Faroqhi 2004) and reinterpretations of what had been seen as exotic and decadent customs such as the harem (for example, Lowe 1991; Melman 1992).

8. Margret Spohn has traced some of the historical sources of popular images of Turks, suggesting that representations drawn from language, religion, music, and litera-ture depict Turks as warlike, barbaric, crude, and aggressive (Spohn 1993; 2002).

9. This phrase has been attributed to Nicholas I of Russia in the mid-nineteenth cen-tury, who called the Ottoman Empire the sick man of Europe as the other European pow-ers gradually weakened it (see de Bellaigue [2001] for a discussion of the attribution).

10. Turner's book pulls together Weber's fragmentary writings on Islam that appear in English in various publications, including Weber's *Economy and Society* (1978).

11. Hildebrandt envisioned the state as a "hero-creation."

12. These descriptions of men's gendered labor practices judge the Turkish man's work orientation in implicit comparison with a Western ideal of sustained work over long hours. The men's activities would seem to reflect age-old practices, a manifestation of "tradition." However, some scholars have pointed out that at least in some regions, it is actually recently changing technologies and markets that have altered the struc-ture of labor relations and created or exacerbated a gender imbalance. According to this explanation, which avoids exoticizing the village man, the marked imbalance that can now be seen in the division of labor between men and women is a phenomenon that has accompanied the introduction of machinery into tasks typically carried out by men, decreasing the number of hours that men must labor in the fields, increasing profits (Delaney 1991: 267–268) but also shifting the balance of power in the household toward men.

13. Erotic fantasies of the harem were a prominent theme in Victorian and pre-Victorian erotica, as in *The Lustful Turk*, first published anonymously in 1828. This was a novel written in the form of an epistolatory travelogue (Marcus 1966).

14. When Lady Montagu separated from her husband, she was left without property, and Craven was forcibly separated from her seven children (Melman 1992: 88).

15. In contrast, Garnett is less admiring of those whom she does not regard as white. After describing how white slave women are often married off to high-status men and achieve equal status with their former owners, she identifies a different outcome for those of African origin: "It is only the negresses who always remain a class apart, and fall not infrequently into penury and want. As a rule, however, they are themselves chiefly to blame for their misfortunes. For, after they have been freed and married, it not infrequently happens that their ungoverned tempers cause them to quarrel with, and separate from, their husbands, when they are obliged to support themselves as best they can by hawking parched peas and such trifles about the streets" (Garnett 1909: 225). She also notes that there is not an admixture of black blood in the lower classes, "because the climate does not seem favourable to the propagation of the coloured races, and the few negro or mulatto children who come into the world seldom survive infancy" (Garnett 1909: 226).

16. Her representations of the Turk stands in stark contrast to representations of the Bedouin, in whom she recognized a kindred love of freedom and individuality that was greater than what was possible in Europe, as well as equality in marriage (Hahn-Hahn 1845, II: 238, 241).

17. She drew a similar contrast based on her observation of women and their slaves: "They seem to treat their slaves very kindly; the black servants sat among their mistresses, and munched away bravely: the slaves are well dressed, and could scarcely be distinguished from their owners, were it not for their sable hue" (Pfeiffer 1852: 42).

18. Though the headscarf and other forms of women's covering have been a symbolic focus, these were not actually banned, except in specific contexts, while several aspects of men's attire such as the fez and the mustache were made illegal.

19. This is a process that has come to be recognized by gender scholars in recent years, especially in Deniz Kandiyoti's pioneering work on Turkish masculinity (see 1994, 1997).

20. Saba Mahmood (2005) has challenged universalizing assumptions about the freedom and agency of the Western liberal subject by examining the subjectivity of devout Muslim women in Egypt.

21. According to Sirman, many professional and academic women of an earlier era had felt that women's equality had already been accomplished by the modernizing secularism promoted by Kemal Atatürk. They were more threatened by Islam and "tradition" and saw the ideals of Kemalism as their only protection (Sirman 1989: 14).

22. Sirman points out that this feminist concern with oppression within the family stemmed directly from the influence of Western feminist theory rather than from Ottoman women's writings (Sirman 1989: 27–28), which were inaccessible because of the Romanization of the Turkish script.

Chapter 2

1. The village, however, is also depicted as a dead end for pragmatic reasons: successful farm life depends on familial continuity from one generation to the next. When this is cut by migration, and children and other close relatives leave for the city, it is impossible to grow old and die there, with no younger generation to take over the heavy work.

2. Some researchers, especially Werner Schiffauer (1991) and Margret Spohn (2002), have captured the rarely heard voices of first-generation male guestworkers, though they problematically reproduce the tradition-modernity dichotomy in their analyses of the transitions these guestworkers experience (see Chapter 3).

3. Even among those who came as guestworkers, many had migrated first to Turkey's major urban centers before moving to Germany.

4. In France, the controversy has centered on students who wish to wear a headscarf in the secular space of the state school (see Scott 2005; Bowen 2006). In Germany, where the state's relationship to secularism is rather different, the debate over a ban on headscarves has mostly been limited to teachers as representatives of the neutral state.

5. Similar themes are echoed by Sigrid Meske (1983).

6. *Die Wolfsbraut* (The Wolf's Bride) (Beiersdorf 1984–85) includes as a central character a young woman working as a cleaning lady in a movie theater. In *Metin* (Draeger 1979), which is focused on a young boy, both mother and father are guestworkers. But even in the early period, there were films about women that focused on their flight from arranged marriages and abusive husbands (for example, *Shirins Hochzeit* [Shirin's Wedding], Sanders-Brahms 1975).

7. The main actor in *Angst essen Seele auf*, El Hedi ben Salem, was Fassbinder's lover at the time the film was made. He was subsequently rejected by Fassbinder, imprisoned for murder, and ultimately committed suicide (Bingham 2003).

8. Time Out Film Guide 13, http://www.timeout.com/film/78594.html).

9. *Gastarbeiterliteratur* (guestworker literature) from the late 1970s was primarily didactic, protesting against inhumane living and working conditions and social discrimination (see Suhr 1989; Horrocks and Kolinsky 1996). Similarly, New German Cinema of the 1970s and early 1980s was intensely concerned with social and political questions (Elsaesser 1989: 52), while the literature of the late 1980s and early 1990s focused on issues of deterritorialization and the loss of identity, drawing on Turkish traditions in order to challenge conventions of German literature (Harnisch, Stokes, and Weidauer 1998: 18).

10. Marxist feminists focused on how material conditions shape the organization of family relations, an approach that had its roots in Engels's *The Origins of the Family, Private Property and the State*, written in 1884. Gillian Howie (2004) has expressed a concern with the turn to "cultural feminism" and its tendency to ignore the material conditions that give rise to exploitation.

11. Tevfik Başer, born and educated in Turkey as a graphics artist and photographer, studied filmmaking in Hamburg, Germany, in his early thirties (Kuheim 2001).

12. I gained access to this film through the archives of the Kreuzberg Museum in Berlin. It seems to be the same film as *Aufbrüche*, which is summarized in English by Trumpener (1989: 29).

13. According to Geertz, "unlike genes and other nonsymbolic information sources, which are only models *for*, not models *of*, cultural patterns have an intrinsic double aspect: they give meaning, that is, objective conceptual form, to social and psychological reality both by shaping themselves to it and by shaping it to themselves" (Geertz 1973: 93).

14. Rand Conger and Glen Elder (1994) have shown that the husband in rural U.S. families under economic pressure is likely to become more hostile and aggressive and the wife more depressed, the husband displacing onto his family the anger he experiences at work. These reactions are consistent with what in Germany is perceived as the Turkish "cultural" pattern of the dominant father and submissive mother.

15. The notion of "cultural defense" was developed in the United States in the mid-1980s in the wake of a number of cases in which defendants invoked the traditions of their culture to explain or mitigate their actions (see Renteln 2004). A number of scholars have criticized the cultural defense for its reliance on "cultural tradition" to legitimate crimes against women (see Okin 1999; Volpp 2000). Anne Phillips (2003) suggests that, on the whole, the cultural defense has not been successfully employed by male defendants to mitigate crimes against women, though there are troubling exceptions.

16. Working in Trinidad, Aisha Khan has argued analogously that "ideologies about mixing are causal forces in social processes" (Khan 2004: 4), because the concept of creolization is used in so many situations and is thus an important cultural practice. Jan French has argued that in certain contexts the concept of *mestizaje* "provides openings for choices about self-identification and political identity-making" (French 2004: 665).

17. For discussions about German-Turkish hyphenated identities, see Caglar (1997) and Kaya (2002).

18. Caglar suggests that Turkish pop music, in contrast, in the 1990s became popular among German-Turkish youth in ways that opened up new spaces that celebrated Turkishness yet disrupted reified identities by referring to "the metropoles and urban spaces, not to Turkey as a cultural system" (Caglar 1998: 256). Alternatively, Turkish pop could be seen to disrupt the Turkish-German dichotomy in another way, representing what is Turkish yet urban and thereby transcending the dichotomy between the rural, parochial Turkish and the cosmopolitan German.

19. Cartel also became popular in Turkey and was taken up by the Turkish media to promote Turkish nationalism (Kaya 2001: 183).

20. "The German- and Turkish-language media seem to agree on one point: 'The new German film is Turkish!'" (Deutsch-türkishe Tendenzen im Film? 2000; see also Trumpener 1989).

21. Yavuz also directed the documentary film *Mein Vater der Gastarbeiter* (My Father the Guestworker), discussed at the beginning of this chapter.

22. According to Anthony Kwame Harrison, "It's the partnership of hip-hop and corporate media that's brought us the negative images and the rap music that people complain most about" (quoted in Roach 2004: 2).

23. Kaya (2001) contrasts this form of hybridity with what he calls the "multiculturalism" of middle-class Turkish youth, whom he sees as preoccupied with identity talk that is heavily influenced by media representations. They take up the folkloristic aspects of ethnic culture that are presented in the multicultural festivals promoted by the *Auslanderbeauftragte* (office in charge of foreigners).

24. As I noted in the introduction, mosque attendance has been rising since 2001 among the Turkish population. In 1990, 37 percent of men reported participating in a religious event at least once a month, while in 2001, the figure was 43 percent and in 2005, 55 percent. For women, the percentage increased from 26 percent in both 1990 and 2001, to 33 percent in 2005 (based on Markus Gangl's tabulations from GSOEP).

25. This statement is based on conversations with the president of IGMG, Mehmet Sabri Erbakan, in 2001 and 2002 and with others involved with reformist Islamic groups.

26. This course was developed by the Institut für Internationale Padagogik und Didaktik for use by future teachers of Islamic education in the public schools.

27. This focus also escapes the seemingly unresolvable conflict between the principle of group rights that underlines the doctrine of multiculturalism and that of individualism grounded in universal human rights.

28. The Netherlands also has a large Turkish immigrant population with demographic characteristics that are generally similar to those in Germany, though their position as a minority in the Dutch national imaginary is quite different from the their place in the German national imaginary. In the Netherlands, Turks are in many respects a "model minority," in contrast to others. For a fuller treatment of this woman's story, see Ewing (2002).

29. For an analysis of the power dynamics within Turkish village families, see Sirman (1990). Nergis's stance might also be justified by many Muslims with whom I spoke. They argued that all money earned by a wife should be hers to manage as she wishes, since the husband is financially responsible for maintaining the family.

30. For an analysis of marital power dynamics among working-class Turkish couples in which the wife works, see Bolak (1997).

Chapter 3

1. The validity of the individual components of this discursive amalgam can itself be questioned. For example, one criticism of Turkish Muslim men has been that they deny autonomy to their wives, sisters, and daughters. Autonomy has been defined in

a number of ways, one of the most straightforward being in terms of behavior that is experienced as willingly enacted and fully endorsed by the actor (Chirkov et al. 2003: 98, after Deci and Ryan 1985). The liberal notion of the autonomous subject as articulated by Immanuel Kant, which is at the heart of Western legal theory, takes the notion of autonomy even further, to mean a moral stance in which decisions to act are based solely on unconstrained free will and rationality (Kant [1948] articulated this point in "Groundwork of the Metaphysic of Morals," first published in 1785). This concept of the decontextualized autonomous subject has been challenged in increasingly sophisticated ways, especially by feminist legal theorists (for example, Abrams 1999) and by those seeking to articulate a number of dimensions that have been confounded in the Western Enlightenment tradition (for example, Chirkov et al. 2003). Influenced by Said's critique of Orientalism (1978), anthropologists have for the most part discarded the influential Geertzian idea (1983) that the Western or modern self is somehow peculiar in its bounded autonomy.

2. Researchers often mine the interview for explicit information about the interviewee's knowledge, opinions, memories, etc., though explicitly articulated statements cannot be taken as reflections of the implicit dimensions of cultural practices, or even as representative of statements that might be made in other settings.

3. Other works on men of Turkish background include those by Kaya (2001) on Turkish-German youth culture in Berlin and Tertilt (1996) on a Turkish street gang in Frankfurt.

4. Studying the effects of migration on the relationship between self and family/group among migrants from a single Turkish village, Schiffauer argued that the experience of migration radically restructured migrants' ways of thinking from a group orientation centered around status and duty within the village to individualism, though his conclusions are vitiated by the fact that the individuals he focused on did not always fit into the typology he had constructed. He explained this discrepancy by arguing that the effects of migration on an individual were conditioned by specific aspects of the individual's position within the family and the nature of his or her relationships with other family members. Schiffauer did, however, disrupt the Germany-Turkey dichotomy by demonstrating that this transformation of the self within the village began in the 1950s, as a result of widespread internal migration to cities such as Istanbul, well before the extensive migration of guestworkers from the village to Germany.

5. Kağitçibaşi also identified an intermediate category of "emotional/psychological interdependence." She sees this category emerging in societies with what she calls "collectivistic cultures of relatedness" in which families become financially independent, as in situations of migration, but remain emotionally interdependent (Kağitçibaşi 2002: 5). Spohn relies heavily on such intermediate categories in her analysis.

6. The translations are my own.

7. I discuss this scene in more detail in Chapter 4.

8. In Germany, all children are tracked into a three-tiered system of secondary schools after the fourth grade, at the young age of ten or eleven. The *Hauptschule* (grades five through nine) and *Realschule* (grades five through ten) prepare children for vocational training, while the *Gymnasium* (grades five through thirteen) prepares students for various types of university. In the school year of 2003–2004, only 6 percent of Turkish students attended a *Gymnasium* (compared with 23 percent of all students in the Western German states) (Söhn and Özcan 2006: 109).

9. This phenomenon of dropping out of secondary school and then returning to qualify for university study several years later is probably not unusual among young men of Turkish background. Though I did not collect systematic data on this issue, I did meet several men in their twenties who had done the same and had become successful professionals.

10. This is the best-selling book version of the documentary film, discussed in Chapter 2.

11. Kaya quoted a similar statement from his research on Turkish-German youth in Berlin, made by an eighteen-year-old Berliner reflecting on a visit to Ankara: "Here we are called yabanci (foreigner), and there in Turkey, in my own country, they call us 'Almanci' [German]" (Kaya 2001: 161). Caglar discusses the negative stereotypes associated with German-Turks in Turkey (Caglar 1994: 98).

12. According to one study of the poor educational attainment of Turkish youth in Germany published in 1978, when Turkish children were just beginning to enter the German school system, "Turkish workers of rural background, similar to Italians from the South and unlike Greeks and Yugoslavs, by and large only encourage the school attendance of their gifted male children, while trying in spite of an absolute prohibition of juvenile employment, to obtain illegal jobs for the less bright boys of the family" (Abadan-Unat 1978: 316–317). Even in rural Turkey, students like Sezai were not all that unusual.

13. It is a manifestation of what scholars such as Rosaldo (1994) and Ong (1996) have called *flexible citizenship*, which is not grounded in a clear national or even cultural identity.

Chapter 4

1. Michael Herzfeld has stressed the fluidity and variability within a single community of practices associated with honor and therefore has argued that the use of *honor* as an analytic category be replaced with a more neutral concept such as *reputation* (Herzfeld 1980: 348). As Robert Paine (1989) argued, honor and self-esteem may rest on successfully negotiating an "agonistic dilemma" between contradictory social values. Carroll Pastner has discussed how among tribal Baluch in Pakistan the evaluation of specific actions as honorable is often subject to debate as "participants in the controversy may calculate honor in a variety of contradictory ways" (Pastner 1988: 249). Interpretations of

Islamic principles are often one of the bases for such calculations, a point that is consistent with the more general principle articulated by a number of "practice theorists" that social action is rarely a matter of following rules (see Bourdieu 1977; Ortner 2006).

2. My translation of a description from the original script for the film (Akin 2004: 32).

3. In Chapter 3, I suggest an alternative interpretation of this scene.

4. Schiffauer's depictions of men whom he knew well over many years illustrate Herzfeld's argument in his discussion of manhood and honor in a society based on sheep stealing that there are many ways of enacting masculinity and honor and alternative models to draw upon, even in a remote Greek village on Crete (1985).

5. Ayse Caglar has suggested that by focusing on "networks of interconnecting practices surrounding objects," as well as "the sentiments, desires and images that these practices evoke," the researcher can avoid the a priori imposition of cultural identities and categories (Caglar 1997: 180). Such an approach also allows us to recognize how people establish and negotiate relationships among these objects, practices, existing cultural categories, and their own desires and fantasies, as I stress here.

6. In an environment in which young men are stigmatized for being Turkish, such practices can also be interpreted as a way of reclaiming their honor by denouncing the honor of German men, who do not defend their women (Kaya 2001). Analogously, in an environment of harsh stigmatization, discrimination, and lack of career opportunity, a street gang may provide companionship, self-esteem, and status through activities such as criminal assaults that are not fundamentally different from status competition in gangs of other ethnicities but mobilize notions of honor that as an idiom resemble rural Turkish practices. But at another level they are political expressions of resistance—such as asserting that German boys don't know how to defend their honor when gang members assault them and steal their leather jackets. Young men who engage in such practices, however, can be seen as violating their family's honor through their criminal behavior and their disregard of the expectations of their parents.

Chapter 5

1. In attendance at the meeting were the school senator, the district mayor of Neu-kölln, representatives of the Bundestag, teachers at the school, parents, and a representative of a Turkish organization. But, as "an Arab man" complained, almost no migrants were present.

2. The tabloid, not identified in the *Tageszeitung* article, was *Bild*. The headline read "Ermordet, weil sie ihr Kopftuch wegwarf" (Murdered because she discarded her headscarf).

3. In Turkish: "Mutlu Sürücü: Kardeşim 5 sene önce başını açtı."

4. A portion of the quotation was, however, reproduced in the German weekly *Die Zeit* (Lau 2005), which took his comments out of the context of his media criticism of the headscarf issue.

5. Biehl was an American reporter working in Germany for *Der Spiegel*.

6. Several months later, a federal court decided to reopen the case against the two older Sürücü brothers, who had been acquitted in the first trial (von Bullion 2007).

7. The term *clan* was also used in several online blogs in response to the sentencing of a Pakistani family for a murder in Denmark several months later: "Danes Sentence Entire Clan for Honour Killing." News sources such as the BBC, however, did not use the term (van Laenen 2006).

8. Van Gogh had made the film with the Dutch politician Ayaan Hirsi Ali, a Somali refugee who had renounced Islam and had earlier fled an arranged marriage. Hirsi Ali, who at the time was a member of the Dutch parliament, was also a self-proclaimed ex-Muslim. She escaped to the Netherlands in 1992 to avoid an arranged marriage. Here is one standard account of her history: at age five she had undergone the ordeal of female genital mutilation, a custom still practiced in many Muslim communities. This and other grievances with Islamic practice lead her to reject her faith and seek to aid other women oppressed by outmoded tradition. Despite the threat to her life, Hirsi Ali refused to back down on what she called her Islam Reform Project: "I am on a mission. And it has only just begun." Islamic extremist Mohamed Bouyeri, a Dutch national of Moroccan descent, shot and stabbed van Gogh repeatedly, even as van Gogh pleaded for mercy. In the wake of the murder, Hirsi Ali asserted publicly that she would make a sequel to *Submission* (*60 Minutes* 2006). In May 2006, she resigned from Parliament after a public uproar following the discovery that she had originally entered the Netherlands with falsified papers, and there was much anguished debate about whether she should be expelled from the country (see BBC News 2006). She left the Netherlands and became a resident fellow at a conservative think tank in Washington, D.C. (Hirsi Ali 2006).

9. The website for the Europäisches Forum für Migrationsstudien (EFMS) (http://web.uni-bamberg.de/~ba6ef3/, accessed December 2007) lists several German government press releases and newspaper articles on the topic.

10. Leicht, like several other writers seeking to disrupt mainstream representations, drew on the work of anthropologist Werner Schiffauer, whom I discuss later in this chapter.

11. Drawing on Roland Barthes's approach to modern myth, Schiffauer (2001) had made an analogous argument about the role of the German press in shaping the evolution of the self-presentation and ideological positioning of Cemaleddin Kaplan, the leader of the Islamist group that broke with Milli Görüş and was banned on December 5, 2001, by the German government in the wake of September 11.

12. Taking up the concept of moral panic, Stuart Hall and Tony Jefferson identified a "signification spiral," in which the perceived potential threat of an issue often becomes associated with a minority group or subculture and escalates through the process of signification (Hall and Jefferson 1976: 77).

13. This is a key feature of moral panics as they were first identified by Stanley Cohen in the early 1970s (Cohen 1980: 40).

14. Linke sees the body as a basic organizing metaphor that focuses on ideas of blood and contagion and identifies a "deep-seated revulsion to racial difference" (Linke 1997: 560) in which the racial subaltern is feminized and associated with disease and dirt and the expulsion of people is "conceptualized as a process of bodily discharge: a form of excretion or elimination" (Linke 2002: 252).

Chapter 6

1. In Velázquez's reflexive scene, the artist is painting a subject, the royal couple, who are located outside the canvas, where the viewer is standing, but who are also reflected in a mirror behind the artist. Both the artist and the rest of the royal family are gazing out at the viewer / royal couple, who gaze back. See Foucault's *Archaeology of Knowledge* (1972) for a rather different use of the complex gazes in this painting.

2. See John Bowen (2006) for a rich account of the headscarf controversy in France.

3. The states of the former East Germany did not have significant immigrant population from Turkey.

4. Article 4 of the Constitution states: "(1) Freedom of faith and of conscience, and freedom to profess a religious or philosophical creed, shall be inviolable. (2) The undisturbed practice of religion shall be guaranteed" (*Basic Law for the Federal Republic of Germany* 2001: 14).

5. The culture minister in the state of Baden-Württemberg, where Ludin had applied for a teaching position, had decided against her on the grounds that wearing a headscarf is not a religious duty for Muslim women and that its contested nature within Islam makes it a political symbol that the state should not endorse.

6. See Article 33, paragraph 4 of the Constitution: "The exercise of sovereign authority on a regular basis shall, as a rule, be entrusted to members of the public service who stand in a relationship of service and loyalty defined by public law" (*Basic Law for the Federal Republic of Germany* 2001: 28).

7. The SPD and Green Party voted against the ban.

8. Gordon (2002) discusses how Nazi leaders, though they rejected what they regarded as the decadence of Weimar culture, promoted and encouraged female dance troupes, which had been a part of this cultural world, because of the controlled and disciplined sexuality their performances projected.

9. In West Germany, restoring the educational system after the war generally involved a return to policies of the Weimar period (Hahn 1998: 113).

10. See Krüger, Krüger, and Treptau (2002) for a history of nudism during the Nazi era.

11. Wessel is based in Frankfurt and is writing a book, *Honor Killings in Our Midst: The Fates of Three Women Who Broke with Tradition.*

12. Historically, Turkish sensibilities surrounding nudity are quite different from American sensibilities, given the Turkish practice of same-sex public baths that was common in urban areas during the Ottoman period.

13. Central Council of Muslims, February 1, 2005; Ute Rasche interviewing Nadeem Elyas.

14. Considerable scholarship on German efforts to reconstitute a national identity in the wake of the Nazi era has focused on the silences that have characterized the postwar era and on the continuities that exist despite efforts to create a break with the past, an issue I discuss more fully in Chapter 7.

Chapter 7

1. The website, http://www.leitkultur.de, was set up on October 25, 2000. I accessed it on May 1, 2002, and again on July 25, 2007. Not all of the early postings remained archived on the site, but many were still there, along with a scattering of more recent ones.

2. See Müller (2006) for a detailed account of the origins of the concept and the differences between the ways that Sternberger and Habermas elaborated it.

3. According to one survey, 46 percent of all those interviewed fully or partly agreed with the statement "Islam is a backward religion," 34 percent with the statement "I am distrustful of people of Islamic religion," and 27 percent with the statement "immigration to Germany should be forbidden for Muslims" (Heitmeyer and Zick 2004). Leaders of such groups as IGMG were sharply critical of Heitmeyer's scholarship for what they viewed as its anti-Muslim cast (personal communications).

4. Conservative Bavarian interior minister Günther Beckstein, for example, had reportedly proposed to expel one hundred Islamic extremists under operation *Aktion Kehraus* (Action Sweep Out) (Spiegel Online 2005).

5. The BBC reported in 2003 that, according to German intelligence, leaders of Kaplan's organization had at one time tried to join forces with Osama bin Laden. Kaplan himself had previously been imprisoned for four years for inciting the murder of a rival (BBC News 2003).

6. In 2004 German police arrested Kaplan and deported him to Turkey, where he was immediately arrested on charges of having planned terrorist attacks against the mausoleum of Atatürk and a mosque in Istanbul in 1998.

7. The head of the Refah Party, Necmettin Erbakan, became prime minister of a coalition government in 1996 but was forced out of power by the military in 1997. There has been a succession of Islamist political parties, which were formed and then banned. The present prime minister of Turkey, Recep Tayyip Erdoğan (2003–), is the head of the Justice and Development Party (AKP), which is an offshoot of Milli Görüş (National Vision) in Turkey and what eventually became IGMG in Germany.

8. As the *Islamische Zeitung* complained, the only other nonviolent group that is the target of surveillance analogous to the attention paid to IGMG is the Church of

Scientology, which BfV began observing in 1997 because it was seen as a dangerous, seductive, secret, and powerful organization that is gradually infiltrating all arenas of power: the media, the courts, and the political process through its ability to mobilize capital. Scientology, like Islamism, challenges Germany's efforts to remain an open democracy while at the same time banning such groups.

9. Personal communication, Mehmet Sabri Eerbakan, president of IGMG, on June 29, 2002.

10. National elections were scheduled for September 22, 2002. Though the general feeling after September 11 was that security threats and the rise of unemployment had displaced immigration as an issue, in the spring of 2002, the federal government had pieced together a proposal for an immigration policy that the CDU/CSU resisted (Leithäuser 2002).

11. The paper issued from a meeting of the executive committee of the CDU, in which the committee also accepted for the first time the face that Germany is a country of immigration. For a discussion of this position paper see Klusmeyer (2001).

12. For example, non–European Union citizens are required to take German-language and integration classes, with the threat of a cut in social benefits or nonrenewal of their residence permit if they do not do so. Furthermore, those who express undemocratic views or hatred or violate the constitutional principles of tolerance and respect for democratic institutions can be deported more easily (Münz 2004).

13. The concept of *culture* as it developed in cultural anthropology in the United States can also be traced back to Herder, via Franz Boas, who was exposed to the German hermeneutical tradition before moving to the United States in 1887.

14. A headline in *Der Spiegel* announced on November 2, 2000: "Begriff 'Leitkultur' kommt nicht ins CDU-Papier" (The Concept "Leitkultur" Doesn't Appear in CDU Paper) (Spiegel Online 2000). It no longer appeared in the foundation paper of the CDU's commission on integration, though it did appear in a position paper on November 6.

15. Tibi himself initially supported Merz's use of the term, according to an article titled "Bassam Tibi Demands German *Leitkultur*" that appeared in the weekly news magazine *Focus* in November 2000, though he subsequently sought to return the concept to its broader, European focus (Tibi 2001; Manz 2004: 494).

16. The Jewish population has been growing in Germany in recent years, a point emphasized by the German government: "The Jewish population in Germany has tripled in the past decade, but there are still only one fifth as many Jews living in Germany today as there were at the beginning of World War II. Jewish sites—historical and communal—are being rebuilt around the country through the efforts of local communities, even as the Jewish community as a whole continues to face threats from small groups of right-wing extremists. Attempts to stamp out these groups for good are based on the recognition that Anti-Semitism and intolerance are attacks not only on individuals, but on the very fabric of democracy" (German Embassy n.d.).

17. Concerns about the legitimacy of the BfV can be seen on its Internet home page: "We would like to inform you about the work of the BfV. Three quarters of the population are persuaded of the necessity of the institution Protection of the Constitution, however, there often are also unclear images about legitimization, function and control of the protection of the constitution. With this offer of information we want to give to all citizens the possibility to get to know more about us" (http://www.verfassungsschutz.de/en).

Epilogue

1. "Gewalt an deutschen Schulen," video clip available at YouTube (http://www.you tube.com/watch?v=1kqnBM_tMZk). This clip appears to have been recorded from a German television newscast.

REFERENCES

Abadan-Unat, Narmin. 1978. "The Modernization of Turkish Women." *Middle East Journal* 32 (3): 291–306.

Abrams, Kathryn. 1999. "From Autonomy to Agency: Feminist Perspectives on Self-Direction." *William and Mary Law Review* 40 (3): 805–846.

Abrams, Philip. 1977. "Notes on the Difficulty of Studying the State." *Journal of Historical Sociology* 1 (1): 58–89.

Abu-Lughod, Lila. 1986. *Veiled Sentiments: Honor and Poetry in a Bedouin Society.* Berkeley: University of California Press.

———. 1993. "Finding a Place for Islam: Egyptian Television Serials and the National Interest." *Public Culture* 5 (3): 493–514.

———. 2002. "Do Muslim Women Really Need Saving? Anthropological Reflections on Cultural Relativism and Its Others." *American Anthropologist* 104 (3): 783–790.

Adelson, Leslie. 1990. "Migrants' Literature or German Literature? TORKAN's *Tufan Brief an einem islamischen Bruder.*" *German Quarterly* 63 (3–4): 382–389.

———. 2003. "Against Between: A Manifesto." In *Zafer Şenocak*, ed. Tom Cheesman and Karin Yeşilada, 130–143. Cardiff: University of Wales Press.

Adorno, T. W. 1986. "What Does Coming to Terms with the Past Mean?" In *Bitburg in Moral and Political Perspective*, ed. G. Hartman, 114–129. Bloomington: Indiana University Press.

Agamben, Giorgio. 1999. *Remnants of Auschwitz: The Witness and the Archive.* Trans. Daniel Heller-Roazen. New York: Zone Books.

Agence France-Presse. 2004. "Turkish Men Scared Off by Housework." September 14. http://www.news.com.au/common/story_page/0,4057,9116417^13762,00.html (accessed January 3, 2005).

Ahmed, Leila. 1992. *Women and Gender in Islam: Historical Roots of a Modern Debate.* New Haven: Yale University Press.

Akin, Fatih. 1998. *Kurz und schmerzlos* (Short and painless; English title: *Short Sharp Shock*). Hamburg: Universal Pictures Video.

———. 2000. *Im Juli* (In July). Koch Lorber Studio.

———. 2004. *Gegen die Wand* (Against the wall; English title: *Head-On*). 121 min. Hamburg: Wueste Film.

Aksan, Virginia. 2007. Review of *Osman's Dream: The Story of the Ottoman Empire*, by Caroline Finkel. H-NET Book Review, posted July 4. http://www.h-net.org/reviews/showrev.cgi?path=209301189534080.

Altinay, Ayse Gul. 2004. *The Myth of the Military Nation: Militarism, Gender, and Education in Turkey*. New York: Palgrave Macmillan.

Anaya, Rudolfo. 1996. "I'm the King: The Macho Image." In *Muy Macho*, ed. Ray Gonzales, 57–73. New York: Anchor Books.

Anderson, Benedict. 1991. *Imagined Communities: Reflections on the Origin and Spread of Nationalism*. New York: Verso.

Appadurai, Arjun. 1996. *Modernity at Large: Cultural Dimensions of Globalization*. Minneapolis: University of Minnesota Press.

Appiah, Anthony. 2006. *Cosmopolitanism: Ethics in a World of Strangers*. New York: Norton.

Arat-Koç, Sedef. 2007. "(Some) Turkish Transnationalism(s) in an Age of Capitalist Globalization and Empire: 'White Turk' Discourse, The New Geopolitics, and Implications for Feminist Transnationalism." *Journal of Middle East Women's Studies* 3 (1): 35–57.

Asad, Talal. 2003. *Formations of the Secular: Christianity, Islam, Modernity. Cultural Memory in the Present*. Stanford: Stanford University Press.

Associated Press. 2002. "Terrorist Arrests in Hamburg." CBS News, July 2.

———. 2004. "Muslim Denies Plane Crash Plot." December 20. http://www.cnn.com/2004/WORLD/europe/12/20/germany.kaplan.ap/index.html (accessed July 12, 2005).

Ateş, Seyran. 2003. *Grosse Reise ins Feuer: die Geschichte einer deutschen Türkin* (Big Journey into Fire: The Story of a German Turkish Woman). Berlin: Rowohlt.

Auster, Paul. 2002. *The Book of Illusions*. New York: Henry Holt.

Bakirdögen, Ayhan, and Tanja Laninger. 2005. "Lebte Hatun Sürücü zu modern? Kripo vermutet, dass Lebenslust des 23jährigen Mordopfers Täter provozierte" (Did Hatun Sürücü Live Too Modern? The Criminal Investigation Department Speculates that the Love for Life of the 23-Year-Old Murder Victim May Have Provoked the Perpetrators). Die Welt.de. February 10. http://www.welt.de/data/2005/02/10/461512.html.

Balibar, Étienne, and Immanuel Wallerstein. 1991. *Race, Nation, Class: Ambiguous Identities* Trans. Chris Turner. London & New York: Verso.

Barbieri, William. 1999. "Group Rights and the Muslim Diaspora." *Human Rights Quarterly* 21 (4): 907–926.

Barthes, Roland. 1972. "Myth Today." In *Mythologies*, trans. Annette Lavers, 109–159. New York: Hill and Wang.

Başer, Tevfik. 1986. *40 Quadratmeter Deutschland* (Forty Square Meters of Germany). 80 min. Hamburg: Studio Hamburg Film Produktion.

Basic Law for the Federal Republic of Germany. 2001. German Bundestag, Administration/Public Relations section. http://www.bundestag.de/htdocs_e/parliament/function /legal/germanbasiclaw.pdf (last accessed December 10, 2007).

Bauer, Patrick. 2005. "Hinter der Schulfassade" (Behind the School Facade). July 13. http://www.taz.de/pt/2005/03/09/a0272.nf/text.

Baumgartner-Karabak, Andrea, and Gisela Landesberger. 1978. *Die verkauften Bräute. Türkische Frauen zwischen Kreuzberg und Anatolien* (Sold Brides: Turkish Women between Kreuzberg and Anatolia). Hamburg: Rowohlt Taschenbuchverlag.

BBC News. 2003. "'Caliph of Cologne' Goes Free." May 28. http://news.bbc.co.uk/1/hi/world/europe/2943080.stm.

———. 2004. "Housework Sermon Sparks Imam Boycott." March 26. http://news.bbc.co.uk/2/hi/europe/3571343.stm.

———. 2006. "Profile: Ayaan Hirsi Ali." June 29. http://news.bbc.co.uk/2/hi/europe/4985636.stm

Beiersdorf, Dagmar. 1984–1985. *Die Wolfsbraut* (The Wolf's Bride). Berlin: NDF.

Bekdil, Burak. 2005. A Matter of Demography. *Turkish Daily News*, December 7. http://www.turkishdailynews.com.tr/article.php?enewsid=30058.

Bellér-Hann, Ildikó, and C. M. Hann. 2000. *Turkish Region: State, Market & Social Identities on the East Black Sea Coast*. Santa Fe: School of American Research Press.

Berlant, Lauren. 1998. "Intimacy: A Special Issue." *Critical Inquiry* 24 (2): 547–566.

Beseke, Ulriche. 2006. "Ihr Bruder hat sie sexuell belästigt" (Her brother had sexually harassed her). Stern TV, April 19. http://www.stern.de/politik/deutschland/:G%FClsah-S.-%FCber-Ehrenmord-Ihr-Bruder/559785.html.

Bhabha, Homi K. 1994. *The Location of Culture*. London: Routledge.

———. 1995. "Are You a Man or a Mouse?" *Constructing Masculinity*, ed. M. Berger, B. Wallis, and S. Watson, 57–68. New York: Routledge.

Biehl, Jody K. 2005. "The Death of a Muslim Woman: The Whore Lived Like a German." Spiegel Online, English site. March 2. http://www.spiegel.de/international/0,1518,344374,00.html (last accessed December 2007).

Bild. 2007. "Horror Hauptschule: Die Ex-Rektorin der berüchtigten Berliner Rütli-Schule packt aus!" (Horror High School: The Ex-Director of Berlin's Infamous Rutli School Speaks Her Mind). May 25. http://www.bild.t-online.de/BTO/news/2007/03/07/horror-hauptschule/ruetli-ex-direktorin-serie-1.html (last accessed December 2007).

Bingham, Adam. 2003. "All That Heaven Allows." *Bright Lights Film Journal* 42. http://www.brightlightsfilm.com/42/ali.htm (last accessed December 2007).

Boddy J. 1991. "Anthropology, Feminism and the Postmodern Context." *Culture* 11 (12): 125–133.

Bohm, Hark. 1988. *Yasemin*. Hamburg: Hamburger Kino Kompanie.

Bolak, Hale Cihan. 1997. "When Wives Are Major Providers: Culture, Gender, and Family Work." *Gender and Society* 11 (4): 409–433.

Boos-Nünning, Ursula, ed. 1990. *Die Türkische Migration in deutschsprachigen Büchern 1961–1984* (Turkish Migration in German Language Books 1961–1984). Opladen: Leske and Budrich.

Borneman, John. 1991. *After the Wall: East Meets West in the New Berlin*. New York: Basic Books.

———. 2004. *Death of the Father: An Anthropology of the End in Political Authority*. New York: Berghahn Books.

Bourdieu, Pierre. 1966. "The Sentiment of Honour in Kabyle Society." In *Honour and Shame: The Values of Mediterranean Society*, ed. Jean G. Péristiany, 191–241. Nature of Human Society Series. Chicago: University of Chicago Press.

———. 1977. *Outline of a Theory of Practice*. Cambridge: Cambridge University Press.

———. 1999. "Rethinking the State: Genesis and Structure of the Bureaucratic Field." In *State/Culture: State Formation after the Cultural Turn*, ed. George Steinmetz, 53–75. Ithaca: Cornell University Press.

Bowen, John R. 2006. *Why the French Don't Like Headscarves: Islam, the State and Public Space*. Princeton: Princeton University Press.

Briggs, Charles L. 1986. *Learning How to Ask: A Sociolinguistic Appraisal of the Role of the Interview in Social Science Research*. Studies in the Social and Cultural Foundations of Language. Cambridge: Cambridge University Press.

Bush, Laura. 2001. "The Taliban's War against Women." Radio Address to the Nation. Crawford, Texas, November 17. http://www.state.gov/g/drl/rls/rm/2001/6206.htm.

Butler, Judith. 1989. *Gender Trouble: Feminism and the Subversion of Identity*. New York: Routledge.

———. 1993. *Bodies That Matter: On the Discursive Limits of "Sex."* New York: Routledge.

Caglar, Asye S. 1994. *German Turks in Berlin: Migration and Their Quest for Social Mobility*. PhD diss., McGill University.

———. 1997. "Hyphenated Identities and the Limits of Culture." In *The Politics of Multiculturalism in New Europe: Racism, Identity and Community*, ed. T. Modood and P. Werbner, 169–205. London: Zed Books.

———. 1998. "Popular Culture: Marginality and Institutional Incorporation." *Cultural Dynamics* 10 (3): 243–261.

Calhoun, Craig. 2002. "Imagining Solidarity: Cosmopolitanism, Constitutional Patriotism, and the Public Sphere." *Public Culture* 14 (1): 147–171.

Certeau, Michel de. 1984. *The Practice of Everyday Life*. Berkeley: University of California Press.

Çetin, Sinan. 1993. *Berlin in Berlin*. Cihangir, Istanbul: Plato Film Production Co.

Cheesman, Tom. 2002. "Akçam—Zaimoğlu—'Kanak Attak': Turkish Lives and Letters in German." *German Lives and Letters* 55 (2): 180–195.

Chirkov, V., R. M. Ryan, Y. Kim, and U. Kaplan. 2003. "Differentiating Autonomy from Individualism and Independence: A Self-Determination Theory Perspective on Internalization of Cultural Orientations and Well-Being." *Journal of Personality and Social Psychology* 84 (1): 97–110.

Çileli, Serap. 2002. *Wir Sind eure Töchter, nicht eure Ehre!* (We Are Your Daughters, Not Your Honor). Michelstadt: Neuthor.

Cohen, Stanley. 1980. *Folk Devils and Moral Panics: The Creation of the Mods and Rockers*. New York: St. Martin's Press.

Collier, Jane, with William Maurer and Lydia Suarez-Navaz. 1995. "Sanctioned Identities: Legal Constructions of Modern Personhood." *Identities: Global Studies in Culture and Power* 2 (1–2): 1–27.

Collins, Patricia Hill. 2004. *Black Sexual Politics: African Americans, Gender, and the New Racism*. New York: Routledge.

Conger, Rand, and Glen H. Elder. 1994. *Families in Troubled Times: Adapting to Change in Rural America*. New York: A. de Gruyter.

Connell, Robert W. 1987. "The Evolving Man." *New Internationalist* 175. http://www.newint.org/issue175/evolving.htm.

———. 1995. *Masculinities*. Berkeley: University of California Press.

Crapanzano, Vincent. 1985. *Tuhami: Portrait of a Moroccan*. Chicago: University of Chicago Press.

Cziesche, Dominik, Dietmar Hipp, Felix Kurz, Barbara Schmid, Matthias Schreiber, Martin Sümening, Silvia Tyburski, and Andreas Ulrich. 2003. "Das Kreuz mit dem Koran" (The Cross with the Quran). *Der Spiegel* 40: 82–97. September 29.

de Beauvior, Simone. 1953. *The Second Sex*. Trans. H. M. Parshley. New York: Alfred A. Knopf.

de Bellaigue, Christopher. 2001. "The Sick Man of Europe." Letter. *New York Review of Books* 48 (11), July 5.

Deci, Edward L., and Richard M. Ryan 1985. *Intrinsic Motivation and Self-Determination in Human Behavior*. New York: Plenum.

Deggerich, Markus, and Holger Stark. 2005. "Germany's 'Project Cleanup' Could Deport Hundreds of Radical Muslims." Spiegel Online International. January 24. http://www.spiegel.de/international/spiegel/0,1518,338766,00.html (last accessed December 2007).

del Castillo Guilbault, Rose. 1996. "Untranslatable Words: 'Macho'" Ponencias Instituto Cultural "Raíces Mexicanas." http://www.folklorico.com/ponencias/macho.html.

Delaney, Carol. 1990. "The Hajj: Sacred and Secular." *American Ethnologist* 17 (3): 513–530.

———. 1991. *The Seed and the Soil: Gender and Cosmology in Turkish Village Society*. Comparative Studies on Muslim Societies, 11. Berkeley: University of California Press.

Demirkubuz, Zeki. 1997. *Masumiyet* (Innocence). 113 min. Turkey: Palermo.

Dempsey, Judy. 2006. "Civic Test in Germany Draws Fire." *International Herald Tribune*, February 14. http://www.iht.com/articles/2006/02/14/news/germany.php.

Dencker, Berit Elizabeth. 2002. "Class and the Construction of the 19th Century German Male Body." *Journal of Historical Sociology* 15 (2): 220–251.

Derin, Seyhan. 1996. *Ben Annemin Kiziyim* (I'm My Mother's Daughter). München: Hans-Böckler-Stiftung.

"Deutsch-türkische Tendenzen im Film?" (German-Turkish Tendencies in Film?) 2000. Das interkulturelle Kino Europas. *Interforum*. October 22. http://www.interforum.net/2000/200_vorworte_D.htm (accessed July 10, 2005).

Deutsche Welle. 2003. "NRW: Kein Kopftuch-Gesetz notwendig." (NRW: No Headscarf Law Necessary). October 10. http://www.wdr.de/themen/panorama/1/kopftuchstreit/konsequenzen_nrw.jhtml (last accessed December 2007).

———. 2005. "German Court: Muslim Students Must Swim." June 1. http://www.dw-world.de/dw/article/0,1564,1602805,00.html.

———. 2006a. "Another German State Bans Headscarf for Teachers." June 1. http://www.dw-world.de/dw/article/0,2144,2040124,00.html (accessed August 11, 2006).

———. 2006b. "German Politicians Outraged by Custody Demands." April 19. http://www.dw-world.de/dw/article/0,2144,1974065,00.html (last accessed December 2007).

———. 2006c "German Court Convicts Turk of 'Honor Killing.'" April 13. http://www.dw-world.de/dw/article/0,2144,1968686,00.html.

Diehl, Claudia, and Rainer Schnell. 2006. "'Reactive Ethnicity' or 'Assimilation'? Statements, Arguments, and First Empirical Evidence for Labor Migrants in Germany." *International Migration Review* 40 (4): 786–816.

Dietrich, Stefan. 2000a. "No Place for Hate." *Frankfurter Allgemeine Zeitung*. October 4. www.djrphd.net/News-Articles/FA-No%20Place%20for%20Hate.doc.

———. 2000b. "Die Inländerfrage" (The Native Question). *Frankfurter Allgemeine Zeitung*. October 25.

Die Welt. 2005. "Türkischer Bund will Tabuthemen in die Diskussion bringen" (The Turkish Federation Wants to Bring Taboo Subjects into the Discussion). February 19. http://www.welt.de/data/2005/02/19/515185.html.

Doeleke, Karl, and Miriam Schröder. 2006. "Reactions to Honor Killing Sentence: 'Not the Signal We Need.'" Speigel Online, August 13. http://www.spiegel.de/politik/deutschland/0,1518,411282,00.html.

Draeger, Thomas. 1979. *Metin*. 82 min. German and Turkish. Berlin: Cikon Filmproduktion.

Elçi, Ismet. 1991. *Düğün / Die Heirat* (The Marriage). 91 min. Berlin: Wolfgang Krenz Filmproduktion.

Elsaesser, Thomas. 1989. *New German Cinema: A History*. New Brunswick: Rutgers University Press.

Erker-Sonnabend, Ulrich. 1987. *Orientalische Fremde: Berichte deutscher Türkeireisender des späten 19. Jahrhunderts* (Oriental Foreigners: Accounts of German Tourists in Turkey in the Late Nineteenth Century). Bochum: Studienverlag N. Brockmeyer.

Esmaili, Golrokh. 2005. "Cultural Misunderstandings at the Sick Bed." *Deutsche Welle*, September 25. http://www.dw-world.de/dw/article/0,1564,1717394,00.html.

Espada, Martín. 1996. "The Puerto Rican Dummy and the Merciful Son." In *Muy Macho: Latino Men Confront their Manhood*, ed. Ray González, 75–89. New York: Anchor Books.

Ewing, Katherine Pratt. 2002. "Images of Order and Authority: Shifting Identities and Legal Consciousness in a Runaway Immigrant Daughter." In *Power and the Self*, ed. J. Mageo and B. Knauft, 93–113. Cambridge: Cambridge University Press.

———. 2003. "Migration, Identity Negotiation and Self Experience." In *Worlds on the Move: Globalization, Migration and Cultural Security*, ed. J. Friedman and S. Randeria, 117–140. London: I. B. Taurus.

Europäisches Forum für Migrationsstudien. 2006a. "Initiative of the Bundesrat Calls for Stricter Punishment of Forced Marriages." EFMS Report, February. http://web.uni-bamberg.de/~ba6ef3/dfeb06_e.htm (last accessed December 2007).

———. 2006b. "Forced Marriages: Debate on Lack of Scientific Approach." EFMS Report, February. http://web.uni-bamberg.de/~ba6ef3/dfeb06_e.htm (last accessed December 2007).

Fanon, Frantz. 1967. *Black Skin, White Masks*. New York: Grove Press.

Faroqhi, Suraiya. 2004. *The Ottoman Empire and the World Around It*. London: I. B. Taurus.

Farzanefar, Amin. 2005. "Cinema between Cultures." *Fikrun wa Fann* 82. Goethe Institute. http://www.goethe.de/mmo/priv/964389-STANDARD.pdf. From *Kino des Orients: Stimmen aus einer Region* (Oriental Cinema: Voices of a Region), by Amin Farzanefar, 233–254. Marburg: Schüren Verlag

Fassbinder, Rainer Werner. 1969. *Katzelmacher* (Cock Artist). 88 min. West Germany: Antiteater-X-Film.

———. 1973. *Angst essen Seele auf* (English title: *Ali: Fear Eats the Soul*). 93 min. Munich: Tango Film.

Federal Ministry of the Interior. 2003. *Annual Report of the Office for the Protection of the Constitution*. http://www.verfassungsschutz.de/en/publications/annual_reports/vsbericht2003_engl.html/vsbericht_2003_engl.pdf.

———. 2005. *Annual Report of the Office for the Protection of the Constitution*. http://www.verfassungsschutz.de/en/en_publications/annual_reports/vsbericht2005_engl.

Fehrenbach, Heide. 1998. "Rehabilitating Fatherland: Race and German Remasculinization." *Signs* 24 (1): 107–127.

Fekete, Liz. 2005. "'Speech Crime' and Deportation." Institute of Race Relations. August 11. http://www.irr.org.uk/2005/august/ak000012.html.

Fenner, Angelica. 2000. "Turkish Cinema in the New Europe: Visualizing Ethnic Conflict in Sinan Cetin's Berlin in Berlin." *Camera Obscura* 15 (2): 105–148.

Fertig, Michael. 2004. *The Societal Integration of Immigrants in Germany*. Essen: RWI.

Finn, Peter. 2000. "Debate over a 'Defining Culture' Roils Germany." *Washington Post*, November 2, A22.

Fleishman, Jeffrey. 2005. "'Honor Killings' Show Culture Clash in Berlin: The Latest Slaying of a Muslim Woman in the German Capital Has Sharpened Debate Over the Place of Immigrants in Europe." *Los Angeles Times*, March 20, A10.

Focus Online. 2006. "Stoiber für Ausweisung der Familie Sürücü" (Stoiber for Expulsion of Sürücü Family). April 19. http://www.focus.de/politik/deutschland/ehrenmord_aid_107814.html.

Foucault, Michel. 1972. *The Archaeology of Knowledge*. New York: Routledge.

———. 1978. *The History of Sexuality*, vol. I. New York: Pantheon Books.

———. 1991. "Governmentality." In *The Foucault Effect: Studies in Governmentality*, ed. G. Burchell, C. Gordon, and P. Miller, trans. Rosi Braidotti, 87–104. Chicago: University of Chicago Press.

———. 1995. *Discipline and Punish: The Birth of the Prison*. New York: Vintage Books.

Frankfurter Allgemeine Zeitung. 2005. "'Honor Killings' Shock Germans." March 18. http://www.faz.net/s/RubA7251875CDBF4074A4CC29C0D3759240/Doc~E1BE13B9EA1EB48898CA88E128AEA5D64~ATpl~Ecommon~Acontent.html.

French, Jan. 2004. "*Mestizaje* and Law Making in Indigenous Identity Formation in Northeast Brazil: After the Conflict Came the History." *American Anthropologist* 106 (4): 663–674.

Friedman, Sara L. 2005. "The Intimacy of State Power: Marriage, Liberation, and Socialist Subjects in Southeast China." *American Ethnologist* 32 (2): 312–327.

Fuhr, Eckhard. 2000. "Was ist Deutsch?" (What Is German?) *Welt Online*. http://www.welt.de/print-welt/article540437/Was_ist_deutsch.html.

Garnett, Lucy M. J. 1909. *Home Life in Turkey*. New York: Macmillan.

Geertz, Clifford. 1973. "Religion as a Cultural System." In *Interpretation of Cultures*, 87–125. New York: Basic Books.

———. 1983. "'From the Natives' Point of View': On the Nature of Anthropological Understanding." In *Local Knowledge: Further Essays in Interpretive Anthropology*, ed. C. Geertz, 55–72. New York: Basic Books.

German Embassy. n.d. "General Figures." Washington, D.C. http://www.germany.info/relaunch/info/publications/infocus/JewishLife/generalfigures.htm (accessed July 23, 2007).

Gförer, Jörg. 1986. *Ganz unten* (At the Bottom of the Heap). 100 min. Cologne: KAOS Film.

Gilmore, David D., ed. 1987. *Honor and Shame and the Unity of the Mediterranean*. Special publication of the American Anthropological Association, No. 22. Washington,

D.C.: American Anthropological Association.

Goffman, Daniel. 2002. *The Ottoman Empire and Early Modern Europe*. Cambridge: Cambridge University Press.

Göktürk, Deniz. 2001. "Turkish Delight—German Fright: Migrant Identities in Transnational Cinemas." In *Mediated Identities*, ed. D. Derman, K. Ross, and N. Dakovic, 131–149. Istanbul: Bilgi University Press.

Goode, Erich, and Nachman Ben-Yehuda. 1994. *Moral Panics: The Social Construction of Deviance*. Oxford and New York: Blackwell.

Gordon, Terri J. 2002. "Fascism and the Female Form: Performance Art in the Third Reich." *Journal of the History of Sexuality* 11 (1–2): 164–200.

Gupta, Akhil. 1995. "Blurred Boundaries: The Discourse of Corruption, the Culture of Politics, and the Imagined State." *American Ethnologist* 22 (2): 375–402.

Gutmann, Matthew C. 1996. *The Meanings of Macho: Being a Man in Mexico City*. Berkeley: University of California Press.

Habermas, Jurgen. 1986. "Defusing the Past: A Politico-Cultural Tract." In *Bitburg in Moral and Political Perspective*, ed. G. Hartman, 43–51. Bloomington: Indiana University Press.

———. 1994. "Struggles for Recognition in the Democratic Constitutional State." In *Multiculturalism*, ed. C. Taylor and A. Gutmann, 107–148. Princeton: Princeton University Press.

Hahn, H. J. 1998. *Education and Society in Germany*. Oxford: Berg.

Hahn-Hahn, Ida. 1845. *Letters of a German Countess: Written During Her Travels in Turkey, Egypt, the Holy Land, Syria, Nubia, &c. in 1843–4*. 3 vols. London: Henry Colburn.

Hall, Stuart. 2000. "Cultural Identity and Diaspora." In *Diaspora and Visual Culture: Representing Africans and Jews*, ed. N. Mirzoeff, 21–33. London: Routledge.

Hall, Stuart, and Tony Jefferson. 1976. *Resistance through Rituals: Youth Subcultures in Post-war Britain*. London: Hutchinson.

Halsband, Robert, ed. 1965. *The Complete Letters of Lady Mary Wortley Montagu*. 3 vols. Oxford: Clarendon Press.

Hansen, Thomas Blom, and Finn Stepputat. 2001. *States of Imagination: Ethnographic Explorations of the Postcolonial State*. Durham: Duke University Press.

Harnisch, Antje, Anne Marie Stokes, and Friedemann Weidauer. 1998. *Fringe Voices: An Anthology of Minority Writing in the Federal Republic of Germany*. Oxford: Berg.

Hawley, Charles. 2006. "A German State Quizzes Muslim Immigrants on Jews, Gays and Swim Lessons." Spiegel Online, January 31. http://www.spiegel.de/international/0,1518,397482,00.html.

Heckmann, Friedrich. 1997. "Patterns of Immigrant Integration in Germany." *EFMS* (*Europaeisches Forum fuer Migrationsstudien*) paper 14. http://web.uni-bamberg.de/~ba6ef3/pdf/efms_p14.pdf.

Heitmeyer, Wilhelm. 1996. "Für türkische Jugendliche in Deutschland spielt der Islam eine wichtige Rolle." (Islam plays an important role for Turkish youth in Germany.) *Die Zeit* 35. http://www.zeit.de/1996/35/heitmey.txt.19960823.xml.

Heitmeyer, Wilhelm, Joachim Müller, and Helmut Schröder. 1997. *Verlockender Fundamentalismus* (Enticing Fundamentalism). Frankfurt am Main: Suhrkamp.

Heitmeyer, Wilhelm, and Andres Zick. 2004. "Anti-Semitism, Islamophobia and Group-Focused Enmity in Germany." Research Note. Institute for Interdisciplinary Research on Conflict and Violence, University of Bielefeld, May.

Herbert, Ulrich, and Karin Hunn. 2001. "Guest Workers and Policy on Guest Workers in the Federal Republic: From the Beginning of Recruitment in 1955 until Its Halt in 1973." In *The Miracle Years: A Cultural History of Germany 1949–1968*, ed. H. Schissler, 187–218. Princeton: Princeton University Press.

Herd, Denise. 1991. "The Paradox of Temperance: Blacks and the Alcohol Question in 19th Century America." In *Drinking Behavior and Belief in Modern History*, ed. S. Barrows and R. Room, 354–375. Berkeley: University of California Press.

Herder, Johann Gottfried von. 1784. *Materials for the Philosophy of the History of Mankind, 1784.* In Internet Modern History Sourcebook, comp. Paul Halsall, trans. Jerome Arkenberg. 1998. http://www.fordham.edu/halsall/mod/1784herder-mankind .html.

Herzfeld, Michael. 1980. "Honour and Shame: Problems in the Comparative Analysis of Moral Systems." *Man* (New Series) 15 (2): 339–351.

———. 1985. *The Poetics of Manhood: Contest and Identity in a Cretan Mountain Village.* Princeton: Princeton University Press.

———. 1987. "'As in Your Own House:' Hospitality, Ethnography, and the Stereotype of Mediterranean Society." In *Honor and Shame and the Unity of the Mediterranean*, ed. D. D. Gilmore, 75–89. Washington, D.C.: American Anthropological Association.

Hessischen Islamforum. 2005. "Muslimische Kinder in der Schule: Informationen und Empfehlungen." (Muslim Children in School: Information and Recommendations.) June 29. http://www.interkultureller-rat.de/Themen/Islamforen/Muslimische_Kinder %20(1).pdf (last accessed December 2007).

Heywood, Colin. 2002. "Wittek and the Austrian Tradition." In *Writing Ottoman History: Documents and Interpretations*, 7–25. Burlington: Ashgate.

Hilbk, Merle. 1998. "Im Glauben eine Heimat finden" (Finding a Home in Faith). *Die Zeit.* http://www.zeit.de/ 1998/31/199831.ludin_.xml (last accessed December 2007).

Hirsi Ali, Ayaan. 2006. American Enterprise Institute. "Women the Future of Freedom." http://www.aei.org/publications/filter.all,pubID.24831/pub_detail.asp (last accessed December 2007).

Hiscott, William. 2005. "'Parallel Societies': A Neologism Gone Bad." Multicultural Center Prague. July. http://www.migrationonline.cz/e-library/?x=1963619 (last accessed December 2007).

hooks, bell. 2003. *We Real Cool: Black Men and Masculinity.* New York: Routledge.

Hooper, John. 2002. "German Right Tries to Capitalise on Arrest of Bomb Suspects." *Guardian*, September 9. http://www.guardian.co.uk/september11/story/0,11209,7981 79,00.html.

Horrocks, David, and Eva Kolinsky. 1996. *Turkish Culture in German Society Today*. Oxford: Berghahn.

Horst, Hartmut, and Eckart Lottman. 1987. *Auf Eigenen Füssen* (On One's Own Feet). Alternative title: *Aufbruche* (Awakenings). Germany: Medien Operative.

Howie, Gillian. 2004. "After Postmodernism: Feminism and Marxism Revisited." Paper for Marx and Philosophy Seminar on "Marx and Gender," December 4. London School of Economics. Unpublished draft. http://www.marxandphilosophy.org.uk/howie2004.doc (accessed June 6, 2006).

Huntington, Samuel P. 1993. "The Clash of Civilizations?" *Foreign Affairs* 72 (3): 22–49

Ifilm Short Videos. 2005. http://www.ifilm.com/ifilmdetail/2655656?htv=12 (accessed June 7, 2005).

Inan, Afet. 1962. *The Emancipation of the Turkish Woman*. Paris: UNESCO.

Iser, Wolfgang. 1993. *The Fictive and the Imaginary: Charting Literary Anthropology*. Baltimore: John Hopkins University Press.

Ivy, Marilyn. 1995. *Discourses of the Vanishing: Modernity, Phantasm, Japan*. Chicago: University of Chicago Press.

Jenkins, Jennifer. 2004. "German Orientalism: Introduction." *Comparative Studies of South Asia, Africa, and the Middle East* 24 (2): 97–100.

Jordan, James. 2003. "Zafer Şenocak's Essays and Early Prose Fiction: From Collective Multiculturalism to Fragmented Cultural Identities." In *Zafer Şenocak*, ed. T. Cheesman and K. Yesilada, 91–105. Cardiff: University of Wales Press.

Kağitçibaşi, Çiğdem. 2005. "Autonomy and Relatedness in Cultural Context: Implications for Self and Family." *Journal of Cross-Cultural Psychology* 36 (4): 403–422.

Kalinowsky, Yvonne, and Norbert Kron. 1999. *Zwischen Kebab und Karriere. Junge Türken in Berlin* (Between Kebab and Career. Young Turks in Berlin). Documentary, 29 min. Germany.

Kandiyoti, Deniz. 1987. "Emancipated but Unliberated? Reflections on the Turkish Case." *Feminist Studies* 13 (2): 317–338.

———. 1994. "The Paradoxes of Masculinity: Some Thoughts on Segregated Societies." In *Dislocating Masculinity: Comparative Ethnographies*, ed. A. Cornwall and N. Lindisfarne, 197–213. London: Routledge.

———. 1997. "Gendering the Modern: On Missing Dimensions in the Study of Turkish Modernity." In *Rethinking Modernity and National Identity in Turkey*, ed. S. Bozdogan and R. Kasaba, 113–132. Seattle: University of Washington Press.

———. 1998a. "Gender, Power and Contestation: Rethinking 'Bargaining with Patriarchy.'" In *Feminist Visions of Development: Gender Analysis and Policy*, ed. C. Jackson and R. Pearson, 135–152. London: Routledge.

———. 1998b. "Some Awkward Questions on Women and Modernity in Turkey." In *Remaking Women: Feminism and Modernity in the Middle East*, ed. L. Abu-Lughod, 270–287. Princeton: Princeton University Press.

Kant, Immanuel. 1948. "Groundwork of the Metaphysic of Morals." In *The Moral Law*, ed. H. J. Paton, 51–70. London: Hutchinson University Library.

Karaömerlioğlu, M. Asim. 1998. "The Village Institutes Experience in Turkey." *British Journal of Middle Eastern Studies* 25 (1): 47–73.

Kaya, Ayhan. 2001. *Sicher in Kreuzberg: Constructing Diasporas*. Bielefeld: Transkript Verlag.

———. 2002. "The Hyphenated Germans: German-Turks." *Private View* (Spring): 36–43.

Kelek, Necla. 2005. *Die fremde Braut. Ein Bericht aus dem Inneren des türkischen Lebens in Deutschland* (The Foreign Bride: An Inside Account of Turkish Life in Germany). Cologne: Kiepenheuer & Witsch.

Khan, Aisha. 2003. "Portraits in the Mirror: Nature, Culture, and Women's Travel Writing in the Caribbean." *Women's Writing* 10 (1): 93–117.

———. 2004. *Callalloo Nation: Metaphors of Race and Religious Identity among South Asians in Trinidad*. Durham: Duke University Press.

Kleinlogel, Cornelia. 1989. *Exotic-Erotik: zur Geschichte des Türkenbildes in der frühen Neuzeit (1452–1800)* (Exotic-Erotic: On the History of the Image of Turks in the Early Modern Period [1452–1800]). Bochumer Schriften zur deutschen Literatur 8. Frankfurt am Main: Peter Lang Verlag.

Klusmeyer, Douglas. 2001. "A 'Guiding Culture' for Immigrants? Integration and Diversity in Germany." *Journal of Ethnic and Migration Studies* 27 (3): 519–532.

Koğacioğlu, Dicle. 2004. "The Tradition Effect: Framing Honor Crimes in Turkey." *Differences: A Journal of Feminist Cultural Studies* 15 (2): 118–151.

Kogan, Irena. 2003. "A Study of Employment Careers of Immigrants in Germany." Working Paper No. 66. Mannheim Zentrum für Europäische Sozialforschung. http://www.mzes.uni-mannheim.de/fs_publikationen_e.html.

Kortepeter, Carl Max. 1991. "German *Zeitung* Literature (as Sources for Ottoman History)." In *The Ottoman Turks: Nomad Kingdom to World Empire*, 151–161. Istanbul: Isis Press.

Kristeva, Julia. 1982. *Powers of Horror: An Essay on Abjection. European Perspectives*. New York: Columbia University Press.

Krüger, Arnd, Fabian Krüger, and Sybille Treptau. 2002. "Nudism in Nazi Germany: Indecent Behavior or Physical Culture for the Well-being of the Nation." *International Journal of the History of Sport* 19 (4): 33–54.

Kuheim, Rosemarie. 2001. "Tevfik Baser." http://www.deutsches-filmhaus.de/bio_reg/b_bio/regiss/baser_tevfik_bio.htm (accessed July 21, 2004).

Kula, Onur Bilge. 1992, 1993. *Alman Kültüründe Türk İmgesi*, 2 vols. Ankara Gündoğan Yayınları.

Kultus, Eva. 1998. *Der Preis der Freiheit: 10 Jahre im Leben einer jungen Frau türiksher Herkunft. Langzeitstudie: der mühsame Prozeß des eigenen Wegs aus einer türkischen Familie* (The Cost of Freedom: Ten Years in the Life of a Young Woman of Turkish Background. A Long-Term Study of the Difficult Process of Finding One's Way Out of a Turkish Family). Frankfurt: IKO-Verlag für Interkulturelle Kommunikation.

Kuran-Burçoğlu, Nedret. 2003. "A Glimpse at Various Stages of the Evolution of the Image of the Turk in Europe: 15th to 21st Centuries." In *Historical Image of the Turk in Europe: 15th Century to the Present: Political and Civilizational Aspects*, ed. Mustafa Soykut, 21–42. Istanbul: Isis Press.

Langenscheidts Grosswörterbuch Deutsch als Fremdsprache. 1998. Berlin: Langenscheidt.

Laninger, Tanja. 2005. "Mord an Türkin—Brüder verhaftet. Hatun Sürücü soll von ihrer eigenen Familie hingerichtet worden sein—Hintergründe weiter unklar" (Murder of a Turkish Woman—Brothers Arrested. Hatun Sürücü May Have Been Executed by Her Own Family—Details Remain Unclear). *Die Welt*, February 15. http://www.welt.de/data/2005/02/15/463980.html.

Lau, Jörg. 2005. "Wie eine Deutsche" (Like a German.) *Die Zeit* 9. http://zeit.de/2005/09/Hatin_S_9fr_9fc_9f_09.

Leggewie, C. 2000. "Integration und Segregation." In *Migrationsreport 2000*, ed. K. J. Bade and R. Münz, 85–108. Frankfurt am Main: Campus.

Leicht, Justus. 2006. "Germany: The Murder of Hatun Sürücü and the Debate over 'Honour Killings.'" World Socialist Web Site, May 17. http://www.wsws.org/articles/2006/may2006/germ-m17.shtml.

Leithäuser, Johannes. 2002. "The Shifting Site of the Immigration Showdown." *Frankfurter Allegmeine Zeitung*. February 19. Reprinted as "Germany: Immigration, Integration," *Migration News* 9: March 4. http://migration.ucdavis.edu/mn/more.php?id=2579_0_4_0.

Levi, Primo. 1986. *Survival in Auschwitz and the Reawakening: Two Memoirs*. New York: Summit Books.

Lewis, Oscar. 1959. *Five Families: Mexican Case Studies in the Culture of Poverty*. New York: Basic Books.

Leyendecker, Hans, and John Goetz. 2007. "Alles versucht, die Rückkehr zu verhindern." *Süddeutsche Zeitung*, January 22. http://www.sueddeutsche.de/deutschland/artikel/958/98860/.

Linke, Uli. 1997. "Gendered Difference, Violent Imagination: Blood, Race, Nation." *American Anthropologist* 99 (3): 559–573.

———. 2002. "Archives of Violence: The Holocaust and the German Politics of Memory." In *Annihilating Difference: The Anthropology of Genocide*, ed. A. Laban Hinton, 229–271. Berkeley: University of California Press.

Lowe, Lisa. 1991. *Critical Terrains: French and British Orientalisms*. Ithaca: Cornell University Press.

Lutz, Helma. 1991. *Welten Verbinden—Türkische Sozialarbeiterinnen in den Niederlanden und der Bundesrepublik Deutschland* (Connecting Worlds: Turkish Social Workers in the Netherlands and the Federal Republic of Germany). Frankfurt/Main: IKO-Verlag.

Magnarella, Paul J. 1998. *Anatolia's Loom: Studies in Turkish Culture, Society, Politics and Law*. Istanbul: Isis Press.

Mahmood, Saba. 2005. *Politics of Piety: The Islamic Revival and the Feminist Subject*. Princeton: Princeton University Press.

Malik, Sarita. 1996. "Beyond 'The Cinema of Duty'? The Pleasures of Hybridity: Black British Film of the 1980's and 1990's." In *Dissolving Views: Key Writings on British Cinema*, ed. A. Higson, 202–215. New York: Cassell.

Mankekar, Purnima. 1999. *Screening Culture, Viewing Politics: An Ethnography of Television, Womanhood and Nation in Postcolonial India*. Durham: Duke University.

Manz, Stefan. 2004. "Constructing a Normative National Identity: The Leitkultur Debate in Germany, 2000/2001." *Journal of Multilingual and Multicultural Development* 25 (5 & 6): 481–496.

Marcus, Steven. 1966. *The Other Victorians*. New York: Basic Books.

Mardin, Serif. 1969. "Power, Civil Society, and Culture in the Ottoman Empire." *Comparative Studies in Society and History* 11 (3): 258–281.

Markell, Patchen. 2000. "Making Affect Safe for Democracy? On 'Constitutional Patriotism.'" *Political Theory* 28 (1): 38–53.

Mattson, Michelle. 1999. "Tatort: The Generation of Public Identity in a German Crime Series." *New German Critique* 78 (Special Issue on German Media Studies): 161–181.

McClintock, Anne. 1997. "'No Longer in a Future Heaven': Gender, Race, Nationalism." In *Dangerous Liaisons: Gender, Nation and Postcolonial Perspectives*, ed. A. McClintock, A. Mufti, and E. Shohat, 89–112. Minneapolis: University of Minnesota Press.

Meeker, Michael E. 1976. "Meaning and Society in the Near East: Examples from the Black Sea Turks and the Levantine Arabs." 2 parts. *International Journal of Middle East Studies* 7 (2): 243–270; 7 (3): 383–422.

——. 2002. *A Nation of Empire: The Ottoman Legacy of Turkish Modernity*. Berkeley: University of California Press.

Meerapfel, Jeanine. 1985. *Die Kümmeltürkin Geht* (The Spice Lady Leaves. English title: *Melek Leaves*). West Germany.

Melman, Billie. 1992. *Women's Orients—English Women and the Middle East, 1718–1918: Sexuality, Religion, and Work*. Ann Arbor: University of Michigan Press.

Merz, Friedrich 2000. "Einwanderung und Identität" (Immigration and Identity). *Welt Online*. October 25. http://www.welt.de/print-welt/article540438/Einwanderung_und_Identitaet.html.

Meske, Sigrid. 1983. *Situationsanalyse türkischer Frauen in der BRD. Unter dem Aspekt ihrer kulturellen Neuorientierungen in der Türkei* (Analyzing the Situation of Turkish Women in the FRG in Light of Their Cultural Reorientation in Turkey). Berlin: Express Edition.

Middle East Media Research Institute (MEMRI). 2005. "Arabische Zeitung über 'Ehrenmorde' in Deutschland" (Arab Newspaper on "Honor Killings" in Germany). May 27. http://www.wadinet.de/news/iraq/newsarticle.php?id=1035.

Militant Islam Monitor. 2006. "Honor Killings in Berlin: Six Muslim Women in Four Months—Murdered by Family Members. April 21. http://www.militantislammonitor .org/article/id/1859.

Mills, Sara. 1991. *Discourses of Difference: An Analysis of Women's Travel Writing and Colonialism*. New York: Routledge.

Mitscherlich, Alexander, and Margerete Mitscherlich. 1975. *The Inability to Mourn: Principles of Collective Behavior*. New York: Grove Press.

Monheim, Gert. "Mord in Namen der Ehre. Der Tod von Hatun Sürücü" (Murder in the Name of Honor: The Death of Hatun Sürücü). Stern TV and RTL. December 7.

Mosse, George L. 1975. *The Nationalization of the Masses: Political Symbolism and Mass Movements in Germany from the Napoleonic Wars through the Third Reich*. New York: Howard Fertig.

Mrozek, Andrea. 2000. "Heavy on the Leitkultur." *Central Europe Review* 2, No. 42 (December 4). http://www.ce-review.org/00/42/mrozek42.html.

Müller, Jan-Werner. 2006. "On the Origins of Constitutional Patriotism." *Contemporary Political Theory* 5: 278–296.

Müller, Peter. 2006. "Fragen der Ehre und des Rechts." *Welt am Sonntag* 16: 7, April 16.

Münz, R., W. Siefert, and R. Ulrich. 1997. *Zuwanderung nach Deutschland: Strukturen, Wirkungen, Perspektiven*. Frankfurt am Main: Campus.

Münz, Rainer. 2004. "New German Law Skirts Comprehensive Immigration Reform." *Migration Information Source*. Washington, D.C.: Migration Policy Institute. http:// www.migrationinformation.org/Feature/display.cfm?ID=241.

Murray, Charles. 1984. *Losing Ground: American Social Policy 1950–1980*. New York: Basic Books.

Naficy, Hamid. 2001. *An Accented Cinema: Exilic and Diasporic Filmmaking*. Princeton: Princeton University Press.

Navaro-Yashin, Yael. 2002. *Faces of the State: Secularism and Public Life in Turkey*. Princeton: Princeton University Press.

Nökel, Siegrid. 2002. *Die Töchter der Gastarbeiter und der Islam: zur Soziologie alltagsweltlicher Anerkennungspolitiken: eine Fallstudie* (The Daughters of Guestworkers and Islam: Toward a Sociology of the Everyday Politics of Recognition: A Case Study). Bielefeld: Transcript.

O'Brien, Peter. 1996. *Beyond the Swastika*. London: Routledge.

Okin, Susan Moller. 1999. "Is Multiculturalism Bad for Women?" In *Is Multiculturalism Bad for Women?* 7–24. Princeton: Princeton University Press.

Onder, Zehra. 1996. "Muslim-Turkish Children in Germany: Sociocultural Problems." *Migration World Magazine* 24 (5): 18–24.

Ong, Aihwa. 1996. "Cultural Citizenship as Subject-Making: Immigrants Negotiate Racial and Cultural Boundaries in the United States." *Current Anthropology* 37 (5): 737–762.

———. 2003. *Buddha Is Hiding: Refugees, Citizenship, the New America.* Berkeley: University of California Press.

Online Newshour with Jim Lehrer. 2002. "Al-Qaida in Germany." October 25. http://www.pbs.org/newshour/bb/terrorism/july-dec02/germanycell_10-25.html.

Ortner, Sherry. 2006. *Anthropology and Social Theory: Culture, Power, and the Acting Subject.* Durham: Duke University Press.

Özbek, Meral. 1997. "Arabesk Culture: A Case of Modernization and Popular Identity." In *Rethinking Modernity and National Identity in Turkey*, ed. S. Bozdogan and R. Kasaba, 211–233. Seattle: University of Washington Press.

Özdamar, Emine Sevgi. 1992. *Das Leben ist eine Karawanserei, hat zwei Türen, aus einer kam ich rein, aus der anderen ging ich raus* (Life Is a Caravanserai with Two Doors, through One of Which I Came, and through One of Which I Left). Cologne: Kiepenheuer & Witsch.

Paine, Robert. 1989. "High-Wire Culture: Comparing Two Agonistic Systems of Self Esteem." *Man* (New Series) 24 (4): 657–672.

Palm, Dorothee. 2000. *Frauen Geschichten: Musliminnen in Deutschland erzählen aus ihrem Leben* (Women's Stories: Muslim Women in Germany Recount Their Lives). Cologne: Teiresias-Verlag.

Parla, Ayşe. 2001. "The 'Honor' of the State: Virginity Exams in Turkey." *Feminist Studies* 27 (1): 65–88.

Pastner, Carroll McC. 1988. "A Case of Honor among the Oasis Baluch of Makran: Controversy and Accommodation." In *Sharīat and Ambiguity in South Asian Islam*, ed. K. P. Ewing, 248–258. Berkeley: University of California Press.

Paterson, Tony. 2005. "How Many More Women Have to Die before This Society Wakes Up?" Telegraph.co.uk, February 27. http://www.telegraph.co.uk/news/main.jhtml?xml=/news/2005/02/27/wturk27.xml.

Péristiany, Jean G., ed. 1966. *Honour and Shame: The Values of Mediterranean Society.* Nature of Human Society Series. Chicago: University of Chicago Press.

Pfeiffer, Ida. 1852. *A Visit to the Holy Land.* 2nd ed. Trans. H. W. Dulcken. London: Ingram, Cooke.

Pflaum, Hans Günther. 2002. *Turkish Cinema Newsletter* http://www.turkfilm.net/arc107.html (accessed February 2, 2004).

Phalnikar, Sonia. 2005. "When Freedom Gets the Death Sentence." *Deutsche Welle* DW-World.de. February 24. http://www.dw-world.de/dw/article/0,1564,1499191_0,00.htm (accessed June 5).

Phillips, Anne. 2003. "When Culture Means Gender: Issues of Cultural Defence in the

English Courts." *Modern Law Review* 66 (4): 510–531.

Pitt-Rivers, Julian. 1966. "Honour and Social Status." In *Honour and Shame: The Values of Mediterranean Society*, ed. J. G. Péristiany, 19–78. Chicago: University of Chicago Press.

Povinelli, Elizabeth A. 2002. "Notes on Gridlock: Genealogy, Intimacy, Sexuality." *Public Culture* 14 (1): 215–238.

Radtke, Frank-Olaf. 1997. "Multiculturalism in Welfare States: The Case of Germany." In *The Ethnicity Reader: Nationalism, Multiculturalism and Migration*, ed. M. Guibernau and J. Rex, 248–256. Cambridge, UK: Polity Press.

Radway, Janice. 1984. *Reading the Romance: Women, Patriarchy, and Popular Literature.* Chapel Hill: University of North Carolina.

Rasche, Uta. 2005. "Unfaire Berichterstattung" (Unfair Coverage). *Frankfurter Allgemeine Zeitung*, April 13. http://fazarchiv.faz.net/; trans. Christina White, "German Edition of 'Hürriyet' Newspaper: Smear Campaign against German-Turkish Female Activists." http://www.qantara.de/webcom/show_article.php/_c-478/_nr-269/i.html.

Reitz, Edgar. *Heimat* (Homeland). 1984. Munich: Edgar Reitz Filmproduktion.

Renteln, Alison Dundes. 2004. *The Cultural Defense.* New York: Oxford University Press.

Review of Religions. 1988. "Editorial: Nudity." Vol. LXXXIII, No. 11. http://www.alislam.org/library/links/nudity.html.

Ritter, Bettina. 2006. "Muslim Students at Berlin Schools Opt Out of Gym Class." *Deutsche Welle*, January 23. http://www.dw-world.de/dw/article/0,2144,1859368,00.html.

Roach, Ronald. 2004. "Decoding Hip-Hop's Cultural Impact: Scholars Are Poised to Take a Close Look at the Influence of Hip-Hop on the Social Identity, Values of Today's Youth." *Black Issues in Higher Education*, April 22. http://findarticles.com/p/articles/mi_m0DXK/is_5_21/ai_n6146619 (last accessed December 2007).

Rodriguez, Roberto, and Patrisia Gonzales. 1997. "Deconstructing Machismo." *San Francisco Chronicle*, June 20. http://www.azteca.net/aztec/literat/macho.html.

Rosaldo, Renato. 1994. "Cultural Citizenship and Educational Democracy." *Cultural Anthropology* 9 (3): 402–411.

RP Online. 2000. "Zuwanderer sollen sich deutscher Kultur anpassen" (Immigrants Should Accept German Culture). October 18. http://www.rp-online.de/app/suche/index.php?page=1&search=Zuwanderer,%20die%20auf%20Dauer%20hier%20leben&sort=&skip=0&shown=2&searchin=rpo.

———. 2006. "Stoiber verlangt Ausweisung der 'Ehrenmord'-Familie." April 19. http://www.rp-online.de/public/article/nachrichten/politik/special/israel/327717.

Said, Edward. 1978. *Orientalism.* New York: Vintage Books.

Sanders-Brahms, Helma. 1975. *Shirins Hochzeit* (Shirin's Wedding). Freiburg im Breisgau: Panta-Rhei-Filmverl.

Santner, E. L. 1990. *Stranded Objects: Mourning, Memory, and Film in Postwar Germany.* Ithaca: Cornell University Press.

Schiffauer, Werner. 1987. *Die Bauern von Subay: Das Leben in einem türkischen Dorf* (The Peasants of Subay: Life in a Turkish Village). Stuttgart: Klett-Cotta.

———. 1991. *Die Migranten aus Subay: Turken in Deutschland. Eine Ethnographie* (Migrants from Subay: Turks in Germany. An Ethnography). Stuttgart: Klett-Cotta.

———. 2000. *Die Gottesmänner: Türkische Islamisten in Deutschland* (Men of God: Turkish Islamists in Germany). Frankfurt: Suhrkamp.

———. 2001. "Production of Fundamentalism: On the Dynamics of Producing the Radically Different." In *Religion and Media*, ed. H. deVries and S. Weber, 435–455. Stanford: Stanford University Press.

———. 2005. "'Deutsche Auslander.' Schlachtfeld Frau" ("German Foreigners." Battlefield Women). *Süddeutsche Zeitung*, February 25. http://www.sueddeutsche.de/kultur/artikel/474/48426/.

Schneider, Jens. 2002. "Discourses of Exclusion: Dominant Self-Definitions and 'The Other' in German Society." *Journal for the Anthropology of Europe* 2 (3): 13–21.

Schomaker, Gilbert. 2005. "Gesetzesinitiative gegen Zwangsheirat" (Legal initiatives against forced marriage). *Die Welt.* June 1. http://www.welt.de/data/2005/06/01/726100.html.

Schütte, Jan. 1987. *Drachenfutter* (Dragon Chow). West Germany: Novoskop Film.

Scott, Joan Wallach. 1989. "Gender: A Useful Category of Historical Analysis." In *Coming to Term*, ed. E. Weed, 81–101. London: Routledge.

———. 2005. "Symptomatic Politics: The Banning of Islamic Head Scarves in French Public Schools." *French Politics, Culture and Society* 23 (3): 106–127.

Semiz, Esat. 2005. "Alman Etnolog Schiffauer: Islam namus cinayetine izin vermez aksine önler." (German Ethnologist Schiffauer: Islam Does Not Give Permission for Honor Killing; On the Contrary, It Forbids It). *Zaman* Germany.

Şenocak, Zafer. 2000. *Atlas of a Tropical Germany: Essays on Politics and Culture, 1990–1998.* Trans. Leslie Adelson. Lincoln: University of Nebraska Press.

Sheridan, Clare. 1926. *A Turkish Kaleidoscope.* London: Duckworth.

Shohat, Ella, and Robert Stam. 1994. "The Imperial Imaginary." In *Unthinking Eurocentrism: Multiculturalism and the Media*, ed. E. Shohat and R. Stam, 100–136. London: Routledge.

Silverman, Kaja. 1992. *Male Subjectivity at the Margins.* New York: Routledge.

Sinha, Mrinalini. 1995. *Colonial Masculinity: The "Manly Englishman" and the "Effeminate Bengali" in the Late Nineteenth Century.* Manchester: Manchester University Press.

Sirman, Nükhet. 1989. "Feminism in Turkey: A Short History." *New Perspectives on Turkey* 3 (1): 1–34.

———. 1990. "State, Village and Gender in Western Turkey." In *Turkish State, Turkish Society*, ed. A. Finkel and N. Sirman, 21–52. London: Routledge.

———. 1993. Review of *The Seed and the Soil: Gender and Cosmology in Turkish Village Society*, by Carol Delaney. *American Anthropologist, New Series* 95 (2): 508–509.

60 Minutes. 2006. "Slaughter and 'Submission': Creator of Dutch Film Vows Sequel despite Muslim Death Threats." August 20. Story originally aired on March 13, 2005. http://www.cbsnews.com/stories/2005/03/11/60minutes/main679609.shtml (last accessed December 2007).

Söhn, Janina, and Veysel Özcan. 2006. "The Educational Attainment of Turkish Migrants in Germany." *Turkish Studies* 7 (1): 101–124.

Souad. 2004. *Burned Alive: A Victim of the Law of Men*. Trans. Judith Armbruster. New York: Warner Books.

Soykut, Mustafa. 2001. *Image of the "Turk" in Italy: A History of the "Other" in Early Modern Europe: 1453–1683*. Berlin: Klaus Schwarz Verlag.

———, ed. 2003. *Historical Image of the Turk in Europe: 15th Century to the Present, Political and Civilisational Aspects*. Istanbul: Isis Press.

Soysal, Levent. 2001. "Diversity of Experience, Experience of Diversity: Turkish Migrant Youth Culture in Berlin." *Cultural Dynamics* 13 (1): 5–28.

Spiegel TV. 2004. "Allahs rechtlose Töchter" (Germany's Lost Daughters). November 15. http://www.spiegel.de/sptv/thema/0,1518,327916,00.html.

Spiegel Online. 2000. "Zuwanderung: Begriff 'Leitkultur' kommt nicht ins CDU-Papier" (Immigration: The Concept "Leitkultur" Doesn't Appear in CDU Paper). November 2. http://service.spiegel.de/digas/find?DID=27789836 (last accessed December 2007).

———. 2004. "Muslim Integration: Germany's Lost Daughters." November 22. http://www.spiegel.de/international/0,1518,329060,00.html (last accessed December 2007).

———. 2005. "Neues Zuwanderungsgesetz: Aktion Kehraus" (The New Immigration Law: A Sweep Out). Issue 4, January 24. http://service.spiegel.de/digas/find?DID=39080828.

———. 2006. "Interview with Leon de Winter: 'The Dutch Are Not Afraid of Islam.'" February 2. http://service.spiegel.de/cache/international/0,1518,398708,00.html (accessed February 23).

Spivak, Gayatri. 1993. "Can the Subaltern Speak?" In *Colonial Discourse and Post-Colonial Theory*, ed. P. Williams and L. Chrisman, 66–111. Hartfordshire: Harvester Wheatsheaf.

Spohn, Margret. 1993. *Alles getürkt* (Everything Turkified). Oldenburg: Bibliotheks-und Informationssystem der Universität Oldenburg.

———. 2002. *Türkische Männer in Deutschland: Familie und Identität. Migranten der ersten Generation erzählen ihre Geschichte* (Turkish Men in Germany: Family and Identity. First Generation Migrants Tell their Stories). Bielefeld: Transcript.

Sternberger, Dorf. 1979. "Verfassungspatriotismus" (Constitutional Patriotism). *Frankfurter Allgemeine Zeitung*, May 23.

Stirling, Paul. 1965. *Turkish Village*. London: Weidenfeld and Nicolson.

Stoler, Ann Laura. 1989. "Making Empire Respectable: The Politics of Race and Sexual Morality in 20th Century Colonial Cultures." *American Ethnologist* 16 (4): 26–51.

————. 1995. *Race and the Education of Desire: Foucault's History of Sexuality and the Colonial Order of Things.* Durham: Duke University Press.

Strathern, Marilyn. 1987. "An Awkward Relationship: The Case of Feminism and Anthropology." *Signs* Special Issue, Reconstructing the Academy 12 (2): 276–292.

Suhr, Heidrun. 1989. "'Auslanderliteratur': Minority Literature in the Federal Republic of Germany." *New German Critique* 46: 71–103.

Suner, Asuman. 2004. "Horror of a Different Kind: Dissonant Voices in the New Turkish Cinema." *Screen* 45 (4): 305–323.

Taylor, Térèse. 2005. "Truth, History, and Honor Killing." A review of *Burned Alive*. http://www.antiwar.com/orig/ttaylor.php?articleid=5801.

Tekeli, Sirin. 1981. "Women in Turkish Politics." In *Women in Turkish Society*, ed. N. Abadan-Unat, 293–310. Leiden: E. J. Brill.

————. 1990. "The Meaning and Limits of Feminist Ideology in Turkey." In *Women, Family and Social Change in Turkey*, ed. F. Özbay, 139–159. Bangkok: UNESCO.

Terkessidis, Mark, and Yasemin Karaksoglu. 2006. "Gerechtigkeit für die Muslime!" (Justice for Muslims!) *Die Zeit* 6. February 1. http://www.zeit.de/2006/06/Petition (last accessed December 2007).

Tertilt, Hermann. 1996. *Turkish Power Boys: Ethnographie einer Jugendbande* (Turkish Power Boys: Ethnography of a Youth Gang). Suhrkamp Taschenbuch 2501. Frankfurt am Main: Suhrkamp.

Tibi, Bassam. 1998. *Europa ohne Identität? Die Krise der multikulturellen Gesellschaft* (Europe without Identity? The Crisis of a Multicultural Society). Munich: C. Bertelsmann Verlag.

————. 2001. "Leitkultur als Wertekonsens. Bilanz einer missglükten Debatte" (*Leitkultur* as Value-Consensus. Post-Mortem on a Failed Debate). In *Aus Politik und Zeitgeschehen (Das Parlament)*, B1–2 / 2001: 23–26.

Toepfer, Karl. 1997. *Empire of Ecstasy: Nudity and Movement in German Body Culture 1910–1935.* Berkeley: University of California Press.

Trumpener, Katie. 1989. "On the Road: Labor, Ethnicity and the New 'New German Cinema' in the Age of the Multinational." *Public Culture* 2 (1): 20–30.

Turan, Ilter. 1982. "Villages, Village Organization and the Government in Rural Development." *Occasional Papers* No. 20. Iowa City: University of Iowa.

Turgul, Yavuz. 1996. *Eskiya* (The Bandit). 121 min. Turkey: K Films.

Turner, Stephen. 1974. *Weber and Islam: A Critical Study.* London: Routledge & Kegan Paul.

van Beveren, Tim. 1986. *Jannan—die Abschiebung* (Jannan—The Deportation). 102 min. West Germany: Filmgalerie.

van Laenen, Filip. 2006. "Danes Sentence Entire Clan for Honour Killing." February 7. *Brussels Journal.* http://www.brusselsjournal.com/node/1143/.

Verdery, Katherine. 1991. *National Ideology under Socialism: Identity and Cultural Politics in Ceausescu's Romania.* Berkeley and Los Angeles: University of California Press.

Vieth-Entus, Susanne, Lars von Törne, and Claudia Keller. 2005. "Support for Honor Killing: Teachers Are Not Surprised." *Tagesspiegel*, February 22.

Volpp, Leti. 2000. "Blaming Culture for Bad Behavior." *Yale Journal of Law and the Humanities* 12 (1): 89–116.

von Bullion, Constanze. 2007. "'Ehrenmord'—Prozess soll erneut vor Gericht" ('Honor Killing'—The Case Should Be Retried). sueddeutsche.de. August 27. http://www. sueddeutsche.de/panorama/artikel/159/129935 (last accessed December 2007).

Wali, Najim. 2005. *Al-Hayat,* May 5. http://www.memri.de/uebersetzungen_analysen/ 2005_02_AMJ/eu_ehrenmorde_27_05_05.pdf.

Wallraff, Günter. 1988. *Ganz unten: Mit einer Dokumentation der Folgen/Günter Wallraff* (At the Bottom of the Heap: With a Documentation of the Consequences). Köln: Kiepenheuer & Witsch.

Watkins, S. Craig. 2005. *Hip Hop Matters: Politics, Pop Culture, and the Struggle for the Soul of a Movement.* Boston: Beacon Press.

Weber, Max. 1978 [1968]. *Economy and Society: An Outline of Interpretive Sociology.* 2 vols. Ed. G. Roth and C. Wittich. Berkeley: University of California Press.

Weidman, Amanda. 2003. "Beyond Honor and Shame: Performing Gender in the Mediterranean." *Anthropological Quarterly* 76 (3): 519–530.

Wentzke, Theo. 2005. "'Demokratisches' Umerziehungsprojekt" (Democratic Reeducation project). *Islamische Zeitung,* May 25.

Werbner, Pnina. 1997. "Introduction: The Dialectics of Cultural Hybridity." In *Debating Cultural Hybridity: Multi-Cultural Identities and the Politics of Anti-Racism,* ed. P. Werbner and T. Modood, 1–26. London: Zed Books.

Wessel, Rhea. 2006a. "A Matter of Honor, Your Honor?" *World Politics Review: A Foreign Policy and National Security Daily,* September 27. http://worldpoliticsreview.com/ article.aspx?id=213.

———. 2006b. "In Germany, Debate over Muslim Headscarf Rages On." *World Politics Review: A Foreign Policy and National Security Daily,* November 29. http://www .worldpoliticsreview.com/article.aspx?id=372.

White, Jenny. 1997. "Turks in the New Germany." *American Anthropologist* 99 (4): 754– 769.

Wiegman, Robyn. 2002. "Intimate Publics: Race, Property, and Personhood." *American Literature* 74 (4): 859–885.

Wikan, Unni. 2002. "Citizenship on Trial: Nadia's Case." In *Engaging Cultural Differences: The Multicultural Challenge in Liberal Democracies,* ed. R. Shweder, M. Minow, and H. R. Markus, 128–143. New York: Russell Sage Foundation.

Wilson, William. 1987. *The Truly Disadvantaged: The Inner City, the Underclass, and Public Policy.* Chicago: University of Chicago Press.

Yavuz, Yüksel. 1994. *Mein Vater der Gastarbeiter* (My Father the Guestworker). 52 min. Germany.

———. 1998. *Aprilkinder* (April Children). 85 min. Absolut Medien. Spielfilme 346.

Young, Robert J. C. 1995. *Colonial Difference: Hybridity in Theory, Culture and Race.* London: Routledge.

Yumul, Arus. 1999. "Scenes of Masculinity from Turkey." *Zeitschrift für Türkeistudien* 12 (1): 107–118.

Yusuf Ali, Abdullah, trans. 1991. *The Meaning of the Holy Qur'an.* Brentwood, Maryland: Amana Corporation.

Zaman. 2005. "Dr. Körting: Sürücü olayının Islam dini ile bir ilgisi yok" (Dr. Körting: There Is No Connection between the Sürücü Incident and the Islamic Faith). March 3.

Žižek, Slavoj 1989. *The Sublime Object of Ideology.* London: Verso.

INDEX

abjection
  in cinema, 70
  defined, 3, 229–30n3
  German national imaginary shaped by,
      9–10
  of Nazism/neo-Nazism, 205, 206
  sense of disgust marking, 196–98
Abu-Lughod, Lila, 32
abuse, removal of children from Turkish
      families due to reports of, 7–8, 66, 135–36
Adorno, Theodor, 216, 217, 219
Afghanistan war, 14, 210, 224
Ahmed, Lila, 222n
Akin, Fatih, 76, 100, 125–30
Aksan, Virginia, 34
al-Qaeda and German Turkish community,
      206–11
Algeria, Kabyle of, 32
Angst essen Seele auf (film), 61–63, 237n7
anthropology. *See* ethnography
anti-Semitism, 94, 206, 210, 215, 246n16
anti-terrorism concerns. *See* post-September
      11 climate
Aprilkinder (film), 75–76
Arabesk music, 123
Arat-Koç, Sedef, 50
Asiz, 131–32
assimilation. *See* immigration, integration,
      and assimilation
Atatürk, Kemal, 44, 45
Ateş, Seyran, 161–64, 166, 175–76, 182
Auf Eigenen Füssen (film), 66–67, 70–71
Auster, Paul, 61
autonomous subject, liberal Western notion
      of, 239–40n1

Ayaan Hirsi Ali, 166, 243n8
Aylin, 52–53, 56, 66, 82–83, 85, 87
Azize-A (rapper), 76

Balibar, Étienne, 227
Başer, Tevfik, and *40 Quadratmeter Deutsch-
      land* 65, 70, 73, 126, 182, 238n11
Basic Law. *See* German constitution or Basic
      Law
Baumgartner-Karabak, Andrea, 57
Bayram, 131–32
Beauvoir, Simone de, 11
Beckstein, Günther, 245n4
Bedouins, 32
Ben Annemin Kiziyim (film), 68–69
Ben-Yehuda, Nachman, 178
Bengali babus, 14
Berlin in Berlin (film), 71–72
Berlin Wall
      fall of. *See* reunification of German state
      guestworkers and building of, 15
BFV. *See* Bundesamt für Verfassungsschutz
Bhabha, Homi, 76
Biehl, Jody, 157
bin Laden, Osama, 207, 209, 245n5
"black Turk," 124, 128
the body
      in film
            hunched posture of Turkish women, 66
            signifier, black body as, 62–63
      in German vs. Muslim culture, 183–84,
            185, 192–96
      headscarves and, 185
      in Muslim Test, 183–84
      as organizing metaphor, 244n14

271